Our War

Our War
Australia during World War I
Brian Lewis

Melbourne University Press
1980

First published 1980
Typeset by The Dova Type Shop, Melbourne
Printed in Australia by Hogbin, Poole (Printers) Pty Ltd, Redfern, N.S.W. for
Melbourne University Press, Carlton, Victoria 3053
U.S.A. and Canada: International Scholarly Book Services, Inc.,
Box 555, Forest Grove, Oregon 97116
Great Britain, Europe, the Middle East, Africa and the Caribbean:
International Book Distributors Ltd (Prentice-Hall International),
66 Wood Lane End, Hemel Hempstead, Hertfordshire HP2 4RG England

National Library of Australia Cataloguing in Publication data

Lewis, Brian Bannatyne, 1906-
    Our war.

    Bibliography.
    ISBN 0 522 84199 6

    1. Australia – Social life and customs.
    2. Australia – History – 1914-1918.
994.04'1

Contents

Illustrations

Maps

Metric Conversion

To prevent anachronisms, imperial measures have been used throughout. Approximate equivalents are as follows.

1 foot = 30.5 cm	1 ounce = 28.3 g	1 calorie = 4.2 J
1 yard = 0.914 m	1 pound = 454 g	
1 mile = 1.61 km	1 ton = 1.02 t	

To convert degrees Fahrenheit to degrees Celsius, subtract 32, multiply by 5 and divide by 9.

Money

There were 12 pence (d) in 1 shilling (s), and 20 shillings in 1 pound (£). When decimal currency was adopted in 1966, 2 dollars were equal to 1 pound.

Preface

Our war, Australia's war, lasted just over four years. It gave us an immense conceit of ourselves.

On 8 September 1914 the German Pacific colonies capitulated to an Australian expeditionary force; in the middle of October 1918 the Australian Imperial Force was pulled out of the line in France after five months' continuous fighting. What a five months they had been: the holding of the victorious advance outside Amiens; the first great advance of the Western allies in the war; and then the smashing of the last German defences. The A.I.F. had been the spearhead of all three.

At the beginning we had believed that war was a sacrament which could only be celebrated by a British hierarchy which had been sanctified by passing through the Royal Military College at Sandhurst. At the end we believed that the priests of war had not been granted special grace nor divine inspiration, that they had shown themselves as dangerous blunderers, smug in their incompetence, men who would have been failures in any other calling. Our leaders, we thought, were efficient and humble men.

Every nation tells itself that its troops are superb. We did. The English grudgingly admitted that they were very good; the Germans acclaimed them as the best on the Western Front.

How good was the A.I.F.? It seems that it was very good, even better than the Canadians who had won many of the successes early in the war. Of the fifty-eight British divisions in France in 1918 ten were from the dominions, four Canadian, five Australian and one New Zealand, and all ten at least ranked with the Guards and the best Scottish divisions. It is impossible to imagine how the great retreat of 1918 could have turned into the final victorious advance without them, and particularly without the Australians: they were feared most by the Germans.

The war made us a nation, a nation which had risen from the defeat

1

at Gallipoli. We had rushed eagerly into the war to get a place on the world stage and the world applauded our performance. Our first voice in international affairs was our delegates at the peace conference.

In 1914 the new Commonwealth had been balanced on the top of a collection of States which still issued their own passports, and their own postage stamps and used British coinage. By 1918 the Commonwealth issued all passports and provided Australian coinage of peculiarly crude design. Stamps of similar crudity had displaced the beautiful State stamps, but they did express our political ideals.

The conservatives wanted King George V on the stamps to be supported by really Australian things—kangaroos, emus and wattle. The Labor Party wanted stamps displaying its political ideal—an empty White Australia with only a stuffed kangaroo in the middle. A Labor politician said that he would rather lick the backside of a kangaroo than that of a king.

In 1914 we spoke of England as 'home'—not Scotland, Ireland, Wales or Australia, but England—and we dreamed of going there. The war took hundreds of thousands of Australians to England. We fought 'England's war'. We lost our reverence for English politicians, generals and troops. When we went to England after the war we went conscious of our superiority.

In 1914 the most important political news published in our papers came from London; after the war it was news of the Commonwealth government that had first place. At the beginning of the war our real Prime Minister had been the British one; by the end we accepted Lloyd George as being clever, but also an opportunist demagogue, and our Billy Hughes had become a much greater figure to us.

We looked to England for inspiration and it was given to us by Rudyard Kipling, our greatest living writer. The *Oxford Book of Quotations* proved it. Kipling had 332 entries, only two fewer than Samuel Johnson; admittedly Shakespeare has nearly eight times as many and even Tennyson and Milton had more, but no living man had so many. Kipling's charming stories and his patriotic verse had prepared us for the war and made it seem inevitable. His writing during the war was savage and bestial; by the end he had become a warped old man and we read him no more.

In 1915 there burst on Australia a single small book which displaced all Kipling's works in our estimation: it was *The Sentimental Bloke*, by C. J. Dennis, of Victoria, who published verse in the Sydney *Bulletin*. The book included serial pieces which had already been published and were already popular, but no other book has made such an impact on Australia. No social evening could avoid a recitation from it and it was quoted more than any other book, apart from the Bible. There were not many quotations but they were used so often that they are part of our language: 'I'm crook; me name is Mud'; ' "Peanuts or lollies" sez the boy upstairs'.

The book ends in 1915 with the Bloke and Doreen and their baby son on a farm in the hills watching sunsets. But I really think he should have enlisted.

In the sequel, *Ginger Mick*, the Bloke visits his unregenerate friend in Melbourne and drinks only lemonade, but he prompts Ginger Mick to enlist by telling him how the 'Uns were drivin' dames an' kids before their guns'. Ginger Mick enlists and is redeemed by lower-class patriotism; he reforms and rises to the rank of corporal on Gallipoli. Then, 'Jist, "Killed in Action", an' beneath, 'is name.' His officer, 'an English toff wiv swanky friends' writes, ' "He was a gallant gentleman".' They buried Ginger near the beach with a sprig of mimosa on the mound, 'the nearest thing in reach/To golden wattle uv 'is native land'.

Narrative verse lost popularity during the war and *Ginger Mick* was the last to really move us. It was never as popular as the *Sentimental Bloke*, despite its patriotism, but it was far more wholesome than what Kipling was writing at the time.

The militarism of 1914 died in 1915. We came to believe that our survival depended on our young men offering themselves to death. 'They died that we might live'.

In those four years of war we showed idealism and selfless sacrifice, stupid credulity and vile hatred. At the beginning we believed everything that we were told; at the end we believed nothing.

In the 1930s we just did not believe that the Germans were treating their Jews as we had treated our Germans during World War I; that they had placed their Brown Shirts above the law as we had put our khaki. Their government instituted the mental harassment of the Jews as ours did of our Germans, but their government went further and encouraged physical maltreatment; ours left it to private enterprise. In Australia during World War I some would have been in favour of deporting all with German names.

We all joined in bitter sectarian hatred but we evolved a new religion accommodating all sects; a religion based not on the sacrifice of Christ but on that of thousands of ordinary men. Cathedrals of the new religion were built in all our capitals and every little place had its own shrine.

All children growing into consciousness during those years were fascinated by the war. It was more important to them than their school, church or their football team; to the old people of today their most vivid childhood memories are of the war.

1914

1
The War Begins

It all started with Fraulein barracking for St Kilda. There she was on Saturday morning with the St Kilda colours in a bow at her neck – red, white and black. Why should she wear those colours? She had never been to a football match during the few months that she had been in Australia.

Max Rosenfelt asked his mother about it. Yes, she was barracking all right, but she was barracking for Germany in a war which was just starting; it just happened that the St Kilda colours were the same as Germany's.

The Rosenfelts were Austrian, but Fraulein was from somewhere in Germany and would teach the children good German instead of soft Austrian. Austria was in the war already and it looked as if Germany would join her against Russia and France and, probably, England. If England went in, we would follow behind her. It meant nothing to us, but that Saturday was 1 August 1914. In Europe, it was still Friday the 31st and Friday was an unlucky day.

Max was my next-door friend, each of us nearly nine. We both knew about St Kilda and the other League teams from cigarette cards with pictures of the star players. I had actually been taken to a League match and seen St Kilda win.

It was easy to climb the side fence into the Rosenfelts' tidy back garden to play with Max and his pretty dark sister, Marie. There was another child of some sort, but it was too young to matter.

Their house was one storey and much smaller than our gaunt two-storey one, but it was luxurious. It had electric light while we had only gas; they had an inside W.C. but ours was remote and chilly in the backyard. Mr Rosenfelt had a car, a Standard with a little enamel Union Jack on its radiator cap; they had plenty of money whereas we had to be careful, but they were nice neighbours.

6

The Saturday paper had been the usual Saturday paper, fatter than the weekday papers and more interesting: it had the funny column by 'Ariel' and my elder brother, Athol, sometimes got something included; it had a magazine section with a couple of grey misty pictures. To a child of nearly nine the news was of no interest, but reading it years later, there was quite a lot about the expected war. European news had bigger headlines than local.

War had been expected and it had been an anxious week in Melbourne with tense crowds outside the newspaper offices in Collins Street waiting for cable news to be put on placards. The crowds had been alarmed and excited; there had been near-rioting by larrikins – members of the vicious Melbourne 'pushes' – and the police had been called in.

The crowds sang 'God Save the King', 'Rule Britannia', 'Sons of the Sea' and 'Soldiers of the King'. Most of these songs were to drop out of use as the expected war went on. 'Sons of the Sea' went first, for although we had our own navy, we expected the British navy to do the hard fighting; I can't remember the words, but it had a silly sort of braying tune. 'Rule Britannia' had decreasing popularity for Britannia did not seem to be ruling the waves very well. 'Soldiers of the King' was never very popular; it smacked of red jackets and colonial wars and we had no share in them.

But 'God Save the King' was sung far more often and became a war-time ritual. The words meant little, no more than the creed repeated in a lot of churches each Sunday. To sing it was the thing to do as a sort of minimal support for the war; anyone who did not stand up and sing was likely to be mauled. The King was an amiable sort of figurehead, part of our property, and we would not like to see him damaged; but if he went, we would get another figurehead after a bit of fuss; it might be just as good and the ship of state would sail on just as well. If you thought about it, it was a bit unnecessary to keep asking God to look after him so often.

That first Sunday of August had a feeling different from all previous Sundays, a feeling of being on the edge of something immense and terrible – but exciting. If England went in, so would we. Andrew Fisher, the Labor leader, had just said so in an election speech: in 'to the last man and the last shilling'.

We had a lot of men in the family; would we be involved? We were short of shillings; would they have to go too?

At ten to eleven we were all ready to go to church. We grouped on the front veranda, the front door shut behind us and we paired off to go down the curved path to the front gate. The eldest in front, Keith and Athol.

Keith may have felt a bit excited for he might well be involved. He was obviously suitable for the army. He was twenty-three, a big hefty fellow, and had got his commission in the University Rifles, once a volunteer unit and now incorporated in the compulsory scheme for all males between the ages of twelve and twenty-three. The scheme had been in full swing for a couple of years and most boys had some idea of what they would meet if they went into the army. Last year Keith had struggled through his university course to get his Certificate of Mining Engineering. He still needed a couple of subjects for his degree, academic mathematical ones; his Tasmanian schooling had been bad in mathematics, and anyway, he did not look like a mathematician. Big and amiable, he got on well with everybody and we all relied on him if we got into trouble, and none of us more than Athol. Keith would fit well in the army.

Athol, eighteen months younger, was very different. He was slight in build with curly black hair, whereas Keith was blond; he was volatile, quick in thought and action. He was in his second-last year of his law course at the University. At school at Launceston he had planned silly pranks and still did at home and at the University. Life for him was fun, but since babyhood he had relied on Keith to cover up for him. If war did come, it was unlikely he would be affected; it could not last beyond Christmas and he was not robust enough for the army. He always dressed more formally than the others and wore a felt hat with a turned-up bound edge, a Homburg, like father. All other felt hats in the family had flat brims.

Ralph, eighteen months younger than Athol, and Phyllis were the next pair. Ralph was short and thickset with curly black hair like father and Athol. At Launceston Grammar all the Lewises were called 'Curly Lewis' because of Athol and Ralph. So dark and curly was their hair that on our first Sunday at the Toorak Presbyterian church it was said we were a family of converted Jews.

Apart from Keith and Athol, all of us younger males wore straw hats on Sunday. Clumsy and uncomfortable and vulnerable to practical jokes, they were fragile and silly in rain and cost a couple of shillings. Owen's had the University band of blue and black diagonal stripes; Ronnie and Neil had the Wesley College purple band with two little gold stripes and a gilt lion in front; mine had a maroon band with a pale-blue 'L' for Lawside, my kindergarten. Even Phyllis was liable to wear a straw hat, but not on Sunday; then she wore a wide floppy hat like mother's. No male straw hats survived the war.

Ralph had planned to be a working geologist in the field and had chosen to go to the Working Men's College, where Dr Pritchard was a world figure in geology, but he was already feeling that a university degree would be valuable and hoped that the family could afford his further study. That humble-sounding Working Men's College has since blossomed into the Royal Melbourne Institute of Technology but even then was superior to the other technical colleges.

Beside Ralph walked Phyllis, nineteen, elfin pretty and very vital; she had done excellently at school and was now in the first year of her arts course at the University. As the only girl among seven boys, she exaggerated her position by deliberate differences. She was very careful in her speech and corrected ours, and she had a more refined vocabulary. A 'lolly shop' was a 'sweet shop' to her and she would ask for two penny ices rather than two wafers or cones. She was as quick and mischievous as Athol, and Ralph was overshadowed between them. She was particularly devoted to her next youngest brother Owen.

The next pair was Owen and Ronnie. Owen, just eighteen, was academically brilliant; he was hard-working and earnest and had none of the frivolity of Athol and Phyllis. He was doing his first-year engineering at the University after being Dux of Wesley a year younger than was regarded as proper. He was the most conventionally pious of us all, but it did not offend us, as he lived up to his beliefs and was particularly gentle to us younger ones.

Typical of him was one Saturday morning when Neil walked the two miles to Chapel Street to sell stamps in bulk to a dealer. There was a miscount and Neil was over-paid. Owen suggested he should put the matter right and Neil walked back the two miles to make a refund.

Owen was of average height and thick-set with honey-coloured hair, not ginger like Neil's. Between them they gave us the name of 'Honey Lewis' at Wesley in contrast to the earlier 'Curly Lewis' of Launceston Grammar.

Beside him was Ronnie, just seventeen and in his first long trousers. He had just graduated from shorts with long black stockings over his knees, a fashion which went out in his time. He too was bright at Wesley and he too was pious but in a rather inhuman sort of way. He was in a lonely position in the family, being four years remote in age from Neil and not sharing in the Tasmanian boarding-school kinship of the five elder ones. He was slight, even slighter than Athol, and the two were regarded as the most delicate of the family. If, by chance, the war lasted beyond Christmas into the years far ahead, Ronnie was the least suitable for the army.

Neil and I were the last pair of the family. Neil, red-haired, just turned twelve, was at Wesley in the Big School. He was a clear year younger than his class-mates, despite having put in an unnecessary year in the Prep to make his age more suitable. He was certain to win a government scholarship and get his fees paid—as had Owen and Ronnie.

He suffered in that his cleverness made him remote in age from his fellows and at a disadvantage in the normal scuffles. He did not enjoy fighting, except with me, and he goaded me into hopeless attacks on him, but he enjoyed watching, and provoked fights for me with outsiders.

I, nearly eight, walked beside him, proud to be old enough to go on the family church parade, proud to walk behind my very own elder brothers, gods on earth, who were kind enough to arrange pleasant surprises for me, remote enough in age to treat me as a toy to tease mother.

We were a big family of boys, only rivalled at church by the Thoms, who, as a family, were slightly older than our average. Sometimes we united with them at the corner of Avondale Road and the twenty or so Thoms and Lewises went down Denbigh Road to church together. I felt smug to be in such an imposing group.

Last in the parade, the climax and the origin of it all; father and mother. Father, fifty-two, was short and broad with thick curly black hair thinning in front and a little walrus moustache. He was a confident man who was doing well, even if his family of eight prevented him making any lavish display of it. Mother, four years younger, was fair and buxom in her black velvet dress.

It was a solemn march to church. More people than usual seemed to be going to church this Sunday; we passed more Methodists and Baptists than we usually did. War seemed probable; even if it was over by Christmas it would be tragic but we were committed to it. An occasional uniform had been seen on the streets of Melbourne during the past week and we glimpsed one on our way to church.

We were proud of ourselves and felt that we had good reason: every one of our big family was doing well. Mother was proudest and would boast to casual strangers of the merits of her eight children, although the number seemed to surprise her. After her marriage she had been disappointed not to have a child in the first three years and had discussed adopting one; it would have been funny if she had.

We entered our pew at the very back of the church, mother and father first and then the rest of us in reverse order of age; heads down to the pew in front for a genuine prayer and no little nods of recognition when we looked up; today was serious.

Mr Millar would soon be out of his vestry and climbing his little special stair to his pulpit and then a very solemn service would begin.

Then from the bright morning through the main doors of the church thundered the glory of war. In heavy army boots and trim khaki, three men in uniform. Yes, they were the Jones boys. Last Sunday in the days of peace they had slipped in quietly behind their father and mother, a rather anonymous family; now they were famous.

What other church in Melbourne had three men in uniform?

We had not known that the three Jones were all instructors in the Compulsory Training Scheme; this Sunday they were two sergeants and one warrant officer, third class. The sergeants were important enough, but the warrant officer was splendid in almost an officer's uniform, with shining leather leggings.

Mr Millar's entrance was hardly noticed.

His first prayer was solemn. War was almost upon us despite his requests of last Sunday. Today his requests were being supported by every Presbyterian church in the State and all the other churches, even the Catholic, and some notice by God was warranted.

Now if God allowed the war to start, Mr Millar expected Him to support our just cause. We were not too sure why it was just, we would be better informed in a week or two. It had looked as if Russia had started it all, but we were hoping that God would not make any hasty decision, as Russia would be on our side this time.

This would be Armageddon with all the first-class nations of Europe at each other's throats. Let us be worthy of the sacrifice asked of us.

A serious sermon and then the benediction, but we were not done yet. 'We will now sing 'God Save the King'' '– and we did, with gusto.

The sentiments of that anthem were very proper, with the King's unpopular cousin, the Tsar of Russia, on his side, and his more unpopular cousin, the Kaiser of Germany, against him.

The war really did come that Sunday and Neil brought home the news. On his way home from Sunday school he had gone on the footbridge at the Armadale station and seen the news on a placard outside the booking office. The station had a telephone to the city; with nothing else open and no Sunday papers, this was the best way of getting the news to those anxious to know it. Germany had declared war on Russia, and France had mobilized.

Monday 3 August, and the *Age* had a four-column spread: GREATEST WAR IN WORLD'S HISTORY. ALL EUROPEAN POWERS INVOLVED. GERMAN DECLARATION AGAINST RUSSIA. GENERAL MOBILISATION IN FRANCE. BRITISH DOMINIONS PREPARE FOR EMERGENCIES. CANADA OFFERS 30 000 TROOPS.

On 4 August: AUSTRALIA JOINS. FLEET AND 20,000 MEN. OFFER BY FEDERAL CABINET. Then there was MANNING THE FORTS. DRILL SHIRKERS SENT HOME. Those shirkers had dodged their compulsory training and now the men who had been guarding them were needed to man the fort at Queenscliff. The searchlights had been continuously lighting up the entrance to the Bay since Friday night.

Wednesday 5 August: BRITAIN INVOLVED. WE CANNOT STAND
ASIDE. OBLIGATION OF HONOUR. BELGIUM UNWAVERING. Phyllis came
home from the University saying that after lectures the classes had stood
and sung 'God Save the King'.

GERMAN SHIPS IN PORT. ORDERS FROM ADMIRALTY. THEY MUST
BE INTERNED. That evening the *Herald* told us what we had done.

We, here in Victoria, had fired the first British shot of the war. At
nine o'clock that morning the new German steamer, the *Pfalz* of 6557
tons, had hurriedly left the Victoria Docks and headed off down the
Bay. She was granted a clearance at Queenscliff and went off through
the Rip to the open sea.

The Queenscliff fort got official instructions and aimed a shot across
her bows: it fell fifty yards astern, but it was enough to make her turn
round and return up the Bay. Not only had we fired the first British
shot, but we had captured the first German ship. It was disappointing
that no recognition of our feat was made in England.

Thursday 6 August and we were officially in.

WAR DECLARED

BRITAIN AND GERMANY.

BELGIUM'S INTEGRITY

MUST BE OBSERVED.

1

No war was ever entered with more honourable motives. We in Australia were protecting the helpless little nations which had no voice in the European debate. We were in to defend Gallant Little Belgium.

Germany had invaded her and so started our war. It was fortunate that the nation which was taking the lead from Britain in commerce and industry should have provoked the war in which it seemed certain she would destroy herself. We fervently accepted that belief which would be a consolation to us in the terrible years ahead and which would still be held more than sixty years later. And it was an impertinent thing for Germany to do. Her group had only half the resources in troops, naval forces and industrial power of the nations which she had attacked.

Yet there had been guesses about Belgium and the coming war. Long before the sides had been picked the *Bulletin* of September 1883 had foreseen the war as a German attack on France through Belgium, with Britain intervening with 50 000 men thrown into Antwerp and Australian troops ordered 'home' to defend the Empire.

There had been more than guesses. When the Germans entered Brussels they found papers left in a hotel by the British military attaché to Belgium. That attaché had been criminally careless; they were plans for an attack on Germany prepared jointly by the General Staffs of Britain, France and Belgium. The Germans published them as evidence of our hypocrisy in claiming that Belgian neutrality had been violated. They were not published in Britain or Australia; if they had been, we would not have believed them. As we believed in God, so we believed in the unspotted innocence of Belgium, raped by the brutal bestiality of Germany; even to hint at doubts would have been blasphemous.

2

The Germans Started It

It started as the usual Balkan war. Russia had been extending her power into eastern Europe by supporting and dominating the new Slav states which had been parts of the Turkish Empire; each of them was continually trying to expand at the expense of its neighbours. Austria was driving south into the Balkans and the two forces met.

Austria had annexed Bosnia and Hercegovina, and Serbia (or Servia as we spelt it then) wanted those provinces. The Bosnians had mixed feelings: they were Slav, but Roman Catholic, and used the Roman alphabet. They were civilized compared with the crude and violent Servians, who were Orthodox and used the Cyrillic alphabet.

The Austrian Crown Prince and his wife visited the newly acquired provinces and were assassinated by a group which had been supplied with arms by Servia and had the hidden support of that nation.

Austria was getting tired of attacks by Servian terrorists and this latest one had been the worst. The world had sympathy with Austria and her poor old Emperor, whose queen had been killed by terrorists and whose heir had died violently; now the heir apparent had been murdered. The world agreed that Servia should be taught a lesson, although it meant Austria being involved in a Balkan war.

Servia, however, was backed by Russia; if Russia supported Servia, then Germany and Italy were bound by treaty to help Austria. A European war was certain if Russia intervened: Russia would pull in France, and Britain might be dragged in as well.

The *Argus* of 27 July: SERVIA DEFIES AUSTRIA. RUSSIA'S ARMY MOBILISING. The same issue had RUSSIA IS READY and added, 'The real causes are deeper. The Austro-Servian differences are the first symptoms of a gigantic Slav-Teuton struggle'. The *Herald* of the same day: RUSSIAN INTERVENTION MEANS ARMAGEDDON. SERVIA HELPLESS ALONE.

The next day it was: OUTLOOK BRIGHTER. BRITAIN'S INFLUENCE FELT. AUSTRIA REASSURES RUSSIA. The text said, 'Germany is certainly working for peace – There is reason to suppose that Great Britain had made it plain that there can be no European war with Great Britain left out'. There was no mention of Belgium. In another column was GREAT BRITAIN ACTS. MEDIATION PROPOSED.

To us here it looked as if it all turned on what Russia did and she could not do much just now. There was a great transport strike there: 150 tram-cars had been burned and wrecked in St Petersburg and 130 000 transport men were on strike. On 29 July they went back to work and Russia could have her war, but the headlines read: PARIS FEELING HOPEFUL. RESTS WITH GERMANY, ANTI-WAR RIOTS IN STREETS, and in Berlin, BRITISH EMBASSY CHEERED. Those Germans were thinking that Britain might be able to prevent the war. The stock exchange thought that war was unlikely and Lloyd's underwriters did a large business at 20 per cent against any of the great powers being at war within six months.

But the machine had started. On 30 July: AUSTRIA DECLARES WAR – we had rather expected that and even approved it, but we did not like RUSSIAN ARMY MOBILISING. The first of the great powers was moving.

It might yet be prevented. The next day we saw: SOCIALISTS CONSIDER ACTION: 'The International Socialist Bureau had discussed, at Brussels, the possibility of common action being taken by the proletariat to avoid extension of the conflict. A general strike and revolutionary action were suggested, but definite decision was postponed'. A pity, that postponement; another Russian transport strike might have had some effect.

On 1 August the headlines read: RUSSIA MOBILISING. 'ABSOLUTE AND GENERAL'. ANXIETY IN BERLIN. 'A COMING CATASTROPHE'. KAISER AND WAR. But there was hope: TRYING TO PRESERVE PEACE. GOOD NEWS IN PARIS. MINISTER'S OPTIMISM. 'We have received', said M. Malvyn of France, 'news from Germany, which we had not dared to hope for'. The German ambassador announced that Germany had not mobilized her army, and that direct negotiations were still going on between Berlin and St Petersburg.

In the same edition was DEPARTURE OF BRITISH FLEET. GREAT JOY IN ST. PETERSBURG. 'St. Petersburg went delirious with joy upon receipt of the news that the British Fleet had left Portland'. So the fleet had left the Channel for the North Sea where its only possible enemy was Germany; the Russians were assuming it would be on their side in the war they seemed bent on having. As yet, there had been no invasion of Belgium.

The French Atlantic fleet had concentrated in the Mediterranean, leaving its west coast defenceless before the German navy–unless it was assumed that the British would protect it in any war with Germany, Belgium or no Belgium.

In the paper of 6 August was the German account of what had happened, and it was to be the last time for years that the German view would be printed. A *White Book* issued in Berlin stated:

> We worked shoulder to shoulder with England in mediation. We forwarded the British proposal that Austria ought, after the invasion of Servia, to dictate her conditions there. We had assured Russia that we would accept this basis. The Kaiser called the Czar's attention to the menacing character of Russia's action [mobilisation], the Czar replied 'I thank thee from the bottom of my heart for thy mediation, which now leaves a gleam of hope–but the troops will not take provocative action while negotiations continue. I give thee my word'. The Kaiser replied 'Mobilisation is rendering mediation nearly illusory–it is still in thy power to avert a world calamity, Russia could well wait the result of my mediation'.

And there was something in what the Kaiser had said. Russian mobilization was placing troops along the German border and the Germans feared the huge Russian armies.

This Berlin *White Book* was the last factual and undoctored item from Germany which our papers would publish.

The British also published a *White Book* but it was a dubious and evasive document. It set out that the 'Foreign Minister, Sir Edward Grey, refused to state the terms for British neutrality', but that 'the neutrality of Belgium would appeal very strongly to public opinion here', but he did not think that 'we could give a promise of neutrality on that condition alone'. Even the promise to respect the integrity of France and her colonies would not move him. He would state no terms.

The Kaiser had behaved tactlessly. Russia seemed bent on fighting Austria–and it might well be that Germany was more than willing to come to the help of her treaty partner. It would have been a very different war if it had been only Russia and Servia against Germany and Austria.

But Britain was firmly committed by treaty and Sir Edward Grey was one of the few people in Britain who knew of it. Parliament did not know, nor did the public, and here in Australia we had no idea what had started our war. There had been more than a decade of fear and dislike of Germany and it was almost a relief to be able to settle things at last. In the excitement there were few balanced enough to make a calm analysis of the *White Book*.

Britain was committed to the greatest war in history and we were committed to Britain, for our shooting near the *Pfalz* had involved us even before war was declared. We had already shown that we were to have a place in this really important war; we hoped that if we did well we would get favourable notice from the great nations who would recognize that we were something more than a remote, inferior and inarticulate piece of Britain.

We and the New Zealanders were tiny peoples dependent on the British navy for survival. We were colonies, and colonies could be seized or exchanged in the power-politics of Europe.

We did not object to a natural thing like war, provided it was kept well away from us; in fact, we were stirred by it. In our early days men had gone from Sydney to fight the Maoris and later men had gone to the Sudan and suffered heavily from alcoholic poisoning; we had put up quite a good show against the Boers, who, after all, were like us in a lot of ways. We were not very worried about the rights and wrongs of wars, but it was comforting to know that we were in the right in this new one.

But we did not like the thought of war on Australian soil; in our early days we had been frightened of French invasions, and later, of the Russians. When father was a boy someone had seen a Russian fleet steaming up Port Phillip Bay and there had been a lot of running about. The battery of guns at Point Ormond, a few miles from Melbourne, had been manned. It was fear of Russia which had prompted the building of our coastal forts and the formation of volunteer forces. In this war our volunteers were to fight on the same side as the French and Russians.

Then we had feared an invasion of 'Leperous Mongols'. We had seen a lot of Chinese on the gold fields and given them as bad a time as we could. Behind them was an immense reservoir of yellow men ready to pour out and submerge White Australia.

Those Japanese had the same coloured skin and had shown themselves quite capable of matching a European power. Japan had the strongest Pacific fleet and we did not trust her treaty with Britain which left the defence of the Pacific to her. We did our best by passing the Defence Acts to provide ourselves with our own army and navy; our navy was now more powerful than any European Pacific squadron. But those forces intended for our defence in the Pacific would be used for the defence of Britain in Europe.

We had a more recent fear. Germany was too young as a nation to have done much good for herself in the colonial scramble but Britain had allowed her in just beside us. German New Guinea was a huge slice next door to our slice and there had already been talk of trouble by Australian prospectors in the back country. German New Guinea was not a ramshackle place, like the near French colonies, but was clean and efficient and the Germans dressed in nice white uniforms.

Very frightening were the German Pacific stamps. They did not show a picture of the Kaiser but of a German warship. The Kaiser encouraged the German Naval Party and her navy was the biggest and most efficient of continental Europe. The Germans had a disconcerting reputation in ship building, machine design and engineering production; even on the Tasmanian mines German machinery was replacing the more massive British and the cheaper, but less reliable, American.

Germany was doing too well at the expense of Britain. Her mercantile marine was expanding and had a reputation for cleanliness and efficiency; it was taking passengers and cargoes from British ships. She was producing more coal and iron than Britain and was predominant in chemical engineering. Britain had built her power on her Industrial Revolution; Germany was now having her own and avoiding Britain's mistakes.

Britain had flourished because of lively individuals building up family businesses, but that was now long ago; family businesses had withered and died with the new limited liability companies and the workers had become anonymous units in impersonal organizations. 'Clogs to clogs in three generations' had taken effect. The grandsons of the old bosses could be sitting in the House of Lords or wearing clogs; nobody worried where they were.

In Germany the companies were bigger and better organized and had government direction and encouragement. The workers had some pride in playing parts in successful ventures; they felt that they were privates in a conquering army, as in Japan today.

Britain, we knew, was leading the world in democracy by adopting some of the social laws of the Australasian colonies of decades earlier. Germany was a royal dictatorship. The workers had social insurance, courts of industrial arbitration and a Workers' Protection Act as old as 1891. The democratic nations had to wait until long after the war to get what Germany had in 1914. Perhaps her paternal dictatorship was more effective than the untidy democracies of Britain, France and the United States.

As individuals and as a nation we preferred the Germans to the French and the Russians, even if we feared them. Their dominant religion was something like the official English one; they were clean in their habits, unlike the French and Russians, and their traditions were more akin. The typical English Christmas which we celebrated in Australia had been a recent import from Germany: Santa Claus, snow, Christmas trees, everything. There was no hiding that our king was really German.

If our war had started ten years earlier we would have been fighting on Germany's side; there would have been the same number of atrocities but committed by other enemies. In 1904 when the Russian Baltic fleet was sailing half-way round the world to destruction by the Japanese, its first battle had been against British trawlers in the North Sea. Britain thought seriously of a war then, but did not have her hand sorted out.

Bismarck had proposed an alliance when Germany was digesting her newly acquired territories; Britain then had been unwilling to accept any European commitment, but in a few years she was. She asked for a treaty in 1898 and 1901 but now Germany would not accept–the new Kaiser may have had a lot to do with that.

Britain was abandoning her isolationist policy. If the two opposing groups of Europe came together temporarily in shared jealousy of her empire, she would be in a bad way. Joseph Chamberlain felt that a European alliance was vital. He would 'prefer adherence to the Triple Alliance of Germany, Austria and Italy', but if it were not forthcoming, then with France and Russia.

With France and Russia, our old enemies? With atheist France tied to 'Holy Russia'? What a bundle, but in we went.

The only time in history when France had done anything creditable was when she had fought on our side to keep Russia out of Turkey. Britain's last mobilization had been in 1877 when Russia had looked like bagging Constantinople, and it had put a new word into our language:

> We don't want to fight,
> But by jingo, if we do,
> We've got the men, we've got the ships,
> And we've got the money too.

Now the rare opponents of the war with Germany were saying that we were 'jingoistic'.

And France? In 1892 Britain and France had edged around each other like two dogs itching for a fight, because France had hoisted the tricolour at Fashoda on the Upper Nile–a place which, we felt, was part of our share of the Turkish Empire. France had been far more insulting than Germany had during the Boer War.

The personal charm of Edward VII had persuaded France to accept us in the Triple Entente and we made it far stronger than the Triple Alliance. In making peace with France we were preparing war with Germany.

If war was coming, it might be as well to get on with it before German industry and sea-power got completely out of hand.

The two sides were ready and waiting. German officers toasted 'Der Tag'–the day when the German navy would sail out to the decisive battle with Britain. In 1900 a popular London play was *An Englishman's Castle*, showing what would happen in a German invasion.

In 1905 when the Entente was very young, Douglas Haig, the man whose complacency would send hundreds of thousands to their futile deaths at the hands of the Germans, wrote to his sister: 'I see that you are excusing yourself for assisting the enemy by travelling on a German-subsidised mail boat'. Later he recorded that Haldane, Minister for War, had no doubt that the expeditionary force he had created existed 'to support France and Russia against Germany, and perhaps Austria'.

We had not liked the French caricatures of Queen Victoria; we now published caricatures of the Kaiser, unkinder than any royal caricatures since those of the Prince Regent. The Kaiser was a figure of fun with his grotesque brushed-up moustaches. He was the most caricatured man before the war and throughout the war, but it was not then convincing; a man could not be a clown and the embodiment of all evil in the same drawing. Histrionic and hysterical, he was a clown, even if he was the most positive figure of European royalty. He gave ranting speeches without consideration of the policy of his ministers, who had to wipe up, as best they could, after him.

To us it was the 'Kaiser's War', right to the end, and when the end came there were screams that he should be extradited from his refuge in Holland to face trial as the arch war-criminal. Lloyd George yelled loudest, although he must have known that the Kaiser had been allowed no responsibility in the war attributed to him. He was the non-playing captain of the team against us.

The teams sized each other up. On the other side were Germany and Austria–Hungary, with Italy in the reserves bound to come into the field when called on. Germany had the most promising players and a lot of them. Since the Franco-Prussian War her population had grown to exceed that of France; her army was regarded as efficient and well-equipped; her industrial machine could effectively support it and now was far better than the French. She had a good navy, about half the size of the British, and, if supported by Italy in the Mediterranean, capable of dealing with France and Russia.

Germany's four State armies were dominated by the Prussian one and it was accepted as exceptionally good. Its numbers were made up of conscripts on a two-year term. Its officers were unusual. In all other countries, including Britain, the officers were aristocrats. In Germany a man became an aristocrat by becoming an officer. An ambitious man could enter the army and expect promotion on showing ability; thus he could secure a place in the highest caste of his country—and it was a notoriously arrogant caste.

The Austria-Hungarian war machine was a pitiful vehicle likely to fall to pieces if jolted. About one-quarter of its army were Austrian Germans, one-quarter Hungarian and the other half odds and ends of various Slavs and Italians—not a good assembly to put against the Russian Slavs, but good enough to handle Servia and a bit more.

Italy had the second-largest Mediterranean navy but nobody took it or the army seriously. Its only noteworthy performance during the war would be to produce Corporal Mussolini.

The other side—our side—had just as quaint a collection of odds and ends. In the south was the tough and experienced Servian army; in the north, the untidy Belgians. We could not do much to help the Belgians when the Germans got at them, but we were able to do something for the more unfortunate Servians. The Latin word 'servus' meant a slave, and Servia was the place that slaves came from. From now on we called her 'Serbia'.

The Russians were a different matter. Once we had feared the Russian navy, particularly in Australia, but now we did not think much of it—not after what the Japanese had done to it in 1905. But the Russian army was invincible in its sheer numbers—even the Germans were frightened of it. The Cossack cavalry were a wild lot with a long history of atrocities behind them, but this time we did not worry because it was only the Germans and Austrians who would suffer. There was also an immense reserve of hardy peasant soldiers inspired to sacrifice themselves for 'Holy Russia' with the Tsar, their 'Little Father', as a divine leader. It was quaintly feudal in that the biggest landowners were assumed to be the best leaders; the second-most powerful man, the Tsar's cousin, the Grand Duke Nicholas, could not escape being made Commander-in-Chief.

But for Russia it would have to be a quick war, for there were no rifles for reinforcements and her industry was too primitive to supply armaments. There were not enough middle-class to handle the complications of modern war.

The hordes of Russians would advance like a swarm of locusts devouring everything in its path; but if the swarm were checked, it would find that it had eaten everything behind it. It would have to keep going forward but it could not go beyond the limits of its sparse railway system, for any captured railway would be of a different gauge. We felt it better to call those locusts 'The Russian Steamroller'.

The French had a navy of sorts but it was secondary to the army and had different ideals. It retained an old hatred of Britain and was solidly Catholic and conservative—even somewhat royalist.

The French were proud of their army with its mixture of archaic and modern. It had been the first to provide sound technical training, although now Germany was doing it better. Its field artillery remained the best of any throughout the war; but the cavalry was Napoleonic, the infantry that of 1870. That year had inspired the nation and the army and both burned to regain Alsace–Lorraine; after all, Protestant, German-speaking Alsace had been seized so long ago that it had become an integral part of Catholic France. The war of 1870 would be resumed using the same methods.

The infantry was to do it; with tremendous élan it would dash through the dull grey German lines, heartened by its scarlet trousers and blue frock-coats, with its officers in white gloves. It all looked splendid enough, but the army command was divided between Catholics and atheists and promotion was affected by belief. A general of the wrong party might find himself shunted off the main line into the Salonika siding.

We did not like either religious extreme and we had been shocked by the condemnation of Colonel Dreyfus as a traitor because he was a Jew. Now we had to learn to forgive the French everything.

We knew that Britain was the most powerful nation in Europe and we identified ourselves with her. At school we learned by heart verses of her greatness – and some of it was fairly recent. 'Eleven men of England a breastwork charged in vain' – but as they died they took twenty of the enemy with them. If it came to a war we would do the same with the Germans. Then there was the uncouth drunken 'Private of the Buffs', 'Who died as firm as Sparta's king because his soul was great'.

Funny that there was not more about the Royal Navy, but I suppose that as it had had no real fighting for over a century, its heroism was too remote. The navy was the 'Senior Service', solid and reliable and far more important to us than the army.

Its dark-blue uniform was rather like the city dress of professional men. It was like a civilian profession also in that it required a long professional training and a middle-class devotion to a chosen career, training which began in childhood for officers, and commonly for ratings too. It was a demanding profession and entailed late marriage and long absences from family life. During the war we would be disappointed in its lack of brilliance, but we did not criticize it as we did the British army.

The army had more glamour with its assortment of gorgeous uniforms, but we had a suspicion that the sparkle had something of tinsel in it.

We might have had doubts but were proud of that army. It was

The Bulletin

Registered at the General Post Office, Sydney, for Transmission by Post as a Newspaper

Vol. 35.—No. 1900.   THURSDAY, AUGUST 13, 1914.   Price 6d.

THE WAR GOD OF EUROPE STRIKES HIS GONG.

small, but it was the only European army in the new war with previous war experience. It was our team in international events. It had won all the little colonial wars and the casualties it had suffered were not enough to worry us. Over similar periods it was far safer to join in a colonial war than it is today to play football in Italy or South America.

The Boer War had been disconcerting when the numbers of the British army had swollen to nearly half a million men in order to beat the Boer farmers, whose army had been estimated as between 25 000 and 50 000. It had not sounded very glorious, but the relief of besieged Mafeking had been splendid, and it could be regarded as a practice game for the big war now starting. The generals who had lost their reputations had been weeded out and our present leaders were those who had survived the purge.

Entry into the army was later than for the navy. A boy could go right through his public school and then find that the army was the only profession which would accept him. Once accepted he could ensure that much of his service was in reach of family and social life – and social prominence was important for promotion, more important than ability for those who made the army their career.

An English officer had to pass the Army entrance examination, not in itself a difficult matter, but some regiments required a good pass. All required a guaranteed personal income; if you had no income only the Indian army was available. The army was a good place to fill in time waiting for your father to die, but it was well to reach the rank of captain in order to retire as a major. It was better to reach lieutenant-colonel; then you would be called Colonel and would be eligible for Master of the Fox Hounds. Many officers bore high-sounding hyphenated surnames, more than in the navy, but these could not be assumed to reflect doubts on paternity.

The infantry was the pick of the army. Of these the Guards were the most socially desirable and expensive; they were not the most intelligent, but they preserved a reputation for being utterly dependable. The Rifle Brigade had a comparable reputation and was considered brighter and as giving a better background for an army career. It demanded a high pass for entry but a lower private income. In 1928 £300 a year was the figure, and I think it was the same in 1914 when money was more valuable. It was more than double the average wage. The guarantee of income could be formal and some officers lived on their pay, but they could not afford to play polo; polo was thought to be an aid to promotion, even in the navy.

Those Rifle Brigade officers of 1928 seemed to be capable and intelligent men but their long civil-service sort of existence may have blunted their initiative. They were sure enough of themselves to have contact with their men and appeared to be more effective than officers of the county regiments. Those of 1914 were possibly of similar calibre but few had survived the war.

The discipline of the county regiments was more formal but less effective; the officers were different and did not have to worry about a good pass for entry. If a man was so dumb that he just scraped a pass, there was only the cavalry left for him; it was the most expensive of all. Both British Commanders-in-Chief of World War I came from the cavalry.

It was important in the army to be born well, but every officer became a gentleman on appointment. Money only two generations old was regarded as vulgar, but the army could gild it. Guinness's stout and Tennant's lager took generations to climb into the House of Lords, but the army got Haig's whisky there in one.

Life in the army just passed by. There was no worry about what to eat or where to sleep; there was nothing much to do, and what there was, pretty useless: guarding things which did not need to be guarded and doing things which did not need to be done. The annual training periods were just repetitions of the previous year; the same at home or in a sister battalion in an overseas station.

An officer might take a couple of years away from his regiment to serve in the West African Rifles, or some such body, or get a job as the aide-de-camp to a colonial governor. If he was really bright and interested, there was the Staff College, and after that a real expectation of something better.

All training was over by lunch-time and the weekends were clear. The officers' mess was like a good country hotel, but much cheaper.

The men did the things they were told to do and time passed. A promising one would get a lance-corporal's stripe and see a future. He might rise to sergeant before his seven-year term was up and that established him as a successful man with real work and responsibility— sergeants were expected to have the common sense and interest which their officers might lack. If a man engaged for a second term he might rise to sergeant-major, showing that he was outstandingly good. He might even hope to be commissioned as captain-quartermaster with entry to the officers' mess, but although the others would go out of their way to be nice to him, he would never feel at home. Those senior N.C.O.s were good, if unimaginative.

This cosy little army was to fight a savage European war. It was highly trained, but for a different sort of war. It was an elaborate and smoothly-running machine but it had the weakness of a machine which could lose a vital part. It was excellent at some things and its musketry was

immensely superior to that of the conscript armies of Europe. It was
sure of what it had been trained to do, but unsure when it met something
outside its training. It did all that was expected of it and was wiped
out doing it. There was glory in its unquestioning self-sacrifice.

That gorgeous army and that splendid navy, directed by the wise
statesmen in London, held our empire together. It was for the great
men of Europe to arrange our war, just as they had organized and managed wars in the past. It was all far above our heads and we were perfectly
content to leave such things to Britain and to follow her without question
or advice. Her soldiers and politicians were trained professionals and
ours were just amateurs who came from anywhere.

All my friends at Lawside kindergarten were old enough to know
that we were part of the greatest empire the world had ever known;
far bigger than the Roman Empire which had done so much good to
Europe. Our Empire was on every continent and doing good all over
the world. They no longer burnt widows in India, nor ate acquaintances
in the Pacific, and there was settled peace where there had been continual
wars. Our Empire had brought prosperity and peace and they played
cricket in Fiji and India; it was a pity about Canada, but even there,
some eccentrics did.

On the cover of our school exercise-books was a map of the world
with the Empire shaded in, and on the wall was the same map to a
much bigger scale with the Empire coloured red. There seemed to be
an awful lot of it. Canada looked huge, but that was because it was
near the North Pole and the map exaggerated its size; it really was not
much bigger than Australia. We knew that much of it was just snow,
even if a lot of Australia was just sand.

We thought colonialism was right and proper and conferred benefits
on colonial people, such as ourselves. We had not yet learned that
colonialism was wrong if there was a sea between the colonies and the
mother country, but right if the colonies were adjoining nations. Our
sea-borne empire would float away, but the vast imperialist expansions
of Russia and the U.S.A. of the nineteenth century would remain because
the colonial cultures had been obliterated.

3
The War at Lawside

When the war started we were rather pleased with ourselves as most large families were, for we had been accepted into our proper and elevated position in Armadale. If father had been worried about the low price of metals in the last few weeks and the effect on mining and his practice, it did not worry us. The price of metals often went up and down; we were solid people.

It was something to live in a big house. Only one near us was of the same size, the Morans' down Kooyong Road on the other side; it was painted a shiny white and ours was dull grey and had not been painted since it was built in the 1890s. It might be interesting to still have the original paint on the cast-iron decoration to the balcony and veranda, but it was only red-brown picked out with dirty yellow, and the Morans' freshly painted house looked much better. It looked prosperous with a long street frontage and a tennis court which could be seen through the hedge.

We had hopeless dreams of a tennis court, hopeless in costing a hundred pounds and hopeless in a rented property; difficult too, for it would obliterate our wash-house and our lonely W.C. and it would be cramped on the back lines.

But with all that, ours was an imposing house and we looked impressive as we set out for church, seven boys and one girl, all in Sunday clothes and clean linen and bright after our Saturday-night bath.

We had two maids, and that put us at the very top of the Armadale social ladder; even the Morans did no better. To have one maid gave prestige, to have two gave prominence.

To have any domestic help was something. The cheapest sort you could have was an elderly indigent female relative; she was very cheap but lived with the family and was kicked around by them as an inferior. Better was a 'lady help', who was just what her title meant; she was a lady and lived with the family and was not kicked around so much, but cost more. Better than either was a companion; she was very superior and might be quite a young girl who wanted to get away from the country. There had to be at least one maid if there was a companion. We knew of no companions in Armadale. The other thing about her was that if any of the young fellows in the house fiddled with her she expected marriage; if it was a maid she would expect the sack.

Of course we had a washer-woman – most people did for at least a half day each week, and she was the worst paid of the local workforce. She was usually a hefty Irish widow, and she needed to be hefty. She would arrive at eight o'clock and already the fire under the copper was lighted and the water boiling; in went the wash and she pulled it out with a stick into the trough alongside, then put it through a wringer on the edge of the trough and into the next one. Then it was all hung out on the clothes-lines until it was dry; then the sheets would be pushed through the mangle and quite often her finger went too, and there would be a fuss. Our Mrs Leach was a good sort and saw out the war years with us.

Mr Marr and his son came to do the garden every Thursday; it was more than the garden could expect, and was more than adequate.

Father carried us and all these people comfortably on his back, for he was doing well. His consulting practice in civil and mining engineering had boomed since he had set up in Melbourne five years before, and expenses had dropped now that everybody lived at home and there were no boarding fees.

I suppose there were debts from the expensive days in Tasmania. There was no reserve and mother was careful, but our food was as good as could be, and we dressed well.

It could not be regarded as extravagant to have two maids with ten in the house and there was plenty of work for them and mother. Perhaps some of it was unnecessary. Every day every room in use had its carpet swept with the Bissell's sweeper or its linoleum wiped over, and only the dining room and drawing room did not demand daily attention.

The chamber pots had to be emptied – that was Milly's job – and the beds made in an elaborate sort of way. Mother's double-bed demanded a complicated ritual: the blankets and top sheet had to be folded over in a series of flat folds, requiring the co-operation of two deft and intelligent people. Dusting everything was another formal ritual.

The preparation of food was necessary and tedious, for little processed food could be bought. There were secondary benefits, for the peelings and odds and ends went into the hens' hot mash each morning and the scrapings from the porridge plates kept Lilah's cat going, supplemen-

ted by the scraps spared from the hens. There was even enough for a
dog at the times when we had one. The three women were busy all
day; only mother had a break of about half an hour in the morning
for her prayers.

We were paying our way; we even thought of buying a house and
had been to look at some. The most likely was a two-storey one with
a tower, but it overlooked the Caulfield race-course and mother thought
that it might have a bad influence on the boys.

War or no war, there was no reason to alter the routine. The calendar
might say that it was winter, but it was the proper week for spring
cleaning, the most uncomfortable week of the year.

Every room had to be cleaned in a set order. All curtains had to be
taken down and put into Monday's wash; all loose rugs and mats were
to be taken up and hung on the clothes-line in the backyard to wait
for some brother to beat them on his return in the afternoon; the fixed
carpets were to be washed and inspected for moths; the paintwork was
washed down and the windows cleaned inside by Lilah, whilst the outside
had to wait for a brother on a ladder. Every book had to be taken out,
dusted and stacked until the shelves had been wiped down, even those
in the two glazed bookcases where little dust could penetrate. Then
it all had to be re-assembled, the books put back and the curtains rehung
in the evening, and again it was some brother's job. The whole house
took the best part of a week and a very trying week it was.

It seemed like spring outside on that first Monday of the war, with
the clear sun after a frosty night. The colony of minahs in the ivy at
the back of the house strutted and scolded; the cheeky sparrows chirped,
and they were a big population with all the horses about in the street
outside; the more sedate thrushes and blackbirds sang in the sun, all
alien birds. The magpie, the only native bird heard in Armadale, dominated them all with his clear bell in the bright morning. A deep
untroubled peace and in Europe the greatest war in history had begun.

The house had quietened down for the morning; father and all the
older ones had banged the front door, each in his turn, and there was
only mother, Lilah, Milly and me left. Mother inspected me; yes, passable,
hands reasonably clean, neck passable too, cap on straight, and so it
was out of the front door, through the front gate which clanged behind
me for another day.

A turn to the right—it could have been to the left, and to school
with the Rosenfelts, but their Fraulein escorted them and that seemed
undignified—so it was to the right and up to the Wattletree Road corner
to wait about until the Allens arrived. This was the third year of waiting
for the Allens.

We were all heading for Lawside kindergarten—'kindergarten' was one of the very few German words to survive through the new war. Two of the Allen girls were real aristocrats, for they were older than I was and age conferred prestige at Lawside. A girl would stay until she was ten or even eleven and a boy would leave when he was nine. Next month I would be nine and next year I would go to Wesley preparatory school and father would pay my fees.

It was not only age which made the Allens aristocratic, it was their number; there were four girls. Moreover, their parents were important. It would have been creditable enough to have a father who wrote important things in the *Argus*, but their mother did too; she wrote the daily 'Vesta' column for ladies.

I waited on the corner for the Allens—they were far too important to be expected to wait for me. My memory is not accurate for I would like to think that this year all the four girls paraded, but there must have been only three: Margaret, the eldest; Patricia, just a bit older than me; then Betty and little Helen on her short fat legs.

They crossed Kooyong Road and along Wattletree Road we went, under the London plane trees with little balls hanging on long stalks from the leafless branches, like the bobbles hanging from the velvet cover of grandmother's little table. On the ground was a carpet of brown leaves which made a happy rustling as we kicked our way through them.

We passed the three shops on the other side of the road: three isolated shops in a sea of houses, built by some optimist in the days of the Land Boom but now so isolated that they struggled for survival; only the lolly shop flourished. It was our shop; we had chosen it on our arrival in Armadale. Owen had organized a test; each of the elder brothers had bought four ounces of cream caramels at the standard price of threepence, and our shop had given two more than its rivals. It was an amiable shop with a fat friendly lady who bustled from the back rooms when the bell above the door tinkled with our entrance.

I had walked with the Allens from my first day at school. Now, with little Helen, they went slowly enough for me to walk along the gutter—not in the gutter, but along it, and that required skill. The gutter had sloping sides, each of two rows of bluestone pitchers sloping down to the flat central row. I could put my feet on the horizontal joint between the two rows; no girl could keep her balance, but I could. The elder Allens pretended not to be impressed.

At the corner of Armadale Street we might be joined by the two Pyke girls, Gelda, my age, and Molly, a year younger. Along we all straggled until Wattletree Road died where it merged at an angle into Dandenong Road, an immensely wide road with trams running between

Lawside Kindergarten, Armadale

central plantations with trees so young that there was a clear view down the slope to St Kilda and the sparkling waters of the Bay. Down the road puffed a soft wind carrying the honey scent of wattles from the country inland.

Here at right angles was Denbigh Road, with our church at the High Street end and Lawside only a few houses from the corner with a couple of children hanging about the side gate; we all entered and broke up into our proper groups. The girls paired off; the most exalted pair of each age-group united and despised all inferior pairs. They linked arms and paraded in the girls' playground, sunnier and far better than the boys'. The boys grouped, rather than paired, and were not exclusive about age; I joined Nelson Paling, Alan Gibbs and Max Rosenfelt.

Every Monday morning was important for we had not seen each other for two days and there was a lot of talk about. One of us had been to the moving pictures and expected an audience.

Lawside looked like every other house in the street, just a one-storey house with a slate roof, and it was only when you went down the drive at the side that it revealed its importance. Across the back, hard against the fence, was the school. It was an imposing weatherboard building entered through a porch. There you took off your street shoes, hung them in a bag on your special peg, and put on the light shoes which had been in the bag. Inside was one big room, and we had not entered many bigger. It was large enough to have the older children separated from the little ones by a clear space for joint activities; light and cheerful, a nice place to go to on Monday morning.

Between the school and the house was the garden and asphalt area in front of the school and there was the wood-slatted octagonal summer-house where some of us had lessons on a good day. Beside it was a flag-pole—no other back garden had one—and on your birthday you were allowed to pull the cord to hoist the Union Jack. There was a particular little garden bed beside it and there Beverley Hetherington had planted forget-me-nots when she left with her parents for a six-month visit to England.

On the other side of the garden was another unusual item for a suburban backyard; not one W.C., but a pair. One faced the garden discreetly masked by a hedge, the other faced dismally into the side paling fence. It got me into trouble in my very first week of school.

When someone had done something anti-social, the whole school was assembled in the central area and the failing was indicated: this time it was the boys only who were kept back, so it was something a boy had done. I had the comfortable smug feeling of innocence in the presence of detected sin, but the feeling evaporated; Miss McAllister seemed to be looking at me. One of the boys had gone to the girls' W.C.—I had not known that there was sexual segregation and that we males had our own inferior W.C. What had seemed to have been an amiable conversation with a seated Patricia had been a misdemeanour.

Each day just after nine o'clock Miss McAllister came out of the back door of the house on the other side of our territory, a brisk person with black hair and a bright complexion; a kindly person but decisive, no fooling about with her. She blew a whistle and the boys and girls merged into their classes, ready to march into school—not that it was very far to go, but we marched. We marched with our hands clasped behind our backs and the elder girls marched best of all; in their eager pursuit of appreciation they raised their knees to a ridiculous height and forced their heads down and their chins out.

Into the school where all our little chairs were set in a block in the centre—that was where we had left them last thing on Friday afternoon. There in front of us was the blackboard, but it was shiny clean; on it was a text in very neat white chalk lettering and around the edge was a fascinating and elaborate red chalk border.

School began. We sang a hymn, and if it was your birthday you were allowed to choose it. Most of us knew our hymns and had our favourites, but some seemed hardly interested and really ignorant, the Pykes and Rosenfelts amongst them. Max Rosenfelt chose 'Onward Christian Soldiers', generally popular, but the sentiment may have been unlikely; Gelda Pyke picked 'Shall we Gather at the River'. Then we knelt by our little chairs for prayer: a brief one by Miss McAllister and then the Lord's Prayer. Then we picked up our chairs—just as in Sunday school—and carried them to our desks.

Our life was in the schoolroom and the playing space in front. The house was aloof from us and only entered by the girls who had piano lessons from the dark Miss Whyte. She was supposed to be fierce and smacked the fingers of the girls with a long pencil when they were unusually clumsy. She taught non-academic subjects in the school, like sewing, and I was very good at it. Miss McAllister lived there too, and so did the grey Miss Whyte, who never appeared in the school. Sometimes she would come out to the flag-pole with the fourth inmate of the house, Darky, a black spaniel, who was very friendly to us whenever we met him. But when the grey Miss Whyte brought him out on official visits he would be wearing a military sort of red jacket and Miss Whyte would tell him to die for his country; down he would go, flat on his back with his legs in the air and there he would stay until she called 'On parade'; then up he would jump, as lively as ever.

The first time I went into that house was through the front door with mother to my first annual break-up party. We had all come along from the official break-up down the street at the Presbyterian Sunday school hall; quite a crowd it was, with all the mothers there. The mothers talked and we played organized games in the two front rooms, dull they were and there was a feeling of constraint, it was like playing in church. Every one of us showed off in front of the elders.

At last that part was over; then along to the very big room with the back door leading to our playground. Here was a long table with a white cloth covered with plates of spectacular cakes, glasses of jelly and sweet things which the grey Miss Whyte had made. The only decent-looking thing was a dish of fried eggs and I wanted one. It turned out to be a half apricot on a dollop of blanc-mange.

There was a strange feeling at Lawside on that first August Monday of the war; every one of us came from homes which were excited about it and we brought that excitement with us to school. The Boer War had meant little to our parents: it could not have been lost and Australia was not really involved. This new war also could not be lost, but it was much bigger and we were in it officially, right from the very start and the German colonies were close to us.

In the first week a change came over us and we boys had a new importance, for it was only the males who were fighting. Soldiers marched and we marched every day; we marched for pleasure, not with hands behind us but hard at our sides, and we stamped our feet, as we were sure soldiers did. The girls surrendered their pre-eminence in marching and concentrated on being Red Cross nurses. In that middle-class community, it was an unlucky girl who did not have a white apron with a red cross on the front, before many days were out.

The orderly division of the playground broke down and it became the joint property of the two sexes. The boys fought their battles in their old playground but went to hospital in the summer-house on the girls' side where the nurses attended to them.

We gathered that the Belgians were holy and beautiful, but we did not know what the Belgians were. We learned that they were people rather like the early Christians, and most of us had been to 'Quo Vadis' and knew what the lions did to Christians. Now the Germans were doing far worse things to the Belgians.

Belgium was 'Gallant Little Belgium' and the people were the 'gallant starving Belgians' and from now on, if we did not finish our porridge we were told how much the Belgians needed it. In February of the next year the *Argus* described how they were getting it: 'Food is not at an extraordinary price. Bread is sold for about 2d a pound–Meat is fairly cheap and plentiful–Milk is about 2½d a quart. Eggs are very scarce, vegetables are cheap: butter is about 1/6d a pound'. But we still saved our pennies for the gallant starving Belgians.

The Germans were unspeakably horrible. We had known Germans and they had seemed nice people, but all the time they had been wicked and we had not recognized it. Marion Schneider had been head-girl not so long ago and it was a shock to know that all the time she had been a secret German. Her name showed it and if we had known that her mother was an unspotted Australian and that her father had been born and lived all his life close by, it would have made no difference.

And old Mr Himmer, who taught music in a house a few doors from the school, he was a German. He had seemed such a jolly old chap who spoke to us as we passed his house; now no one would answer him if he spoke to them. Those foreign surnames were all German unless they ended in 'i' or 'o'.

Max had a German name but it did not seem to worry him or affect his position at school. He was Austrian, and although Austria was on Germany's side, they were not fighting England, not yet.

In fact, Max seemed to feel rather superior to us. He came from Europe with its glittering Kings and Emperors whose soldiers fought real wars, not sordid amateur ones like ours in South Africa, and they fought them in splendid uniforms, not like the dull khaki forced on us by those amateur Boers.

His Austrians dressed in spotless white and his Hungarians galloped along with flashing sabres, nothing meanly utilitarian like our troops.

They were far more attractive than the French infantry with scarlet trousers and blue frock-coats, or the Belgians in a similar get-up, but with top-hats instead of the French peaked caps. The French cavalry was good: they had shining helmets, like our firemen, but trailing a brush of horse-hair and they wore shining breast-plates, but even they were vulgar compared to Max's Austrians.

My ideas of war came from the *Boys' Own Paper* where a young officer, pathetically but not mortally wounded, was propped with his back against a tree with a bandage around his head and one arm in a sling – for war-wounds were confined to gashes on the head and holes in the arm – whilst he was touchingly comforted by one of his faithful men. Those wounds, suffered for the glory of his country, seemed a small price to pay for being transformed into an interesting hero.

We were not completely ignorant of military affairs at Lawside because last year Jack Wilkinson had been a fellow student and his father was Colonel Wilkinson and lived in Denbigh Road quite near the school. They were a martial family: Jack was hoping to go into the Australian navy as a thirteen-year-old trainee officer, and Colonel Wilkinson was important – I think he was the top army engineer.

Quite recently I had had direct contact with the Australian army.

Last birthday Alan Gibbs had been given a tricycle and I badly wanted one. I had got it last Christmas. Uncle Sam sent an annual Christmas gift to mother of £5; it was divided amongst the family and my share was five shillings but mother made up the rest and I got a tricycle costing fifteen shillings. Maybe it was not as good as Alan's: the big front wheel was badly set and cut into the enclosing fork; but still, it was a trike.

One Saturday afternoon Neil and I met another eight-year-old on his trike, and Neil arranged a race for us down the slope of Kooyong Road from Wattletree Road, my rival on the footpath on the other side of the road and me on ours. Off I went, down the six-foot strip of asphalt, and I had reached maximum acceleration when out stepped Major and Mrs Johnston from their front gate.

Major Johnston may have retired from the army but he was still a fine erect soldierly figure, with a well-pressed grey suit, grey Homburg, a flower in his buttonhole, gloves and a walking stick. Mrs Johnston was ample and fluffy with a wide hat and veil and a sunshade. They were out for their usual 3.30 promenade.

There was not a chance of missing them and I went slap into Mrs Johnston's backside. She was very outspoken. The major was very considerate and excused me to her and calmed her down and we parted friends. It had been almost worth it to have had this consideration from such a fine man, through contact with his wife.

If Max, Alan Gibbs or Nelson Paling came home with me after school, sometimes we got out the flat red box with the soldiers in it. It was the final depot for all the soldiers of the six elder brothers and many of them were casualties. It was not so bad if a man had lost a head, a bit of match inserted into the lead hollow of the head would keep it in place, but there was no cure for an arm, leg or rifle lost in action. Most of them were infantry and quite cheap by the dozen, but it was not a really imposing army with its medley of red uniforms and the maimed ones serving as second-line troops. They seemed a silly lot to us, all standing up and shooting from the shoulder and so exposing themselves in a reckless way. It might be reasonable against natives but silly against the Germans. I doubt if the war added much to their popularity, but they were the only toy soldiers we had.

We excused the cavalry more. Their bright but chipped uniforms were less out of place. They were far more expensive, and they often had an arm which moved and held a sword or a lance—the lance did not last at all well, and usually the arm itself just hung down and trailed its weapon, for the hinge was not rigid or permanent. Sometimes the arm had come right off and had to be balanced on the lead stump. Those soldiers never seemed convincing; they had been made archaic by the new war and they were only a wet-day army.

We preferred the Daisy air gun: it cost five shillings and most boys between eight and fourteen had one. It fired round lead pellets by compressed air; the compression was made by bending the rifle at its hinge above the stock and you dropped a pellet down the barrel. They looked like miniature rifles. They could sting quite a bit at short distances and could damage an eye, so we did not shoot at each other, only at bottles or sparrows.

There was dangerous ammunition available, but at great cost. Threepence would buy a dart, a vicious point of metal with a fringe of soft hair which just fitted the barrel when it was broken for loading. Darts could easily blind an eye. They travelled much further than pellets but their cost made them rare.

Once we threw away ninepence. A man was mending the roof of the Gregsons' shed and we were able to shoot three darts into his backside across the Rosenfelts' garden before he realized what had hit him. We did not grudge him his three darts. Neil shot a couple into my buttocks as I climbed up the ivy at the back of the house, but we salvaged those.

When a boy became fourteen he hoped to have a pea-rifle, a .22 calibre gun which was a real rifle in all its essentials, lethal to rabbits and to other boys, particularly if you bought the more expensive 'long' cartridges. They carried too far to be used in backyards and had to be taken to the country beyond the tram terminus where there might be a sitting rabbit; those .22s killed many times more rabbits than boys. Rifles and pseudo-rifles were the most popular war-time toys and they were more; the boys who shot the .22s in 1914 were getting their first training for rifle shooting in France in 1918.

Everybody wanted to do something about the war and the obvious thing to do was to provide money, preferably somebody else's; even we children could do that. Miss McAllister gave each of us a little canvas bag with a string around its neck for pennies; all our pennies would go towards something or other, probably it was those Belgians. It would be a glorious thing to present the fattest bag on Monday morning, but I was at a disadvantage. The others at home seemed to be unconcerned and the only regular penny I got was on Saturday morning after mother had inspected the back paths to be sure they had been properly swept, and even then I would not get it unless I had dried the spoons and forks at washing up. I never had a chance against those children of more lavish families.

By the end of the first week we all carried flags to school. Everybody seemed to produce a flag from somewhere and quite a reasonably sized Union Jack could be bought for threepence.

In the streets flags were everywhere. They flew from buildings in the city, cars carried them, and even our baker's cart had a little one beside the driver; they blossomed from previously bare poles in front gardens—it would be suspicious to have a flag-pole and no flag.

The most patriotic flag of all was carried by a girl riding on a horse; nothing could be more patriotic than a girl with a big Union Jack and she rode astride, like Joan of Arc, and not side-saddle like a lady.

Funny how the idea lasted. In 1942 when the second war was still fun in Australia, girls rode horses in Perth carrying flags, but Australian ones. In 1914 the Union Jack was the commonest flag for this was England's war. In any case, the Union Jack was the easiest to buy and we were doubtful about what colour the Australian flag really was. The red one was commoner than the blue; it was our merchant navy flag, just like the British one but with our stars on it. Later it was decided that the blue one was official and looked nicer, but then nobody seemed to know or care; anyway, it was a new thing with no glorious history behind it. It was as new as our patched-up Commonwealth and we cared little more about its flag than we had about our State flags in the old days. The Union Jack was good enough for us.

There were a few French flags about, they must have been pre-war stock, far more common were Belgian flags; no one had seen one before August, but now they were the most respectable of foreign flags. They had vertical stripes of red, yellow and black; they must have been put into production locally in the first days of the war. The colours stood out against the red, white and blue of Britain and France and the blue and white of Russia; but although Russia was our ally her flag was rare, we did not seem to want to display it.

Not only flags; there were bugles. Bugles had been an annoyance for years; some young fellow in the Cadets or Citizen Forces would practise on his bugle in his backyard. Now he could blow it in the streets of Melbourne and the suburbs. Best of all was to ride in a car with a big Union Jack, blowing away on a bugle.

The war changed our scrapbooks. Nearly every one of us had one and we would show it to the others when they came round to play after school, and sometimes we would take it to school.

They were big books with blank sheets of rough paper inside and we collected things to stick into them; then on a wet Saturday afternoon we would be kept quiet by pasting in the things which we had amassed.

At home we had the scrapbooks from the parents' younger days; the one from father's family was not his personal one and had suffered from childish witticisms, but mother's was superb. They both still exist. The centre of each page was something important, usually a coloured picture or a panel with a suitable poem. On one page of mother's book a delightful original drawing by Chevalier, very free and very different from his constipated paintings. As surrounding decoration mother had pasted dried flowers, ferns and sea-weed, as well as tiny bright pictures, just like the ones we had. An interesting thing was that her book had pages from her own mother's scrapbook bound in. The tiny pictures were even smaller than ours and quite as bright. Amongst the flowers and fat children were two little groups, each of a Prussian soldier killing a Frenchman, thus giving a hint of English sentiment during the Franco-Prussian War.

Neil's and my scrapbooks were very crude in comparison. There was a coloured picture in the centre of each page, usually from the Christmas supplement of an English journal, surrounded by the usual decorations. At Lock's shop in High Street a penny would buy a length of assorted tiny pictures in bright colours: angels, cherubs and sexless babies, parrots, sleeping cats, cottages under oak trees and an occasional soldier in a bright uniform. If our luck was in, there would be a bottle of glue available; otherwise it would have to be flour paste; we were not very good at making it and it was messy and the pictures often dropped out afterwards.

The war made our scrapbooks colourless. Of course they had to be about the war. The only appropriate coloured pictures were of Red Cross nurses and you could have only one of them, so it had to be a battle-ship in action in black-and-white taken from the *Illustrated London News*. Soldiers and sailors were all we could stick around it, and the only ones available were hopelessly old-fashioned in their bright uniforms. We got tired of our scrapbooks.

Ellison Harvie, who had left Lawside the previous year, did better. She was a serious scholarly type who later became the most successful woman architect in Melbourne, and her capacity already showed. Her scrapbook was not a collection of decorations, but an anthology of war poetry gathered from English and Australian journals. Its most significant item was the history of Ginger Mick, a Melbourne larrikin, who was moved to enlist and was refined and ennobled by the army until he finally died heroically for his country. Her book lasted out the whole war and for fifty years after.

Scrapbooks were not the only things which girls managed better than us males. We felt inferior. The war brought unrest and rebellion. We, the depressed minority at Lawside, rose against our oppressors. We had always done silly things to annoy the girls; now we did aggressive things.

In the lighter discipline of Sunday school it had always been our ambition to tie a girl's hair around the top rung of her chair, but none of us had tried it at Lawside. I managed it and tied Patricia Allen's hair around very effectively, a thing I would never have attempted in the days of peace.

Although we resented the girls as a group, each of us had his girl. My girl was Joan, a pretty little thing with auburn hair and brown eyes. One eye was of glass because she had been in a car accident, but she was so remote that I only knew about her eye years after.

Alan Gibbs' girl was Tasma, an unusual name, and her brother was Cleve. Their father had done well out of the Cleveland mine in Tasmania.

The last lesson on Friday afternoon was a story read to us by Miss McAllister, to all of us in our rows of chairs in the centre of the school-room. The story started. Tasma was sitting behind Alan. Alan tilted back his chair, reached out his arms behind his head and pulled down Tasma's head and kissed her.

Alan was sent out. I made a fuss about the treatment of my friend and was also sent out. We were by ourselves in shared disgrace. We put on our street shoes in the entrance porch and then got all the other bags of street shoes and threw them over the back fence.

We knew they would catch up with us in time but it would be longer if we did not go home, so we went to Nelson Paling's house and played there. It was a long time before we were found, and it was important that we should be found as the others needed their street shoes over the weekend. But I don't think anything very drastic happened to us.

4

The Grown-ups' War

Saturday 12 September: Melbourne showed its enthusiasm and jubilation over the news of 'Australia's bold attack on New Guinea and the Allied victory in Europe'. We held a Patriotic Carnival in aid of the Patriotic Fund in the Exhibition Building, but there was only room for 40 000 and many thousands failed to gain admission. A great procession went to it through the city. Five hundred men of the new forces, 1000 from the Rifle Clubs, then those Boy Scouts and the Imperial and Victorian Associations, then costers, donkeys and clowns and stockriders from all parts of the State: two miles of procession. The troops drew up in the arena under the arc lights, then in came the Boy Scouts, semaphoring and Morse signalling, boxing, wrestling, drilling and tent-pitching, rushing about everywhere with stretchers and ambulances. Yes, it would be something to be one of those Boy Scouts.

Melba had started doing things. She had given a concert and £1390 had gone to the Patriotic Fund. She would keep giving concerts and doing other things, like raffling vegetables from her country home, for a couple of years before she got a bit tired of it all.

Bazaars were very popular in the first years of the war; bazaars to raise money for the Red Cross or the Belgians. The first I went to was in the Beaumaris Hotel. I walked to it from the Stevens' house at Mentone with their elderly, dwarfish and subnormal maid – but she was a good sort. Dusty and very much out-of-place we must have looked in a very social gathering. We did not have the money to buy anything much, but our entrance money allowed us to hear someone almost as important as Melba sing patriotic songs. The second bazaar was in the grounds of a big house in Toorak and it was much better. People had given things for the bazaar and the penny bran-pie dip turned out to be a good investment.

This new war of ours was really exciting and stimulating, it gave us a sudden zest. It was far better than the football; not everybody was interested in the League games, but everybody was interested in the war and we got the progress score every day in the morning paper and every day it became clearer that we were winning easily.

The League teams of the war were playing in Europe. We were only in the reserves but we hoped and we expected that our own team would be allowed on the field before the end of the match. We Australians did not know very much about the rules, but every time the other side scored, we yelled 'foul'. We called the umpire's attention to the fouls every Sunday at church. We hoped that the great nations would recognize and appreciate our keenness and notice that we had already scored; it might not be a great matter in comparison with theirs, but it was spectacular.

We had won the first British victory of the war. On 8 September the German Pacific colonies capitulated to an Australian expeditionary force after a battle in which quite a lot of people were killed. The isolated colony of Samoa had already surrendered to the New Zealanders, but it was just one isolated colony and there had been no fighting. There was no fuss made about the Australian victory in the English papers and hardly a mention of it in our own, but it seemed very creditable to have organized a combined naval and military expedition in such a short time, particularly as we thought that the Japanese intended to capture all the German Pacific possessions. It was certainly the first British victory and the first sizeable bit of German territory captured: immense areas of land compared to the little backyards that thousands were already being killed for in France.

The Germans had their warships of the Pacific Squadron somewhere, but we did not know where, and they had wireless to direct them. Wireless was a very new thing. Only a few years ago the only contact had been by cable and the British controlled the cables. Now wireless could be received and transmitted by ships. In 1900 the range of wireless had been 200 miles but ten years later it was 6000 miles. The Germans had wireless stations all over the place which could communicate with Berlin and with each other and with German warships at sea. Britain asked Australia to knock out the ones near us.

Victoria naval reservists were called up to the depot at Williamstown, only a few miles from the city. A couple of days later a special train came into the depot, loaded them all on board, and took them to Sydney. There they joined the South Australian, Queensland and New South Wales contingents on board the *Berrima*, a requisitioned P. & O. liner, all in the greatest secrecy.

Secrecy? The *Berrima* steamed down Sydney Harbour with an Australian naval force as a guard against the German Pacific Squadron, down the Harbour through hundreds of yachts dressed with flags, and steamers sounding their sirens. They sailed to Palm Island off the Queensland coast opposite Townsville. They spent a week there dyeing their white naval uniforms jungle green and doing jungle training and musketry.

The Victorian contingent did best at musketry, and best of the Victorians was Chief Petty Officer Hooks of Melbourne. When the first landing was made in boats from the destroyers, the Victorians manned them and Hooks was in the bows. He was the first man ashore, the first man in hostile territory of the war—the New Zealanders in Samoa had landed after capitulation.

There was no opposition to the landing, just a quiet beach with a stone jetty and a Chinese store and a straight road leading inland. Hooks went up that road again sixty years later and remembered it all.

It was half-light on landing and the party stopped for breakfast at daybreak. They were fired on; they scattered and found a couple of Germans. Two Australians shot at the same time and both of them hit the same German in the wrist. The doctor came up and amputated the hand as the man stood up, and on they went. The doctor pulled off his red-cross brassard and went in as a combatant; he was the first Australian officer to be killed in the war. A map had been captured and they had some idea of the opposition and where the wireless station was. Along the road two Germans were in foxholes waiting to detonate a mine in the road; they had no trouble there, and on they went. At dark they returned to the shore and a bigger party went on next day and got to the wireless station and took the surrender of the German Pacific forces. On his return sixty years later Hooks saw the graves and the monument to the seven men killed—the Germans lost more, mostly their native police. On the monument also were fifty other names: the crew of Australian submarine, E.1. which had disappeared at that time. Round those graves of the first casualties of the first war were hundreds of graves of those who died in World War II.

Later in the war New Guinea would have been exciting news, for victories were scarce, but at that time it hardly got a line in any newspaper. The only substantial reference was later when a military officer was charged with looting—it was something petty, like stamps from the post-office.

Whilst all this was very creditable, we recognized that it was a small matter compared to the great things happening in Europe. Our maritime escapade was tiny compared to the great naval events. We all knew that England and Europe had twice been saved in a great war by the English ships; we knew all about Drake and Nelson and expected a great naval victory which would decide the war.

We got our naval victory. In the first week of the war we read of a great naval battle that had been fought; the Germans had been trounced and had lost nineteen warships. Now we were still waiting for details and confirmation and we kept on waiting. It was the first paper victory of the war.

Then we felt much better: we heard that three German light cruisers had been sunk. There was no delay or doubt this time, they had really been sunk. But whilst we were feeling good, the Germans torpedoed three great battleships and the score was very much in their favour.

Then there was another naval victory, and in some ways it was a pity, because the French had won it. Our war-time bible, the London *Times*, confirmed the news which was printed in the *Argus*. The French had captured the German battleship *Goeben* and the cruiser *Breslau* and sunk the gunboat *Panther*.

Three days later the same ships were being chased around again; but they were cornered, there was no hope of their escape, the Mediterranean was packed with British and French warships and a British flotilla had been waiting for two years for just this chance. But the two big British ships superior to the *Goeben* went off for the day to Salonika and the *Goeben* sank two smaller ones and got clear away to the neutral waters of Turkey.

The Turks had two big ships building in English shipyards and they were now ready and the Turkish crews were in England to take them over. Those ships were important to Turkey, for they would master the Russian Black Sea fleet. Four million pounds had already been paid for them and much of the money had been raised by public appeal. Turkey was still neutral but the British seized the ships and the Turks were furious.

The *Goeben* was in the Dardanelles and there was a thought that Turkey might buy her and her companion. Although our papers thought it was unlikely, Turkey did buy them; but she gave the assurance that they were not for use against Russia. The *Goeben* became the *Sultan Yamiz*. One day she steamed up the Bosporus and came to a stop in front of the Russian ambassador's house on the waterfront; the sailors came on deck in German naval uniform and gave him a concert of German national songs; then, putting on fezzes, they sailed away. Turkey came in on Germany's side on 3 November.

The French had captured the *Goeben*; now the Russians destroyed her. She was left as a burning hulk after a Russian attack, so they said, but somehow she survived the war as the flagship of the Turkish navy and kept giving trouble to the Russians.

Things were disappointing at sea. The German armed merchantmen were all eventually sunk, but not before they had sunk a far greater tonnage of Allied vessels. Admiral Spey's little squadron ran about the south Atlantic and sank two bigger British warships and the last of the Germans was only cleaned up as she lay at anchor in Chilean neutral waters; we would not have liked it if the Germans had done that to one of ours.

Our warships kept blowing themselves up or getting torpedoed. Drake seemed to have changed sides.

We said Britannia ruled the waves, yet in December German cruisers crossed the North Sea and shelled Scarborough and Hartlepool and 120 civilians were killed. We were very indignant at the slaughter of civilians and took quick revenge. We retaliated with the 'most tremendous bombardment of the war' on the enemy coast—well, not the German coast, but the coast of German-occupied Belgium and any civilians killed were under German protection.

The Russians had a second naval success. They sank the German cruiser *Emden* off the China coast and she remained sunk for six weeks. Then she appeared in the Bay of Bengal and immediately sank five British merchant ships. Her men were very considerate to the crews and took them on board until they could be transferred to a ship which was spared to take them away to safety. When they left, they cheered the *Emden*.

She sailed through the shoal waters outside Penang without a pilot and sank a Russian warship and a French destroyer safely anchored in the harbour; a lot of local ladies who had been enjoying Russian hospitality overnight were drowned.

Shipping around the coast of India was paralysed by the *Emden*: she sank ship after ship, including a dredge headed for Tasmania for dredging the Tamar below Launceston. She was impertinent enough to shell the harbour at Madras, not so far from the British naval base at Trincomalee.

Things were going well in the real war in Europe. Gallant little Belgium was resisting bravely and fighting back. She recaptured Liège and inflicted tremendous losses on the Germans and they were on the verge of mutiny; but Liège remained in German hands. The Germans were retreating in disorder through Belgium, but our maps seemed to show that they were still advancing.

Sir George Reid, our High Commissioner in London, always sent out really good news. This time it was that Brussels had been recaptured by a combined Anglo-French force of 75 000 men. This cheered us up, but we heard no more about it. He also said that a force of Russians were assisting the Belgians. This was quite as credible as the tale that Cossacks had been seen on the French front.

Our own British troops were in France and had won a victory on their first engagement. Well, perhaps not quite a victory, but they had made a very creditable retreat, a very promising opening to their efforts—just like the evacuation of Dunkirk in the next war. Bad staff work had put them in an exposed position and they had been able to retreat just in time—the Retreat from Mons. It had been a near-run thing and they only got away with divine assistance. It is a pity that we only heard about it a year later; it would have been very heartening at the time.

The German cavalry were just about to finish them off when God looked out of his little window in the sky and saw that his side was in bad trouble. At once he sent down a battalion of angels and the Germans reeled back in dismay.

If we had heard about the appearance of the angels at the time it would have given us an early assurance that we were fighting on the side of God and right and were receiving the same consideration as the Israelites did on their crossing of the Red Sea. There had not been many miracles lately and this was a really modern one. Later in the war, Lock's newsagency and stationery shop in High Street had a big coloured picture of the British troops and the angels in the sky above them, and in the distance, the discomfited Germans.

It would be comforting to have authentic proof of the appearance of those angels. In Manchester Dr Horton, a leading Congregationalist minister, could vouch for them, and Congregationalists were very conservative about angels: 'the story repeated by so many witnesses that if anything can be established by contemporary evidence, it is established'. This was not the only ecclesiastical confirmation. The Reverend J. Best in his sermon at Ballarat read a letter from an eye-witness describing the angel host; two independent clerical supporters and still there were doubts. It was said that the story had no more substance than the story of the Russian army in France; that it was only a development of a story in a London journal of the British soldiers invoking St George, who arranged that the archers of Agincourt should come to the support of us and our new ally, their old enemy. A couple of months later the Sydney *Bulletin* had an article. Private Robert Cleave of the Cheshire Regiment was prepared to swear he had seen the angels, and he did so before a J.P. His military record was searched. He had been called up the day before the battle of Mons and was in barracks in Chester at the time. But the miracle was still believed, and is to this day.

The British and French were winning victory after victory and some little river or hamlet became known all over the world. But the victory seemed to evaporate in a week or two and the names dropped back into obscurity. Some revived a couple of years later when the fighting moved back to them: not as the places of old victories, but as names of ill-omen.

That early fighting was savage; later there would never be such a high proportion of casualties in relation to the number of men engaged. The small British expeditionary force was being crippled although it was all regular army and the officers were all gentlemen.

Lord Esher, a crony of the King, wrote 'that there will come a day when the flower of our manhood will have been gathered by the reaper, and when the casualty lists will contain none but plebeian names'. Only officers' names appeared in the lists and things looked so serious that some plebeians might become officers.

Those officers may have been young fellows with no qualification for command except their privileged social position, but they died as their inevitable duty, following the tradition which made them expose themselves to danger, even unnecessary danger, as an example to their men. They were very exposed anyway, with their very distinctive uniforms and their swords; yes, their swords. The infantry officers in the very early days had swords and it was months before it was realized that they were poor weapons against machine-guns.

On the walls of the village churches of England are mural tablets to them, each to some young chap from the big house who fell in some very respectable regiment, aged twenty-four or so. Outside the south door of the church or at the village cross-road is the village memorial, a slim octagonal cross with a crusader's sword set on it and on panels around the base are the names of those from the village who served, as privates, with an occasional N.C.O. and a rare officer. The number of those shown as killed is surprisingly low compared to Australian memorials.

In 1914 the British officers came from country estates, and the men from the cities. Later the officers were plebeians from the suburbs and towns and the men from everywhere.

'The Russian Steamroller' was moving forward. We thought that was splendid and we liked the pictures of it squashing the Germans. The Russians were in East Prussia besieging Königsberg and also doing very well against the Austrians. They were behaving far better than expected and had promised to restore the integrity of Poland, the whole of Poland including the Austrian and German bits, and they were going so far as to hint that they would grant Jews equal civil and political rights. It was very encouraging.

At the end of August it was STRAIGHT TO BERLIN and a couple of weeks later, WAY OPEN TO VIENNA. CAPITAL MAY BE REACHED BY MIDDLE OF OCTOBER: 'The Eastern campaign has so far developed with practically uniform success for the Russian arms'. Then they had a victory at Tannenberg and five weeks later, we saw pictures of the mass graves of Germans killed.

As the weeks went by we gathered that the Germans were not really worried about their defeat, and it certainly did not show on our maps: in fact the place-names where we were fighting were further east, into Russia.

We were given no hint that the Germans, out-numbered two to one, had annihilated two Russian corps and captured 125 000 prisoners and 500 guns at the Battle of Tannenberg, or that in the following month at the Masurian Lakes, in east Prussia, they had got another 125 000 prisoners and 150 guns. The Russian Minister for War said that the German claims of victory were ridiculous.

Still more Russian successes: FOE'S GREATEST REVERSE. DEFEAT OF ENEMY PROVES COMPLETE. GERMAN POSITION HOPELESS: 'The Russians do not hesitate to say that German generalship has broken down, and that German strategy is so bookish everywhere it has failed to survive'. ·

We had some regret that the war was being won by Russia, for we could produce no very encouraging news from France. It had seemed pretty good at the beginning when French territory was intact and the French were into Alsace. Then the Germans were in France, having got through Belgium quicker than they had expected.

The Germans were certainly in France; suddenly they were just outside Paris. Then there was a victory for the 'Allies', a new word meaning everybody on our side. This one, the Battle of the Marne, really was a victory, although at the time we did not think much of it: it was too near Paris, and the victory we hoped for would be near Berlin. The French were able to gather superior forces, twenty-seven divisions against thirteen, and throw back the Germans from the Marne to the Aisne. It was a genuine big victory, the only one we would win on the Western Front until the middle of 1918.

We expected that the tide of war had turned and that the Germans would be chased back to their own border and beyond, but they stayed on the Aisne. Both sides dug continuous lines of trenches from the Belgian coast to the Swiss Alps, and there they stayed, shooting at each other.

We could trust our generals. The imperturbable Joffre of the French had not panicked when his armies were tumbling back, and now he would lead them into Germany. We had an even surer trust in our massive and equally imperturbable Lord Kitchener, who directed us from the War Office in London. We felt that we partly owned him, for he had visited Australia to advise on defence and the military training scheme, and soon he would be looking at us with his bulbous eyes above his handle-bar moustache and pointing at us and suggesting that our country needed us. Those posters would be everywhere.

We knew little about Sir John French, our commander in France, but now we read that he was A SECOND MARLBOROUGH and that it was really he and his troops who were responsible for the German retreat from the Marne; we surely could rely on him. We could, but his second-in-command did not and was intriguing for his position.

Sir Douglas Haig kept a diary so that posterity could fully appreciate him and his efforts. 'I know in my own heart that French is quite unfit for this great command. I am determined to behave as I did in the South African war, namely, to be thoroughly loyal and do my duty as a subordinate should.'

Within weeks he recorded that he had told Lord Haldane, Minister for War, that French had made a mess of the first engagement; then he passed on his views to Lord Kitchener; then he and Sir Henry Wilson, Secretary for War, had decided it was time to make a change.

Haig was a personal friend of the King and felt it his duty to tell him that French did not have the capacity or 'military knowledge sufficiently thorough to enable him to discharge properly the very difficult duties'. He arranged for his views on his superior to be put before the Prime Minister and Cabinet. He leaked out that he had lent French two thousand pounds and the repayment had been slow. If all these things were not enough, he could count on the rat-bag *Daily Mail* and its owner, Lord Northcliffe. He got what he wanted in the end.

Now there was to be war in the air. We knew it would come and expected that it would be interesting. The French had used balloons when they were besieged in Paris and we had used them for observation in South Africa, but we thought airships would be far more effective. They were cigar-shaped balloons with an engine and propeller which could take them where they were needed – with luck and no head-winds. The major nations had experimented with them in a vague sort of way, but only Germany had done any good.

Count von Zeppelin had built big rigid airships with engines and propellers in different parts of them and they could fly high and fast. They had already dropped bombs on Antwerp and would be able to fly across the Channel. There was little that could be done about them; they could fly so high that it would be a lucky gun which could shoot them down; it would take a long time for one of the new aeroplanes to get up to their level, and even then there was not much it could do. Shooting into them would not be much good and the only real hope would be to crash-land on them. The big trouble with them was that they were filled with hydrogen and it was highly flammable – perhaps incendiary bullets would make a difference, if they could be produced.

Aeroplanes seemed much more promising and already they were more effective than when Blériot first flew the Channel in 1909. A German bi-plane had stayed up in the air for a record time of twenty-four hours and an American was planning to cross the Atlantic in July 1914. His plane would not take off with its stipulated load, but he hoped that adjustments would ensure a successful flight. A race from London to Paris and back had produced a speed of sixty-three miles an hour. Planes were obviously going to be of importance and the armies all had them. They could take off from fields quite close to the fighting and get a bird's-eye view of what the enemy was up to and then fly back with the information, but they must be ready to defend themselves against enemy planes.

They were actually fighting in the air. A British plane came out of a cloud and saw a German plane immediately below; it swooped down to within revolver range and the pilot emptied all chambers into the German before entering the clouds again. He thought he might have brought the German down, as he saw a lot of Tommies surrounding what looked to be a German plane. Another time a Belgian plane flew straight into the side of a German plane and cut it in half.

Our High Commissioner in London, Sir George Reid, who cabled out the very latest and the most incredible stories, reported that a German army surgeon said that two Allied airmen had shot fifty steel arrows at German soldiers in camp and scored thirteen casualties.

Now he also let us know that the Russians had sent an army of 250 000 men to France, in addition to the first lot he had reported in Belgium.

We were not too sure of the next story in the papers, but we hoped it was true. A Dane reported that 150 000 Japanese were coming across Asia to join in the conquest of east Germany; he had seen the troop-trains at a railway junction in Siberia. That number would have needed a lot of troop-trains.

Britain had accepted our offer of 20 000 men at the very start of the war and they were all in camp by the end of August. Most of them were what was asked for – men with previous military experience in the Citizen Forces or some other military body. They had shaken down into place by the end of the month.

Another 6000 were offered on 3 September, over and above reinforcements and replacements for the first lot, and Colonel Monash was put in command of the new brigade. Others of Monash's rank had fought in the South African war but there was little questioning of his appointment.

Enlistment was now more open and previous military experience was
not required. Men came in from the country to the enlistment centres
in the State capitals and it was noticed that the new recruits were superior
in physique to the first intake. The minimum height was 5 feet 6 inches,
but the new men were generally far taller and they were hefty. But no
matter how splendid a specimen he was, a man was rejected if he depended
on false teeth. Men offered to bring along one or two spare plates with
them if only they were accepted, and someone wrote to the *Argus* suggesting that the army itself should set up a repository of false teeth in some
convenient place.

My brother Keith put his name down for the Engineers ready for
enlistment when he was required.

It was 25 September, not so many weeks since the new troops had
gone into camp. Now they were to go overseas, to England, we thought.
They marched through Melbourne in the drizzling rain up to Parliament
House where the Governor-General took the salute.

Less than two months had made the recruits into an army: it was
a completely new sort of army, but we had doubts whether it was a
proper sort of army.

There were no flags, no bright uniforms, all just khaki, a sombre
procession of baggy uniforms. We knew that in other States the same
sort of men were marching in the same sort of uniform, the Australian
uniform. It was very like the uniforms on the monuments to those
who had gone to the Boer War, but that already seemed to have been
a little war. Only 16 500 men had gone to that one, but now there
were 20 000 leaving soon and more to follow.

We had already seen many uniforms about the streets, but they had
usually been those of the Senior Cadets. They had the same breeches
covering the knees and the same puttees below, but the Senior Cadets
had worn a Garibaldi shirt tucked into the top of the breeches and a
leather belt, an adolescent development of the juvenile Boy Scout uniform. The uniforms in the parade looked adult.

The A.I.F. had baggy jackets with four big pockets, a sort of military
Norfolk jacket; the units which had something to do with horses, like
the artillery, had leather leggings and wide riding breeches and carried
their ammunition in a bandolier slung over the left shoulder; the infantry
had twin-sets of ammunition pouches worn as a sort of brassière.

All wore slouch hats, the brim turned up on the left out of the way
of a sloped rifle. Our State troops before federation had had slouch hats
of different sorts but these were all the same. By the end of the Boer
War most of the British troops had been issued with slouch hats; the
Boers had them too, but they turned up theirs on the right and that

seemed a silly thing to do. From now on those slouch hats were to be distinctively Australian.

There was nothing colourful at all. These soldiers did not have bright badges like those worn by the Citizen Forces who had taken them over from the Volunteers. They were just one badge in two different sizes and it was a dark bronze colour – the Rising Sun. This was a very distinctive Australian badge, but it did not start out that way.

When a badge was needed for the Australian Imperial Force someone had suggested a trophy of arms, a semi-circle of swords or bayonets captured from the French or Russians, like the ones on the walls of military clubs and army messes. But by the time the manufacturer produced a sample, the radiating swords looked like the rays of the rising sun. It was accepted as something really Australian; the Canadians could have their Maple Leaf and the New Zealanders their Kiwi – it never got off the ground, anyway; but the Rising Sun was ours and very good for a rising country.

There was nothing gloriously martial about the procession; it looked almost ominous in an easy-going sort of way. We began to think that the uniform might be an efficient sort of dress for a war which already seemed to demand efficiency. But we really did like the only bit of nonsense – the emu plumes in the hats of the Light Horse. They lacked colour, but they hinted of traditional glory and were distinctly Australian.

Off they went and soon we knew that they had sailed and that a convoy had assembled to bring troops from New Zealand and the other States. A convoy was needed, for the German cruiser *Emden* was still loose in the Indian Ocean.

It was a relief to read in the *Argus* that the *Emden* had been captured at last. She had surrendered after only one shot had been fired at her by a British cruiser; those Germans knew that it was useless to try to fight the Royal Navy, but we had expected that she would have made a fight of it. Then it turned out that the report was false and she was still loose about the place.

It was to be expected that the 'Six' – the six associated public schools of Victoria – would set an example, and so they should, for they were patterned on the English public schools where every boy was expected to go into the army as soon as it would take him, and he would go in expecting his commission as a right. It would be some time before a boy from the English grammar schools would be accepted as a 'temporary gentleman'.

The schools all had cadet corps, but at the English public schools they were called Officers' Training Corps, the O.T.C. This applied to all the public schools, even the cheapest, whose fees were less than one-third of the most expensive.

Our public school fees were higher than the other schools and assumed superiority but did not expect commissions for their boys. Their cadets were called cadets and had been absorbed into the compulsory training scheme as companies of the local battalion and wore the same uniform. They did their drills on Wednesday afternoons instead of in the evenings and Saturday afternoons, but had no other privileges.

When a boy left school at eighteen he went along with his parents' consent and joined up as a private. The rule was that all A.I.F. enlistments had to be twenty-three before becoming officers. It turned out to be a bad rule, for many potential officers were killed before they got a chance of leading. Once a man had been in action, the age limit was relaxed, but even then it was more important to have ability than to have been at a public school.

The University was quite as patriotic. The students had started off well by singing 'God Save the King' after lectures on the eve of the war. Many had rushed off to enlist and abandoned their courses; others decided to wait to complete their examinations in three months' time, hoping that the war would still be available to them. Everybody started drilling and rifle-shooting, not only the young chaps looking forward to the army, but professors, lecturers and laboratory assistants; they all drilled as a patriotic duty. The women started knitting socks and making shirts and pyjamas for the Red Cross.

Now that the first lot had left and the second was training in camp, there was a feeling that more men should be ready to go, even if the war was over before they got to it. Keith was restive because he had not been called up for the Engineers.

The Compulsory Training scheme gained popularity and some who had completed their term returned as volunteers. Junior Cadets of twelve, Senior Cadets of fourteen and Citizen Forces of seventeen and up, all willingly attended their boring sessions of drill.

It was not completely silly. Drill compresses a group into a team because the individual members share the common boredom. Drill was still accepted as the most important part of military training and had survived from the times when lines of men stood up and shot in unison at other lines. We did not fully realize that those days were over.

Too much drill stifled initiative and the instinct for survival. Its value lay in the resentment it caused, because men developed the initiative to avoid it. The Boers had been rotten at drill but they had been good soldiers.

But now drill could not be avoided with decency. If parades were missed and the offender brought before a magistrate, he would be told that it was only because of the Australian navy and the men now drilling that the Germans were not yet in Australia. The magistrate's view was rarely questioned.

The war changed the songs we sang around the house. The elder brothers sang the words, if not the tunes, from American and London musicals: 'Gilbert the filbert, the knut with the K, the pride of Piccadilly, the blasé roué'. None of us had seen Piccadilly, but it belonged to us; we were part of England and London was our political Jerusalem.

There was another song and I am sure I never knew the original words: 'The cow sat in the rice-pan and the monkey loved the cat'. The others sang it but mother hinted that I should not. Years later and knowing about monkeys and their unusual tolerance I was able to understand mother's reservations.

There was the 'Ta-Ra-Ra-Ra-Ra-Ra of the British Grenadiers', cheerful, martial and pre-war, but it was pushed aside by 'It's a long way to Tipperary'. That was a war song with more of the spirit of the 'Marseillaise' than had 'God Save the King'. It belonged to this new war. The words? An Irish soldier sang how far it was to his Irish Molly-O. Natural enough, but why should he be so concerned with Piccadilly and Leicester Square? It did not make sense, but it was the great national song of the early war years. It pushed the old musicals to the side, as it was to be pushed aside in its turn by a greater song.

In the second week of the war that song was first sung on the stage of the Melbourne Gaiety Theatre. It was 'Australia will be There', written by a local for the new Australian nation and it lasted out the war:

> Rally round the banner of your country,
> Take the field with brothers o'er the foam.
> On land or sea, wherever you be,
> Keep your eye on Germany. [No other song even mentioned Germany.]
> No, no, no, no, Australia will be there-ere-ere
> Australia will be there.

And if the war lasted long enough, we might be there and then England would recognize how anxious to help we had been and would be grateful to us.

Those national anthems. It might be all very well if you had a couple of allies but when you had five or six and all their anthems were played on important occasions it got ridiculous. The 'Marseillaise' was inevitable, and even our family recognized the tune, but who really cared what the Japanese, Serbian, or even the Belgian anthem was? The Russian was a splendid hymn with a stately tune, but it was not in our hymnbook—a pity because the Russians were likely to win the war all by themselves and we would like to show our appreciation.

We were in trouble with one of our hymns. The most popular German anthem was 'Deutschland uber Alles'; we used the tune for 'Saviour if of Zion's City' and that was one of our best-liked hymns. Many knew the origin of the tune and the hymn fell into disuse.

The war was a boon for baritones. The moving pictures had not quite killed concert parties; even the pictures sometimes had a patriotic song, but the concert parties were stuffed with them. A concert party from Melbourne would hire the local hall for Saturday night and the entrance charges would more than cover the cost of the weekend.

The best war songs were all for baritones. It was at Mornington where I was given a free seat that I heard the trumpeter going through from Reveille to Lights Out, from the lighted tents of the early morning to the unhearing dead on the battle-field. This was war at its patriotic and pathetic best.

That trumpeter was a windy sort of fellow and he became more and more out of place in the new serious war. His song died.

The baritone's second number lasted out the war:

> There's a long, long trail a-winding into the land of dreams,
> Where the nightingales are singing, and a white moon beams.

Those were the opening lines of sloppy stuff, for none of us had heard a nightingale and all the verses were just as banal. But the paltry song, written before the war, was touched by it; it became high emotional poetry—just the last lines of the chorus:

> There's a long, long night of waiting
> Until my dreams come true;
> Till the day when I'll go walking down
> That long, long trail with you.

In the coming years after our prayers at night, in the timeless gap between waking and sleep, our spirits would go out across the empty seas and over the strange lands to those at the front and we trusted that our prayers would protect them until they came home safely again and once more walked with us.

Later came

> Keep the home fires burning, while your hearts are yearning,
> Though your lads are far away they dream of home;
> There's a silver lining through the dark clouds shining;
> Turn the dark clouds inside out, till the boys come home.

We had read enough of the London theatre to know that its writer, Ivor Novello, was a prominent actor, a producer and author of plays, a gifted man, young and handsome. If he was as patriotic as his song, he would have been in France with the others of his age-group. It rang hollow. More real was

> What's the use of worrying, it never was worthwhile,
> So pack up your troubles in your old kit-bag
> And smile, smile, smile.

In that song the soldiers had nonchalantly lighted their 'fags' and we knew that it was the soldier-slang for cigarettes, and felt that we were sharing their adventure.

They were two of the more common propaganda songs and they heartened us in the early years of the war but they too rang hollow by the end of 1916. Then we could no longer believe that those thousands driven to slaughter in hopeless attacks were like happy groups of Boy Scouts setting out on a Saturday-afternoon jaunt, and we were beginning to doubt if those massacres really had been glorious Allied victories.

We still preferred 'The long, long trail' with its couple of lines which chance had given a profound meaning to us.

'God Save the King' was sung at every assembly of twenty or more people, and if that was not enough for a big occasion, we went on to 'Rule Britannia, Britannia Rules the Waves'—the original version and not the more usual 'No more Chinamen allowed in New South Wales'. It had dwindling popularity as we began to wonder if Britannia really did rule the waves.

Late in the year, November I think it was, we did as most other families did. We pinned up a map of the Eastern and Western Fronts; ours went above the sofa in the breakfast room. It was a combined map in colour published by the *Herald*, and with it went a lot of pins with coloured tops. I've forgotten what colour the Russian pins were, but I think our pins were red and the French ones blue; the Germans were certainly black—they would be, they were a most unattractive lot.

Those of us who had read the *Argus* before breakfast already knew of today's victory or yesterday's re-hashed one, but moving the pins was a morning ritual done by father after breakfast; he would find the funny Slav names on the map and move the pins.

Often it was puzzling; there had been a great victory, but the black pins moved forward, not back. There was real movement on the Austrian sector in the right direction but it seemed all wrong at the end of the year when the victorious Russian pins tumbled back to Russia, right out of East Prussia and across Poland.

Of course the map of the Western Front was to a much larger scale, but even so, there was no spectacular movement. Perhaps the pins moved a little bit forward, but in a day or two they were back where they had started. Every time the pins moved, hundreds of thousands of Germans were killed. We were pleased about that, but we would have liked the red pins to move forward.

5
Our Germans

It was a splendid war to be in. We had come in loyally behind England and England was in because she had guaranteed little Belgium's neutrality by treaty: a photograph of the scrap of paper had been published in our papers. It was funny that we had not heard of that treaty in the weeks when there had been worries about the war starting.

Now the Belgians were resisting gallantly. Arms and ammunition had been issued to civilians and they were shooting Germans; a boy had assassinated Count von Bülow and got away on that general's horse, and King Albert of the Belgians had knighted him and he had been allowed to keep the horse and the general's pocketbook. It was gallant of the Belgians to assassinate, but the Germans did not like it.

Belgian women were forced to go thirteen miles to bury German dead in a forest which the French were shelling and they were forced to carry the corpses until they fell exhausted and then they were kicked and bayoneted. Belgian girls of good family were outraged in the presence of their mothers. At Lawside we did not know what 'outraged' meant, but it seemed that it was a very nasty thing which the Germans did to Belgians. Belgian boys had their arms cut off and were forced to walk over their fathers' bodies, or to carry their decapitated heads—a difficult thing to do with no hands—and their sisters went raving mad as a result. Not only boys, girls too. A letter from the Channel Islands told about a girl. 'One mite is here minus both hands. The Germans cut her mother's head off and gave it to the child to carry. When she dropped it, they cut off her hands'.

The last war atrocities of fourteen years ago had had no notice in the English papers, but they had been published in America and Europe. Rudyard Kipling had been visiting the Boer front and was one of a party which had chivalrously given two Boer farm women a hundred yards' start before shooting at them, so the foreign papers said. And

we had invented a new war term, 'concentration camps'. We had put
Boer women and children into camps to isolate them from their menfolk
and they had died like flies. Those concentration camps got a bad world
press.

In the distant past there had been all sorts of French war atrocities
and Russian ones had been far more recent. Now it was only the Germans
who committed atrocities and we bestowed all vices on them and conferred all virtues on the Belgians. At least, we could raise money for
them.

Of all the sixty or so appeals listed in the *Argus*, the most popular
were those for the Belgians. Federal Parliament voted £100 000 out of
consolidated revenue for them and only one troublesome member asked
what it would be used for. He had a point, for only one little corner
of Belgium was outside German occupation.

Not only could we raise money for the Belgians; we could do something about the Germans, for we had quite a lot of them living amongst
us in Australia.

At the beginning of August 1914 the Germans were the most respected
group in the community, even more respected than the Scots. By the
end of August they were the most despised and hated.

Our Germans were solid business and professional people and German
names were always high on the list of charitable appeals. Solid, too,
were the German farming areas around Melbourne and in the Western
District; you could tell at once that you were in a German area by the
tidy farms and the tamed landscape.

In South Australia was the smiling Barossa Valley, a solidly German
area where German was still spoken in the second and third generations
and where religion had a profound influence on life. But now the speaking of German there was forbidden and the Lutheran schools were closed
and it was felt that something should be done about the German place-
names.

As well as being our best farmers Germans dominated our music,
and music was a social grace; it was praiseworthy to be accepted into
a lieder group. They gave recitals and concerts and were music teachers.
Lower in the social scale were the German bands which paraded the
streets of Melbourne on every weekday; only on Sunday could non-
German music be heard when the Salvation Army took over.

Our Germans were painfully efficient and diligent, but they were
also gently comical. Those pictures of fat amiable Germans with great
pots of beer, Meerschaum pipes and plump little dogs: those were our
Germans at the beginning of August. At the end of the month they
had replaced the Chinese as the prime butt of our malice.

The Chinese were industrious, like the Germans, but ever since the goldrush days we had feared them. At one time about one-fifth of the workforce in Australia had been Chinese, but that was long ago. Now they were market gardeners and furniture makers and they ran the best laundries, but we still feared them, for behind them was China, an immense reservoir ready to pour out its 'Yellow Peril' and submerge White Australia.

The Chinese were good Australian citizens despite their treatment, but we liked them none the better for that; they smoked opium and we smoked tobacco and we said that they had the most unusual vices. The Germans were equally good citizens, and as far as we knew, had no characteristic vices—indeed, on casual inspection, they seemed to look like us and behave like us; but now we found that they were savage and inhuman. The Sydney *Bulletin* full-page cartoons were no longer of rat-faced Chinese but of ape-faced Germans marching through Belgium with babies stuck on their bayonets.

We turned on our Germans, just as in the later years the Germans turned on their Jewish fellow-citizens, but their views were formed by years of semi-official propaganda; we formed ours spontaneously here, as in England.

The stevedores, never a notably patriotic group, beat up Germans, whether they had been naturalized or not. As they were not particularly well informed, they gave the same treatment to Scandinavians and Russians.

Most Germans were sacked. One isolated and unusual action is recorded: the Methodist parson at Port Melbourne was concerned with the plight of the families of Germans thrown out of work and wrote to the *Argus* telling of their difficulties. The wealthier Germans of Melbourne responded and he was told to draw on them for rent and food for the suddenly unemployed. He thought 'that every generous-spirited Britisher would be glad to know'. They were not.

About this time I was sent off one Saturday afternoon to buy something for Saturday's tea. I went to the shop opposite the Armadale Station entrance in Cheel Street, another isolated shop which never prospered; now it was a small-goods shop as it could not be a 'delicatessen' during the war. I asked for German sausage; the shop had none, but it did have 'Belgian' sausage. As I was being served a lady in a fur coat waited with her dachshund on a lead. In came a couple of eighteen-year-olds and kicked the dog—'horrible German dog'—and its owner could do nothing to protect it from patriotism.

Once in Australia we used to have frankfurters—I can't remember them, for after 1914, they became saveloys. Later the Frankfurter Company in Sydney was raided and destroyed by men in military training, although there was no German employed and no German capital involved.

Mother user to take a Seidlitz powder when she was not feeling too good. They went off the market, but we went to Mr Klein's chemist shop at the corner of High Street, even though he was a German.

Firms put advertisements in the papers saying that they were not German and had no German connections. Wunderlich was really Swiss, but it had a German name. Even the purely English companies' advertisements became patriotic. Pears soap had aways been very superior and respectable; now it was even better for it was 'preferred by the brave women who tend our wounded heroes'. If Red Cross nurses preferred it, that was good enough for us.

We had German friends, just as every other family in Australia had.

When the family lived at Derby in Tasmania there was Dr Von Se, an excellent doctor who had replaced one who had qualified at an American correspondence school. One day Athol fell about fifteen feet and landed on his head; he had fractured his skull, or something of the sort, and when he was carried back to Derby he was put to bed in Dr Von Se's house in absolute quiet away from the noises of home. It probably saved his life and we were deeply grateful to the doctor. We also liked him as a man and we thought that here, deep in the Tasmanian bush, we had an excellent doctor and a trusty friend. When we moved to Lottah mother asked for Dr Von Se whenever she was having a baby, so he was a frequent visitor to the house.

Now that we lived in Melbourne, we had other close German friends— Uncle Chris and Aunty Dora Kussmaul. Father had met Uncle Chris first when they were young engineers working for the Melbourne Board of Works, probably on the tunnelling for the sewers of Melbourne. They kept up their friendship and when Ralph was a little boy he asked Uncle Chris what he would do if there was a war with Germany. Uncle Chris was naturalized; he said that this was now his country and he would fight to defend it but that he would not go overseas to fight the Germans.

They had no children of their own and Neil and I often went to stay in their tidy house in Camberwell during our school holidays and we picked up a bit of German when we were there.

Uncle Chris had a silver beard and I got him mixed up with Santa Claus and Professor Kernot, father's old professor, whose bearded portrait hung in the study. Uncle Chris was a kindly man and gave me my first pocket-knife on my fifth birthday when I was staying with them. I still have the scar on my left index finger.

When the war started he was sixty-three and had been with the Melbourne and Metropolitan Board of Works for over thirty years and had reached the top post of designing engineer. He had been a naturalized British subject for thirty-two years, but he was regarded as a German and his position was made intolerable. He may have been over-sensitive, but he felt deeply hurt by the attitude of his friends of a generation. He was given provisional leave for six months. His case was discussed by the Officers' and Servants' Committee of the Board on 25 November. He was granted six months' sick leave, one month of it on full pay and another on half pay and the rest unpaid. His post as designing engineer would be abolished, and this after thirty-two years' service.

Commissioner Gehan said he would have preferred to see him summarily dismissed, although he admired his ability. Commissioner A'Beckett said that in the past they had taken a man for his ability irrespective of his birth, and an unnamed Commissioner interjected, 'Yes, and more shame on us'.

A month later it was confirmed. He would be given three months' salary in lieu of notice and his service would be regarded as having ceased at the end of the previous year. Commissioner Bell objected: if Mr Kussmaul received consideration, German labourers who had been dismissed should be given some compensation.

Uncle Chris was deeply hurt. He had chosen to become a British subject but his old friends of British birth now ignored him and would not admit to having ever known him. If ever a man died of sorrow, it was Uncle Chris; he died that year.

Aunty Dora took me with her to a monumental mason to settle what should be cut on his grave-stone. Around him were those of British birth with British names; but she had his full German name inscribed and I don't think the stone was ever defaced.

I had never heard Uncle Chris say anything unpatriotic, but now Aunty Dora exulted at the news of German victories, although she was Australian-born and her brother was in the A.I.F. He became Major Sanders and no one noticed that he had a German name.

I am still proud of mother and father. Although father was having a difficult time with his work he did a very unpopular thing by writing to the *Argus* in support of Uncle Chris; mother saw more of Aunty Dora than before and she often came to our house. The next year we had enough money to rent a holiday house at Mornington for 7s 6d a week, and Aunty Dora came with us. It was all very well for mother to be nice to her, but I was very embarrassed to have to go to the post-office to ask for letters for Mrs Kussmaul.

Probably because of our old friendship with Uncle Chris and Aunty

Dora, we knew more Germans than did most people, and we persisted in seeing them during the war. We could not visit the middle-aged ones for they all had been interned; their children, who had been born in Australia and were British citizens, were only sacked.

Mr Hartung, the music teacher in Malvern who had lived in Australia for thirty-five years, was very upset by the outbreak of war and lost most of his pupils. The police came and searched his house. As he was then sixty-eight he was not regarded as dangerous and was not interned, but every one of his letters was opened and read by the censor throughout the war.

One day he went to visit his old friend, Edouard Scharf, the concert pianist and Conservatorium teacher; he rang the door-bell and hammered on the door, but got no attention. He went down the side of the house, and through a window saw old Scharf playing vigorously at the piano and not a sound coming out. In the absence of pupils he was learning piano concertos by heart and already knew 150. He had fitted a 'celeste' pedal which interposed a strip of felt between the hammer and the strings; otherwise, he said, he would go mad.

They were not the only ones to suffer in Malvern. Mr Bechervaise, of a prolific Channel Islands family, was reckoned to have a German name and his windows were broken.

Gus Ampt was a friend of my elder brothers. He had been born and lived all his life in Melbourne. He was a brilliant scientist but was sacked at the beginning of the war. Orme Masson, the Professor of Chemistry, gave him a job in his department and protected him throughout the disgraceful witchhunt which the Council of the University mounted against all with German names. There were only a few like Masson in the University.

J. W. Lindt, our most famous photographer, was German; we had met him at the Kussmauls'. His photo of an old German labourer with his pot of beer in the Narbethong pub ('I always have one at eleven') was made into a poster and was so appealing that it became the totem of the brewery. If it had been known that the photographer and his subject were both German, it would have done the brewery no good at all.

Lindt had left Germany when he was sixteen, before the Franco-Prussian war of 1870—a war in which British opinion supported Germany. He built Lindt's Hermitage, a guesthouse on the top of the Black Spur, forty miles from Melbourne. He must have remembered the resorts in the Black Forest, for he made the Hermitage similar. There were tiny houses all over the place, even up trees, and little streams curling among the ferns, and all this in the tremendous gum trees, 3000 feet up on the top of a pass in the mountains.

He was an old man in 1914 and had been naturalized for over fifty years, but he did a foolhardy thing; he wrote to the *Argus* suggesting that all the Germans he knew were good and loyal subjects. It brought attention to him and it was said that he had a secret wireless transmitter for sending messages to German vessels at sea.

One Sunday when the guesthouse was at its busiest and lunch was being served, the security police made a sudden raid. They searched every room, including the guests' rooms, and they questioned everybody. They were looking for wireless equipment and a maid helped them; she took them up the hill to a wire clothes-line.

The raid was reported in the papers, but nothing was said about the negative result and the harm was done. Good Australians would not visit the place any more and it closed.

Mother had an arrangement with Mrs Stevens, who lived near the sea at Mentone. Mother had been bluffed into providing lunch each day for young Elmsley Stevens who came up by train to a school in Armadale; in return, it was reasonable that I should stay in Mentone in the holidays. They were rather superior people and I spent my time with their subnormal servant, and the two dogs.

Mentone had a long wooden pier sticking out into the sea. It was not big like the one at Mordialloc, the next railway station along, but it was still a pier, and the roads of Mentone converged on it. On a triangular block overlooking the pier an old chap had built himself a wooden-framed two-storey shop and covered it with asbestos sheets, and he had a foreign name. On his roof he had a telescope and for a penny you could look through it across the bay. This made him into a German spy who looked at the shipping.

The local adolescents had smashed his windows and he had boarded them up, but it was possible to smash the asbestos sheets if you went to enough trouble. The poor old bloke was living by himself besieged in his barricaded shop. I had threepence, which was a lot of money, and out of contrariness decided that I would support him by buying a threepenny Tobler chocolate bar from him. I knocked on the shut door and then heard bolts being shot and chains jangling; the door opened a few inches and I asked for my chocolate. I was as frightened as the old chap; I doubt if my purchase really made him any happier.

Many felt that the University was pro-German and it had certainly started the war badly. The British Association for the Advancement of Science was a most highly respectable body and its members came on a visit to most of the Australian States. There had been no war when they embarked and the universities of Australia prepared an academic fuss--honorary degrees for everybody. In the middle of August, Melbourne University included Sir Edouard Schaefer and Johannes Walther in its issue of honorary degrees.

That was not all. It had not sacked those of German birth, even if they had not been naturalized, and it had given a job to Gus Ampt, an Australian of German descent.

In parliament a member said that he held a letter from a prominent Melbourne solicitor saying that he had drawn up a revocation of a bequest of £15 000 to the University because of the German influence there.

The Conservatorium of Music had Germans on the staff, including old Edouard Scharf, perhaps the most prominent instrumentalist in the State. He had not been naturalized although he had lived most of his musical life in Melbourne; the Council held that there was no objection to his acting as an examiner, even though he was a German national.

He wrote to Council stating that he had never said anything disloyal, and he was corroborated by the Acting Professor and members of the staff. Council ruled that the Registrar should write to him on the necessity for circumspection regarding his attitude to the war. Then in December Council was informed that he had lost his German citizenship so the poor old chap had no country, but the University still regarded him as an enemy.

Another trouble with the Conservatorium was that it was said to be playing the works of German composers; Beethoven and Brahms were regarded as the most objectionable. It was not actually forbidden to play their works, but most people refrained.

On the University Council the loudest anti-Germans were Dr Leeper, Warden of Trinity College, and Adamson, the Headmaster of Wesley. Leeper was wild Irish, but Protestant, and for a long time had been president of the Loyal Irish Association of Victoria--but was it so loyal? A large proportion of its members supported armed defiance of the policy of the Crown in regard to Irish Home Rule; vehement patriotism and disloyalty were mingled.

Dr Leeper stated in Council that he had heard it reported that Dr von Dechend had exulted over the disaster to British cruisers in the presence of his class. The matter was left in the hands of the Vice-Chancellor, who, at the next meeting, submitted Dr von Dechend's emphatic and unequivocal denial and a letter from his students confirming it. Nothing for Dr Leeper that time.

The Vice-Chancellor said that there were a good many Germans at the University and he did not intend to interfere with them as long as they maintained an attitude of strict neutrality. They seemed to be thoroughly Australian in spirit, and in his opinion, there was no need for action.

The tolerant group at the University had some success. Australians of German descent were not sacked, but means were found of hindering their promotion, even if like E. J. Hartung, they had volunteered for the army and had been rejected on medical grounds.

The military raided the University and went through the rolls of students. Colonel R. Wallace said:

> We have not the slightest intention of interfering with the studies at the University of Germans, or the children of Germans born in Australia. The military visit to the University yesterday was for the purpose of investigating the affairs of certain members of the professorial staff. While the investigating party was at the University, the roll of student names was looked over, but this was merely in keeping with the system we have adopted.

All our German friends had a bad time, but the Rosenfelts next door seemed hardly disturbed. When somebody said that the people next door had a German name, we could explain that they were Austrian, not German, and that seemed to make the German name respectable.

We were not actually fighting the Austrians and had had some sympathy with them before the war; now the Russians were fighting them and they were getting worsted. We heard nothing of any Austrian atrocities but we had a memory of the Russians and their atrocities of more than a century ago; we had fought them in the Crimean War and come near to fighting them since. It might even be that those crude Russians were committing atrocities on the Austrians. In fact, it was reassuring to find that people with German names were not really German after all. I don't think anything much unpleasant happened to the Rosenfelts. I can't remember any of their windows being broken or of hearing any shouting in the street outside their house at night.

Scandinavians had a worse time. No one knew much about them, except that their countries were very close to Germany and they had German sorts of names. We knew that they were not on our side and that they might be German sympathizers: they might be Germans using a weak disguise; they might well be German spies.

Phyllis's friend at the University, Dolly Tonks, had a Norwegian father and this was enough to get her the same treatment as a German. It was really far better to be Austrian.

6
Religion and Drink

The new inventions of wireless and aeroplanes had little effect on our war in Australia, but two old problems grew increasingly important: drink and Ireland. We got drier and drier as the war went on and our attitude to the Irish changed from tolerance to hostility. Our attitude to both was affected by what happened overseas.

Drink had been a subject of continuous debate since the gold rush; then it united the extremes of Catholicism and Protestantism in opposition to it. Father Geoghegan, our first priest, had tried to wean the Irish from the bottle and the Methodists had tried to dash it from the lips; now they were reinforced by the Salvation Army and the Baptists and had followers in all the Protestant Churches. As a reaction, the Irish Catholics began to regard temperance as a Protestant heresy—and they owned a lot of pubs.

The Womens' Christian Temperance Union came out in full cry and it pictured starving wives and children shivering at home whilst father swilled his week's earnings in a pub. They got reinforcement from overseas.

In Russia, of all places, the Tsar closed the vodka shops and his army fighting the Germans was officially stone-cold sober. It was an example for us and our men should be the same. Wet canteens in the military camps were shut down at the beginning of October 1914.

Then our King George announced that no strong drink would be on his table whilst the war was on; the Governor of Western Australia did the same and saved a lot of his expense account. A whole lot of individuals followed the King's example. In Melbourne at the University people signed a pledge saying that they would touch alcohol only if it was medically prescribed.

The Churches were all in favour of temperance, and that seemed reasonable, but Prohibition was another matter. The Catholics were neutral but all the others were officially in favour. From the Methodists to the left they were solid; the Church of England and the Presbyterians had a sizeable minority against.

The imposing purple cassock of a Church of England bishop seemed to call for port after dinner and a good half of the Presbyterian ministers we had known had expected to be offered whisky when they came to our house.

One of the most respected Presbyterians was Dr MacFarlane, the Vice-Chancellor of the University and Master of Ormond College, the Presbyterian residential college. When all were assembled in Hall for dinner, the Doctor's man would enter and place a decanter of whisky in front of him and it would be passed along the high table.

The Methodist Queen's College was officially arid, but the Master, Dr Sugden, was a balanced man and did not pry into what happened in the students' rooms—unless it was silly and then he came down hard. Church of England Trinity was quite as tolerant as Ormond and there was even beer on the tables in Hall. The Roman Catholics had no college as yet.

I can remember that the Presbyterians had a 'Temperance Sunday' every now and then, but a good third would go home for their claret at Sunday lunch.

Sunday school was another matter. The Superintendent, Mr Schneider, was not very concerned but the Senior Elder, Mr McNab, was. He intruded into Sunday school when it was a matter of learning the catechism or the problem of drink. Our lesson would be on the evils of drink and the children were expected to sign the pledge. We eight- and nine-year-olds had been able to write our names for some years now and we got a gorgeous certificate if we signed the pledge, the sort of thing that looked very well on the wall, as good as 'God is Love' in white letters with flowers behind it on a green velvety background. Alan Gibbs and I split on the issue; he got a certificate but I did not.

In Canada and the U.S.A. provinces and areas voted under 'local option' for the closing of saloons. Most of the U.S.A. was for closure and there was even talk of total prohibition for the whole country; Canada was much less enthusiastic. We tried the same voting here, with even less success than Canada, but we followed England in talking about curtailing the trading hours.

The tide of drink continued to ebb throughout the war and only started to rise again when peace returned, except in the U.S.A. where it sank to total national prohibition. If the war was not very serious for that nation, at least its secondary effects were.

Our Catholics, and that meant the bulk of the Irish, differed from the rest of us on the question of drink, but they differed within themselves and were in two defined groups.

Our folk-heroes had all been Irish. Peter Lalor of the Eureka Stockade, O'Hara Burke of the bungled Burke and Wills expedition, and Ned Kelly. Ned Kelly typified the under-privileged Irish who rebelled against authority and used violence – we should like to have been able to exclude them from our war, for they thought quite differently from us. But some of them had a wayward charm.

We had a sneaking approval of their disdain for our starched superiors and there were a lot of things about Ned Kelly that we liked. The story is possibly true that Ned gave a shilling to the boy, John Monash, who was impressed by him. Our Aunt Katie had met Ned and thought that he was a courteous young man. It may have some significance that, when Ned's gang came on a police party, they allowed a Scottish trooper to get away but killed the three Irish policemen, and that Ned was condemned to death by an Irish judge, one of the Irish gentry.

We had our Irish aristocrats who were united in their pride of Ireland. They were both Catholics and Protestants, and that combined group provided our leaders out of proportion to their number.

In the first days of settlement there was Redmond Barry, the judge who sentenced Ned Kelly. He was a Protestant, who was very busy founding ambitious and great things – like the Art Gallery, the Public Library and the University, all of which were established within twenty years of the first settlement.

Barry was Chancellor of the University from its foundation in 1854 until his death in 1880. His Warden of the Senate, later Vice-Chancellor, was John Madden, an Irish Catholic, who studied at the University on his first arrival and was to end up as Chief Justice.

Gavan Duffy was a Catholic who had been mixed up in an ineffective rebellion in Ireland. He was very superior, for he had sat in the House of Commons. Now every second judge and K.C. seemed to be called Madden or Gavan Duffy.

Then there were the Higgins brothers whose father had been Protestant and an Irish Nationalist. Judge Higgins had established the theory of a minimum wage for all workers; his brother, an engineer, was a close friend of father's. I think it was his son Esmond, who, like the Gavan Duffy of his generation, enlisted to fight for the nation which their grandfathers had rebelled against.

Then there was Captain Lalor, who became as great a folk-hero as Peter Lalor of the Eureka Stockade. He was in the first landing at Gallipoli, when, armed with a family sword, he led a little group to the top of the ridge which dominated both shores of the peninsula; but his little lot was shot down by a small detachment of Turks, and that was the last seen of them.

There was a great gulf fixed between our Irish leaders and the other Irish, who also comprised both Catholic and Protestant but whose political views were as divergent as their religious beliefs; they fought violently with each other.

The Catholics were by far the more numerous and most were lower-paid workers; they were anti-English and regarded our Australian war as an English war. Our federal government was Labor, but pro-war, so the Catholics were anti-government, but still pro-Labor. As they dominated the left-wing unions, they were able to express themselves in strikes which hindered our war effort.

Like the Irish Nationalists at Westminster, our Irish aristocrats shunned violence; the others approved of it. It had been one of them, a Fenian, who in Sydney had nearly assassinated Prince Alfred, the son of our great Queen Victoria, on the first royal visit to Australia in 1867. We were very embarrassed that such a thing could happen in loyal Australia and we tried to atone for it by building the Prince Alfred Hospital in Melbourne, although it had happened in Sydney.

The big occasion when the Irish showed their strength was the annual St Patrick's Day march through the city; only the Catholics marched, the Protestant Irish barracked and scuffled on the footpath. It was a more imposing march than the Eight Hours Day Procession when the trade unions displayed their power. Quite a lot marched in both processions.

The other sort of Irish, the Ulster Protestants, had their much smaller demonstration on Orange Day, but it was quite a minor affair and seemed to be held only to annoy the Catholics. Freemasonry was largely a Protestant Irish movement and now the Irish Catholics and Freemasons were at each others' throats in the public service; the police force was dominated by the Irish Catholics.

We, the majority, had always been puzzled by the Catholic Church: now because of what the Church was beginning to say on political matters, we began listening also to the propaganda of the Ulster Protestants. We could buy the most remarkable books about what happened in nunneries.

We had always preferred the vague amorphous shape of the Church of England and its limpid English to the sharp form of the Catholic Church saying the same thing in unintelligible Latin, but we did not think much of the imported Anglican archbishops, with one single splendid exception.

There had been a whole procession of them: schoolmasters who might never have become headmasters had come out here as archbishops; small men with the complacency of their opinion that theirs was the Established Church and with an intolerance which we were now beginning to attribute to the Catholics.

We had always had a much greater personal regard for the Roman Catholic archbishops; there had been only two of them. Archbishop Goold was the first in 1847; and he was a man of learning and a real gentleman. He had lasted until 1886 when Archbishop Carr took over, another gentleman, as cultured as his predecessor. Both men had preserved a benevolent harmony in a community which distrusted the Catholic Church.

In 1913 Archbishop Carr was getting on in years and was given a Coadjutor Archbishop, Daniel Mannix, who started giving trouble as soon as he arrived. He addressed meetings advocating government support for Catholic schools; this might have been all very well, but it was in violent opposition to the established Labor policy of secular education—and the Irish were very strong in the Labor Party. When war came he opposed the British war effort, and this was in violent opposition to the views of our Irish gentry. He was certainly the most incisive churchman ever in Australia and was a brilliant and logical speaker, but his opinions were very wrong, or so we thought, and so did many Catholics. In 1915 a deputation of prominent Catholics waited on Archbishop Carr and asked him to curb Mannix's 'disloyal utterances'. In 1917 Sir Frank Madden, a Catholic and the Speaker of the Victorian Legislative Assembly, called for his deportation.

Mannix was the cultured voice of the riff-raff Irish against the war and against enlistment; that was bad enough, but to make it worse, he spoke better than his opponents.

As a generalization, the dominant Irish voice in Australia was pro-war until the middle of 1916; by the end of that year it was anti-war and anti-England and it was most clearly expressed by Archbishop Mannix of Melbourne.

We were proud of our British army and about one-fifth of its numbers were Irish; many of the proudest and most respected regiments were Irish. We had read about those rather charming and eccentric Irish soldiers in Kipling's books on India and we had imported a lot of Irish sergeants to train our new Citizen Forces.

For a century our greatest military figures had been Irish: there had been Wellington and after him Garnet Wolsey, then Lord Roberts; now we had Lord Kitchener, an immense figure comparable with Wellington. They were all Irish to us for we could not be expected to differentiate between the Irish and the Anglo-Irish; we relied on the British army and the Irish in it.

We were intensely interested in Irish politics and our papers gave them fuller coverage than did the English papers—not only because of the large numbers of Irish in the population, but because Ireland's place in the Empire affected our position, and any gain for Ireland might be a gain for us. Generally, we were sympathetic to Home Rule.

In 1914 Ireland was on the brink of gaining Home Rule and we approved. Although the bulk of us were Protestant, only a rabid fringe supported the Protestants of Ulster who would fight rather than be incorporated with the Catholic south.

In Ulster arms were being landed and openly distributed; the south naturally responded and imported arms also. On a Sunday morning a great procession moved out of Dublin to land 2500 rifles from a yacht in the bay. Like so many Irish affairs it was over-theatrical and the column tried to look as military as it could, with a signals corps, catering corps and ambulances. It all might have been good fun, but on the return journey the police tried to stop it and there was bloodshed—four killed and a lot wounded. The play-drama had become real drama.

What had happened and what was going to happen would have a great effect on Ireland and a great effect on us. It would affect what we did in the war and it would strongly affect our political views—and it still does.

It seemed to the Irish, and to us, that the decision of the elected British parliament was being challenged by the Establishment: that arms would not be permitted in the south but allowed into the north to arm mutineers against the Crown.

At the military centre of the Curragh, Brigadier-General Gough, commanding the 3rd Cavalry Brigade, and other officers, sent in their papers rather than accept the chance that they would be ordered to take action against the Ulstermen. Their action did not damage their military careers and they were supported by prominent military leaders, such as Lord Roberts.

Then the *Age* of 21 September: HOME RULE FOR IRELAND. BILL RECEIVES ROYAL ASSENT. SUSPENSORY BILL CARRIED. So Ireland had Home Rule at last, despite the violent opposition from the north. The Suspensory Bill was to delay action for 'twelve months or until the termination of the war'—not such a silly thing when there was so much else to think about and things might simmer down.

Redmond, the leader of the Irish Nationalists in the Commons, cabled the news to Dr N. O'Donnell, chairman of the Home Rule organization in Victoria, who replied 'Joyful tidings most welcome—yourself and party have realised fondest hopes of Irish race and merit eternal gratitude'.

The Irish Nationalists had won their long fight: they had nearly won in Gladstone's time but the Conservative-dominated House of Lords had thrown out the Liberal Bill of the Commons.

The Nationalists were the most consistent group in the Commons, Catholic and Protestant bound together by the single aim of Home Rule for Ireland. There were never enough of them to win without the support of one of the two big parties, but they were numerous enough to be a nuisance, and often to hold the balance of power. They were not above flirting with both parties to gain their end, but the Liberals were more congenial to them. They were a lively and impertinent lot and supplied most of the parliamentary wit and humour.

One of the most prominent was an Australian, Arthur Lynch, a very famous man in England but exciting little notice here. I fancy that our conservative press did not like his radical views nor the things he did. Years later he was particularly kind to me in London and I got to know him well.

He had become friendly with father and the aunts when he was a Melbourne University student; there were so few students that they all knew each other socially. He had been born near Ballarat of an Irish father and Scottish mother; his father had been with Peter Lalor at the Eureka Stockade, a treasonable affair. Arthur was to carry treason into the second generation, but in both cases it was an amiable sort of treason. He was a big hefty man, a fine figure, one of the rare sort which is immediately attractive to both men and women; an obviously brilliant man, but there was little heat in the flame of his brilliance. He got his M.A. at Melbourne and then graduated in engineering; not so hard in those days when science and mathematical subjects were common to both courses—John Monash did the same. Lynch left Melbourne in 1888 and went to Berlin to study the new psychology, then to Paris to study the new electrical engineering; later he completed medical studies in London.

Pretty Aunt Katie, later brown and stringy, but then fair, with a soft radiance, had thought she was in love with him and talked of working her way to Europe as a governess to join him and it had been hard to discourage her. Aunt Rosie, clever and pretty enough, but not nearly as pretty as Aunt Katie, wrote to him and tried to get him for herself. Kept in her papers was Lynch's gentle discouragement: 'Think of me, if you ever think of me at all, as one inhabiting a world whose revolutions are all apart from yours and then you will be able freely to remember me for my best. To Katie, I beg you will remember me most kindly, as indeed to all the others'. Neither of them got him and neither ever had any real chance of doing so, but it was the start of a battle between them which lasted out their lives and involved our family.

Lynch went to South Africa as a correspondent and met General Botha, the Boer leader, with the result that he was made a colonel in the Boer army and raised one of the two brigades of Irish who fought for the Boers.

After the war he went to France and the U.S.A. and in his absence he was elected to the British parliament as an Irish Nationalist. On his arrival in England to take his seat he was arrested, but his trial was delayed as it was not the sort of thing to have going on during the coronation of Edward VII. Eventually he was found guilty of treason and condemned to death.

He was very hurt about it all, as the peace treaty had provided an amnesty for those who had fought for the Boers, and anyway, he was an Australian. His sentence was commuted to life imprisonment and he served a year before being released. He was elected to parliament again in 1909 and remained there as long as Ireland had a share in Westminster. In 1914 he was as loyal as the other Irish Nationalists and the British made him a colonel to raise troops in Ireland, but I doubt if he did very well.

In 1928 Arthur Lynch was living comfortably in a flat in Hampstead and being battened on by drunken and unsuccessful journalists from Fleet Street. He had written a whole stack of books, some in French and some in modern Greek, but I don't think they were widely read. When I met him he was writing a book to refute Einstein's theory of relativity.

He had become very patriotic once Home Rule seemed certain but he yet remained a Republican, and there were not many of them about. It was all very well to be Republican in his father's time at the Eureka Stockade, but the mood in Australia had changed with the fears of Asian invasion and our reliance on the Royal Navy. The royal house was growing in popularity in England and Australia. King George V was our war mascot.

Lynch told the most fantastic and unbelievable stories about royalty. A country doctor in England had been visited by two men; one seemed very subservient to the other, who, on examination, was found to have contracted a very discreditable complaint. No names had been mentioned but the doctor was no fool; he secured a personal interview with Queen Victoria and suggested that the illness of her eldest grandson should be hushed up. It was. The doctor was made Royal Physician and ended up in the House of Lords. Lynch had other stories just as remarkable.

Arthur Lynch

Arthur Lynch appeared to be almost quixotic in his integrity and
it is hard to appreciate his tolerance of Lord Northcliffe, the owner

Aunt Katie as Arthur Lynch knew her in Australia

of the *Daily Mail* and the manipulator of public opinion and politicians. Lynch became his mouthpiece in parliament.

In 1914 he was at the peak of his career as the most romantic figure in British politics, for many of the public were coming round to his views on the Boer War. Northcliffe asked him for an article on some

East African tribe which had suddenly become prominent. Lynch had no experience of the tribe but knew the neighbouring tribe; one was Moslem and the other pagan. He was asked to write on the tribe he knew. His article was published in the *Daily Mail* but the tribal names were transposed. Lynch was affronted, but he continued to work hand-in-glove with Northcliffe.

7
Traitors and Spies

It was very disappointing that we were in this important war and yet nothing very important was happening here. At least we had spies, maybe not so many as in England, but we were sure we had some if only we could find them. They were about the place in England and our papers reprinted articles about them from the London press.

The spies not only spied; they also built concrete gun emplacements all over the country. One was near a London railway junction, another was near Edinburgh, overlooking the Firth of Forth. Of course the spies were also in Belgium and France and a couple of seaside villas near Ostend were demolished because their concrete floors were said to have been placed there ready for guns. One emplacement was found in Canada overlooking Montreal. We did our best but the only ones found were a couple of concrete cricket pitches in the country.

There were treacherous German pigeons. Within the first few days of the war, British patrols had captured several fishing boats with pigeons on board, ready to fly back to Germany with messages flashed to them from the cliffs of England. INFORMATION FOR GERMANY. CARRIED BY PIGEONS. William Whitehead, a hotel owner in Dover, was arrested and charged. Every time a naval unit moved out of harbour, his pigeons flew off to tell the Germans about it. Peter Duhl, a man with a German name, was sentenced for six months for letting his pigeons out in a London suburb.

Those German pigeons temporarily resident in England might be sagacious birds, but those in Australia were far more energetic. In November 1914 the Defence Department issued an order forbidding pigeons to fly without an official permit—a touching picture, all those pigeons lining up for permission to take off on their morning flight. The Defence Department justified the order: 'German residents anxious to communicate with their fellow countrymen have been using carrier pigeons'. These pigeons could fly as much as five hundred miles a day, so off they would go and take messages to Germany, and probably wait for a while and then return here with the reply. We believed it all at the time, and if you have any doubts, you can look up the *Argus* of November 1914.

We had never liked our pigeons very much, they were messy in their habits and now their loyalty was in question. We got rid of them.

German spies were far more dangerous than pigeons and thousands had been planted in all countries ready for the war. They had found lots of them in Belgium, France and England and it was certain that some were ready and waiting in Australia.

In Belgium they were disguised as priests and Boy Scouts. This was disturbing as we had thought that nothing could be more patriotic than a Boy Scout. In the first week of the war 3000 spies had been arrested in Belgium and 100 shot.

France had spies too. Four days after the war began, fifty had been caught in Paris and ordered to be shot. Then, outside Lille, fifteen spies masquerading as Frenchmen were cornered up a factory chimney. They were shot down from 'their grimy perches, whilst screaming their allegiance to France'. It must have been risky being a chimney-jack in France in 1914.

Another group crossed three hundred miles of France in a motor-car with a load of bombs for use in destroying railways; they were captured outside Rouen. Those must have been remarkable bombs, to have been capable of destroying the railways, for when the British retreated in 1940 they had hundreds of tons of explosive but did not manage to destroy the railways behind them.

The spies were also busy in England. Two were caught in a hotel near Euston Station, they had rifles; but they got off. It turned out that they were only Irish. Spies used motor-cars; they shot at troop-trains; later they used their car headlights to guide Zeppelin raiders. Lord Harewood, Lord-Lieutenant of Yorkshire, said it was German spies who flashed signals from the cliffs to fishing boats whose pigeons carried the messages on to Germany.

The authorities were slower in England; 500 spies were arrested but only 90 were detained. It was November before the first was shot, and then it was done with proper ceremony in the Tower of London. It all lacked the happy spontaneity of France and Belgium.

What was happening in England was a warning to us. The *Age* published a letter to Mr Bechervaise of the Geelong Harbour Trust from his sister in England. She had met 'a lady who had a friend and the friend had a German governess and thought much of her and was horrified when the police came to search her room and found incriminating documents and a bomb as well'. If those Germans in England were spies it was certain that a lot of people here with German names were spies.

No one was quite certain what a spy did. Generally he was expected to have a bomb, a big round one like a plum-pudding, and a fringe of whiskers, like a Russian anarchist, but the Germans were clever and might have other disguises.

Wireless was a new thing and its powers were unknown; our spies would certainly have a wireless set. If a wireless set was found, a German spy would not be far away. All wireless sets owned by people with German names were seized. Even the solidest and most substantial people were suspect. Someone told on Hugo Wertheim, the big musical publisher in Collins Street, and his house was searched, but if he really did have a set, he had hidden it and he escaped arrest.

We were accused of being German spies. We, the Lewises, of 41 Kooyong Road, Armadale, and we had not a drop of German blood in our veins. The eldest brothers had put up a punching ball in the stable, and the Gregsons, two doors away, heard its rat-tat-tat on its board and knew at once that it was a German spy making bombs.

Any German might be a spy; every shop with a German name over it was searched and every German home was ransacked. They might get up to anything. Fortunately we had the new military to protect us. Dressed in new uniforms and armed with loaded rifles they guarded our streets against Germans. In Sydney a milkman on his cart and two men in a car were wounded when they did not heed challenges. A girl in Melbourne was wounded in her bed by a shot aimed by a sentry at someone he thought was suspicious.

We knew that all Germans were our enemies, even if they had lived here for years, that was to be expected, but some Australians were probably traitors. In November the *Argus* and the other papers told how the military went after them.

Sunday in Collins Street, nothing moving in the sabbath calm. At Collins House, no. 360, were the headquarters of Broken Hill Proprietary, North Broken Hill, Broken Hill South and W. S. Robinson, all the most solid and reputable concerns. To suggest that Collins House was a nest of traitors was like hinting that Scots' Church along the street was a house of ill-fame; but this was war-time.

On that Sunday morning a big detachment of military, with rifles, bayonets, and shining officers, swept up to Collins House. They did not wait to ring the bell or for the iron grille across the porch to be opened; they climbed over that, but the main door stopped them. They hammered at it until the terrified caretaker opened it. They pushed past him and up to the offices of the companies and set sentries with fixed bayonets in front of each. The caretaker telephoned the company secretaries and directors who came into town; the sentries barred their way to their offices until their identities had been established, then they were allowed to enter to open the safes under close scrutiny and the papers were removed. The offices remained under guard for the rest of the day.

The raid had been made 'not in expectation of discovering any armaments or possible secret contrabands of war, but to find information of the disposal of metals and transactions with London companies under German influence'. It had been instigated by the Attorney-General, W. M. Hughes, later the belligerent Prime Minister, and Senator Pearce, Minister for Defence. The latter was still hunting spies in the last years of the war, when he demanded action by the military on spies who were communicating with each other by coded messages in newspaper advertisements.

It must have been disappointing to Senator Pearce that after all his efforts and all the excitement, no case of German espionage was discovered here during the war.

The *Herald* of 15 October: COLONEL AND BAYONETS SAID TO RAID 'WOMAN VOTER'. CENSOR CRITICISED.

> Senator Mullan asked the Minister for Defence whether it was a fact that, by the direction of the Military Censor, a military guard with fixed bayonets, and led by a colonel, made a raid on the office of *The Woman Voter*, Melbourne? Did he consider that such an overwhelming display of force was necessary seeing that the newspaper involved was being conducted by three respected female residents of Melbourne? Would the Minister prevent a repetition of this stupid military despotism at a time when we were liberally providing men and money to destroy it in another country? Senator Pearce replied that it was true that a military guard had been placed over the paper referred to.

We had never heard of the *Woman Voter* and it cannot have been a very dangerous journal, but we knew of the 'three respectable female residents of Melbourne'. They were the Goldstein sisters.

'Goldstein' might appear to be a foreign name, but it wasn't. It was one of those names, like Brockhoff and Woinarski, which were so important to us that they had become part of our Australia. The Goldsteins were intellectuals and philanthropists. Vida, the eldest, was strikingly beautiful; I have an idea that I met her with Phyllis and was rather frightened.

They were not even exotic enough to be Jewish. The grandfather had left Poland for Ireland and become a Unitarian; the father had run to Australia and married a girl from a very respectable Western District family. He joined the volunteer Garrison Artillery, just like John Monash, and became a lieutenant-colonel. He was prominent in all sorts of reform movements and founded farm settlements in Gippsland for the unemployed.

The family was intellectual and respectable; they went to Scots' Church, and that was the peak of respectability. When the minister, Dr Strong, was expelled because of his broad views, they followed him into his new Australian Church, and that was very intellectual. They lived in the very respectable suburb of South Yarra.

Their *Woman Voter* advanced radical causes and women's rights, things like the establishment of the Women's Hospital, but they gave that one up when they became Christian Scientists.

Vida stood for parliament a couple of times and did surprisingly well when she stood for the safe conservative seat of Kooyong, later Menzies' easy chair; she polled 9629 votes against Sir Robert Best's 17 175.

In 1914 the group was joined by Adela Pankhurst, the daughter of the English suffragette leader. The Pankhursts had been pacifist during the Boer War; they had abandoned pacifism in 1914, but not Adela, who persisted in Melbourne. Her meetings were regularly broken up by men in uniform, who had popular, if not official, support.

John Monash had been military censor early in 1914, but he does not seem to be the sort of man who would order the raid. He was very tolerant and would know that the German-sounding 'Goldstein' was no more German than his own name and that they were more remote from Germany than he was. Monash's father had been a German national, and he himself still spoke fluent German.

Whoever the military censor was he must have felt that the feminist and pacifist views of the *Woman Voter* were traitorous.

We thought that our army was making a fool of itself by an irresponsible and absurd parade of military power.

8

Visit to Grandmother

From the first days of the war right to the end, Neil and I were able to supply extra war news to our friends at school. We got it from grand-mother's magazines and the letters from her niece in London.

Father's mother lived in a small house near the Malvern station and, every four weeks or so, Neil and I had to visit her on Saturday morning, putting on tidy clothes and sacrificing part of the best day of the week. We did not look forward to those visits.

She looked a nice kindly old lady, with a gentle Scottish accent, apple-cheeked with blue eyes and a little black widow's cap on her white hair. I think she was happy to put on that cap for she never thought much of grandfather. He had died six years before, lonely in lodgings in Carlton, unvisited by his wife and daughters during his illness.

We went to the front door and one of the aunts let us in. Two of them lived with grandmother. Rosie taught mathematics at various girls' schools, which she kept changing after a row with the headmistress. She was a good teacher and was always sure of another job; she kept on teaching until she was nearly eighty. She had done well as an early mathematical student at the University but had to give up her course in third year when grandfather lost his money. Lily had worked at the State Observatory but had been forced to live at home to keep house for her mother and sister. The aunts had been pretty girls but now they were sour.

Phyllis had been forced to live with them for a year to go to school in Melbourne before we moved from Tasmania; on each return trip she prayed that she would die, rather than face them again. Mother, Phyllis and I formed the group most unpopular with the aunts; therefore we had the support of Aunt Katie, who lived by herself.

It was a small house, so small that it did not have a drawing room for ceremonial visits; we were received in the living room on the left side of the front door. There sat grandmother and we kissed her without enthusiasm; we certainly would not kiss those two aunts.

On the side of the fireplace opposite to grandmother's chair was a little octagonal table with a velvet cover with bobbles hanging from its edges. It was the family altar. On it was a single vase of flowers and three photographs in silvered frames. One was of father looking fish-like in his academic gown after graduation; he was proud of it and we had another copy at home. The second was of Con Abbott, grandmother's niece, one of the Menzies girls, who wrote from London every couple of weeks and told of a lot of things about the war which were not in the papers. Her letters still survive. The third was of our cousin Florence who lived in Sydney and was then the most popular of the grandchildren and was always being cited as an example to us. We did not think much of her.

The progress of the war changed that table. The old photograph of Major Monash in his Garrison Artillery uniform came down from the mantelpiece: John Monash, an old family friend, with fierce waxed moustaches and his hands clasped over his sword. He graduated to the table when he became Colonel Monash, appointed to lead the second contingent from Australia. A month later Keith had a photo in uniform and he got a place—previously he had not been at all popular. Then Florence moved to the mantelpiece, she had lost popularity and never got back; so unpopular did she become that eventually she went even from the mantelpiece.

In 1916 Athol, Ralph and Owen all got uniforms and a place on the table. Phyllis, most unpopular of all, got her M.A. and could not be refused a place. Then Ronnie and Neil did so well in their examinations that they were crowded on. I was the only one of the family never to be honoured. The table became so jammed with topical photos that Con Abbott was moved to the mantelpiece and only got down for a couple of weeks during her visit to Melbourne in 1917.

By this table Neil and I sat uneasily and made formal conversation and then were allowed to look at London *Punch* and the *Illustrated London News*. *Punch* we saw occasionally at the dentist's but here we could look at numbers we had missed. Its jokes were no longer the naive things which uniformed maids said to their smartly dressed mistresses; now they were the ingenuous things which privates said to officers in riding breeches. The *Illustrated London News* was far more interesting. Its photos were far better than those in the *Argus* and *Herald* and they were all about the war.

Con Abbott's letters from England were vivid and personal to us. She told that she was glad Australia was sending her men, they would come in useful and she 'hears they are to be used in England as garrison troops—this poor little isle must have some left to protect it'. She was surprised that none of Aunt Rosie's nephews had wished to go, 'for in England there were a few shirkers and they had a bad time of it—and what a glorious chance if they come through all right for distinction, and if they don't it is a noble death.' Aunt Rosie passed on Con's sentiments to the elder brothers.

When the next war came in 1939 Con's attitude had changed. Two of her nephews were in jobs, which, she hoped, would be protected and, with luck, neither would have to join up.

After about an hour our visit neared its end and the only good part was still to come. Grandmother suggested that we might like a piece of cake. We would. It was rich fruit cake, kept on the sideboard beside the claret decanter, and we were offered claret too. It tasted good and made me, just nine, feel very mature.

Con Abbott in a letter to Aunt Rosie told about the spy she caught. She was in the Park Royal Hotel in London and her favourite nephew, Lindsay, was playing billiards when they saw a man drop a paper.

> Lindsay told me to sit on it as it was a plan, so I never budged and when everyone left we saw it was a plan of the water-works as they have been trying to put Anthrax and Typhoid germs in the water. I told Lindsay to take it to the police, they had a search and found the man, but I don't know what they have done with him, anyway they found that the chart was important—they have made up the wildest stories about the mystery of Park Royal Hotel and how the villain was trapped.

Her next letter gave more information. It was a printed plan of a reservoir in Wales left by a rural-council engineer who had been in London on some council business.

That Lindsay.

> At the end of August his name was in all the English papers, as the hero of the West End Cinema raid, that is one of the biggest cinemas in London and Lindsay found it was run by Germans, so he and some pals stood up before the war pictures were shown and Lindsay told the people that it was a German concern and the audience ought to leave the hall and not support Germans showing our war pictures and making money out of them: there was a terrible scene in the house and the British boys got the best of it—two days after it was brought up in Parliament, and then the accounts of a British boy's courageous fight made us laugh.

I don't think we smashed up any cinemas in Melbourne, but at least we did wreck the Swiss pastry-cook's shop in Prahran.

Con's hotel was near Kensington Gardens and there an Army Services Depot was set up just after the war started; cars were bought and commandeered and gathered there. Every day they were driven out by men in khaki taking their officers to lunch at the Ritz.

The officers were very dashing and had become sudden heroes. Even the men had their charm. They may have only been pawns in the game, but they were necessary; simple obedient men, like well-trained dogs, but they could talk to their masters and they were given the condescending name of 'Tommies'.

The depot was fascinating, real officers and men right in the heart of London and much more fascinating than the Zoo. Con saw two lots of royalty visiting it, and she went too. In September she even went to see Tommies in hospital and they loved telling her of their adventures; neither party worried that they had not been to France.

Con Abbott was very proud of Lindsay, her 'Soldier Boy' nephew. He got to France with a commission in 1914 and survived the war. Keith also survived the war; Con thought the two would like to meet when it was all over and invited them both to lunch, but it did not work out as well as she hoped. Her soldier-boy's job in France throughout the war had been with some London buses which had been sent over for transport behind the lines; it was dangerous work, with so little street lighting.

This was a very male war. The males could wear uniforms, from the Boy Scouts up, the Senior Cadets, the Citizen Forces and of course the army, though there were not many of them yet—only the permanent military establishment and the instructors in the Compulsory Training Scheme. There were no uniforms for females, not even the Red Cross, so all they could do was make things for the men. In England too the women were sewing and knitting. Con Abbott wrote on 18 August from the Park Royal Hotel in London:

> Everyone here is busy making a lot of useless things for the poor soldiers—one can't turn round without seeing women knitting cholera belts or bed socks, such prickly looking scrubby things—I came home yesterday and found a man's night shirt on my bed all cut out for sewing with 'Mrs Abbott's work' written on it—and immediately took it along to a poor sailor's wife to give her the chance of making a little money instead of attempting to spoil it myself.

Women felt they must do something, but cholera belts? In the few weeks when the British had been in France there had not been a case of cholera, but they would be ready if it came. Bed socks: they knitted them, but who wanted to wear them? But knitting was expected of women.

Two years later there was a genuine demand for socks in the sodden
trenches of Flanders and France, but long before then, women knitted
socks—and in Australia there was a surplus of good wool. They knitted
socks at every opportunity and in all places. In church there was a division
of opinion, but the majority view was that it was proper to knit during
the sermon.

Phyllis was knitting socks on the dummy of a cable tram on her
way from Flinders Street station to the University and dropped her ball
of wool on to the road. A chivalrous man tried to retrieve it for her,
but the more he pulled, the more the ball unwound. The dummy was
festooned with khaki wool by the time the tram got to the University
and she had to go on to the next stop before she got it all back.

Everybody could do something to help win the war. Money was the
thing, money for the Belgians or the Red Cross. If you couldn't give
money you still might be able to buy things which otherwise you would
not buy, and you could make things for raffles. Raffles became respectable provided the proceeds went to a patriotic fund; they swept the
country.

Mr Pyke, who lived in the house behind us (the one with the good
grapes on the roof of the shed), was a good amateur joiner and he made
a splendid doll's house ready for raffling. His elder daughter, Gelda,
sewed the blanket and sheets for a tiny doll's bed with a big red cross
on the coverlet.

We had always done charitable things at church; now we did patriotic
things. As well as sewing things for the missions at the Dorcas Society,
we formed a Red Cross society and it, too, made things and sent parcels
to the men overseas. It lasted the war until the Armistice; then it dispersed
its funds by giving a book to each returned man and father painted
the inscription inside each—he had plenty of time to do it. Ralph still
has his, a book on Lord Kitchener:

ARMADALE PRESBYTERIAN RED CROSS SOCIETY TO RALPH LEWIS.
In appreciation of gallant services rendered to Australia and the
Empire, with the Seasons Greetings. December 1918.

And we nine-year-olds who suffered every four weeks at the Missionary
Children's League and Mission Band, we eased up on our efforts for
the missions, and with our grubby little fingers, we wound strips of
linen for bandages for our men.

The family was in no position to buy much, but every now and then
we had to take a raffle ticket, although I don't think we ever won anything. When flag-days and button-days became common, one of us
might be shamed into paying a shilling for a button; when we got

home, it was passed on to someone else going out and the single outlay might be enough for two or three of us.

We had been very proud of ourselves: we had been proud of father's success and reputation; we had been proud to have three of the family at the University and two at Wesley and I was to go there next year. Then it all tumbled down. The outbreak of war made a complete muddle of the entire mining industry and dried up the flow of capital for any new works.

There was no immediate possibility of any mining consulting work for father, nor indeed, of any engineering consulting work. His only regular income was a retainer from the Anchor Mine, but it was a low-grade mine, particularly dependent on the price of tin, and tin was at a ridiculous price. The Tasmanian government gave a loan to keep the miners employed, but the price did not rise, so the government foreclosed and sold off the machinery in a market which did not want mining machinery. There was no hope of the Anchor Mine ever raising more capital to open again when things got better. Father's retainer went with the mine.

The cold wind of penury blew and we took in sail. Mr Marr and his son no longer came to do the garden, but this seemed little loss and we quite enjoyed the slight extra load spread between so many. Milly got another job quite easily and came to see us on her day out; Mrs Leach, the charlady, stayed on and so did Lilah. There could be no thought of Lilah leaving; not only was she as good a cook as mother, but she was one of the family and would have stayed whether she was paid or not. She went out with us on family occasions, like going to the moving pictures to see 'Quo Vadis'. Although she was one of the family, she sat in the kitchen and it was all hers; even mother, her close friend, respected her territory. Lilah was much more comfortable than we were: the kitchen stove was lighted at least three times a week and the kitchen was the warmest room in the house. We had one little fire in the study, and the brothers did their homework wrapped in rugs in the dismal breakfast room.

We had rather more washing-up and drying-up to do. Even Athol made his own bed, and that meant things were serious. But there was absolutely no hardship, except for Phyllis in her first year of University, for there were some jobs which were regarded as essentially female. Before she left in the morning she cut the lunches for those at school. Although we thought a lot of Phyllis, we did not think so much of her lunches.

There was no hope of moving into a smaller house for our rent was particularly light and we more than filled the house and would do so until 1916 when the four elder ones were in the army. Food seemed as good as ever, but I suppose we were more careful. We still had our claret at Sunday lunch, but it was strictly a one-glass drink; mother and father still had an occasional whisky before going to bed. We had no real hardship and could not grumble, but mother was anxious as we were living on borrowed money. The E.S. and A. Bank at the corner of High Street and Glenferrie Road was particularly understanding.

We were able to realize one asset. We had a car. In what was called the garage beside the stable, there really was a car, but it just sat there in the dark. It was an Argyle and it was a car of some note, as it had won the first reliability trial from Sydney to Melbourne in 1905 before father bought it secondhand. He justified his purchase on the grounds that it made him more mobile and would save time when he left Lottah on consulting work, but it did not work out well as the hills around us were too steep for it. It followed us to Melbourne and just sat there, although once on a Saturday afternoon Keith and Athol got it going and drove around Armadale.

We had got used to it just being there and had a sort of affection for it as an extravagance now beyond us. It was a clumsy car like an old-fashioned battleship, with fearsome great brass headlights and a detachable canopy roof held up by iron bars. Only one door it had, no doors to the front seat, just one for the back seats, central, right at the back with a step up to it like the ones on bakers' carts. It earned nothing and it had to go. We advertised it and off it went to become a spraying machine for an orchard. Fifty pounds I think it brought us, enough to keep us going for weeks. There seemed to be nothing else to sell.

We lived carefully but had no discomfort. We had enough good clothes to keep us going and the younger ones could expect the elders' clothes to be passed down to them. As the youngest in our new condition I had to finish up everything, but it was not all bad. In the end I got Keith's bicycle and his running shoes. But there was no overcoat available when I needed one at the end of 1914.

In the old days it would have been just a matter of going to Mr Preece's tailor shop in High Street, just up on our side from Chapel Street. Ordinary sort of people who wore a suit to work would have it made by a tailor and it was not much more expensive than the crude ready-mades. Mr Preece had made my clothes in the past, even when I was quite small. Owen had taken me down to Mr Preece one Saturday morning to be fitted and I was very angry when he and Owen laughed at me, just because the pants I was wearing were wrong way round and that little flap was at the back.

Father and the elder brothers had superior suits made in Melbourne by Mr Craigie, who had prospered and had his establishment in Little

Collins Street. He had made grandfather's suits and grandfather had helped him to set up in Melbourne. When Athol had his first son he took him in to Mr Craigie, then a very dignified gentleman, but he insisted on doing the cutting himself; it was something to have clothed four generations.

Now my new overcoat had to be a ready-made and mother took me in to town one Saturday morning. Town for mother consisted of Ball and Welch, quite a fashionable shop within sight of Flinders Street station, and George and George just a block away behind it. Mother also could recognize the town hall as she passed it on her way from one shop to the other, and she probably would have recognized any part of Collins Street between the Assembly Hall and Elizabeth Street, but beyond those limits she was likely to get lost if she strayed.

To George and George first, but all little boys' coats were far too expensive. Ball and Welch then, but there they were just as expensive and the matter would have to wait. But on the way out on the remnants counter on the right-hand side of the door was a coat of just the right size and it was only fifteen shillings, well within the budget. I hated it on first sight, I objected, but mother bought it.

Why that overcoat was so cheap and why it was on the remnants counter was its colour. It was a misty sky blue and was the most revolting coat in all Melbourne.

Two days later, on the very next Monday, as I ran around the playground at Lawside, the coat caught on a nail and got a tremendous tear. I went home at lunch-time utterly dejected. That horrible coat had cost good money and now it was ruined and another coat would be a drain on the family funds. At least, we would have regarded it as ruined a few months ago; now it was to be mended, that horrible-coloured coat was to have a great humiliating mend on one side. It was a couple of years before I inherited a respectable family coat from Neil, but the next year at the Armadale State School nobody seemed to worry about the colour at all; it was something to have an overcoat.

Father's income did not suddenly die, it faded until there was no justification for his office in Queen Street and he gradually abandoned it, but letters were still addressed to it as late as 1918. Miss Alexander, his secretary, got another job, but remained a family friend and visited occasionally, just as Milly did.

Father's big roller-top desk was brought home and jammed into the crowded study and mother took over his old one. The Hammond typewriter came home too, and it was very welcome to us all. It was a funny sort of typewriter with all the letters on a semicircular strip and the keys did not strike directly on the paper, but moved the strip into position opposite the striker. Its charm was that the semicircular strip could be taken off and another with a different type-face put on, and we could type in Gothic lettering or script.

Now that there was nobody to answer his office telephone there was justification in keeping our home one as being necessary for his work, not that there was much work. That telephone was good fun. Every Saturday morning a couple of the elder brothers would wait around until eleven o'clock and then rush for the phone. It was the weekly testing ring. 'Is that Malvern 1207? Testing ring only.' But the girl would not get away easily and she would be forced to put up with silly conversation. And the brothers would be very sympathetic when somebody rang up for J. B. Lewis, the dentist.

Things were bad for father; he seemed to shrink. He had been rather a remote and romantic figure, often away from home on adventurous journeys: to King Island, the west coast of Tasmania, the back of New South Wales; or to Cooktown, in the north of Queensland, and from there by horse-coach and horseback to the wolfram field. Some of us would see him off by train or boat, or we might be allowed to meet him on Sunday morning when he came back from Tasmania. We would be allowed to miss church and go into Melbourne on the Sunday church train and walk along to the Tasmanian boat, but there was no train home and we would go all the way in a cab, a four-wheeler with a step at the back, like our Argyle car.

Now all he could do was to sit in his study and read. Mother found him a nuisance when she came in to brush the carpet and do the dusting.

The leadership of the family passed to mother; she now had the responsibility and was firm and decisive about how we spent what money we had. In the past she may have already made up her mind and then referred to father for the decision she wanted. Now she took the decision without reference to him, for she thought he was not ruthless enough.

It was alway splendid when father agreed to paint a picture for me; it was always a castle, he liked doing castles, impossibly romantic castles on the top of steep hills with spiky roofs to their towers, all meticulously painted in water-colours. Or, for his own pleasure he would set out poetry on a big sheet of paper, or even a vellum, and use gothic lettering with little pictures scattered around the edge, like those illuminated addresses they presented to people when they retired. He enjoyed it and we had half a dozen framed and hanging in the drawing room. Often he gave mother one for her birthday.

Now he had plenty of time for his painting. He felt it too trivial for a regular occupation and he gave it up; he could sense that mother resented him being in the study all the time. His old position had been so dignified that he had done nothing about the place; now he helped clear things away after meals and he even pottered about the garden. That got him out of the way and did no harm to the garden.

We started growing vegetables as a way of saving expense, but our sandy soil was not very good. The only thing that flourished was New Zealand spinach, a ground-creeping succulent which tasted vaguely like spinach when it was boiled up. It tasted quite good for a while, but it was like the widow's cruse, it never failed; there was always New Zealand spinach in the garden. Soon it tasted horrible and did so for the rest of the war and, for that matter, still does.

Time hung heavily for father at home. He still got an odd trip, but trips were very rare throughout the war, and he took on jobs which would have been too undignified for him in the past—like supervising the University examinations at the end of the year. This lasted for two weeks and brought in some money, and at least, it kept him out of the house.

He seemed ashamed of himself in his forced futility and unconsciously our attitude changed. The dashing and romantic father of peace-time began to look like some old bloke who pottered about the place.

Things were going very differently for his oldest and closest friend. John Monash had been his particular companion at the University and was an old family friend who now wrote occasionally to father and grandmother. His career had been close and parallel to father's and on three occasions there had been talk of partnership.

They may have seen each other as boys at Scotch College, but it was at University where they became close friends. Father was doing engineering, and Monash, a couple of years younger, was doing arts. Monash had a great affection for grandmother and father found the Monash home to be a kindly place with interesting people.

Father was working for David Munro and Co., and getting time off to attend lectures. The firm was the biggest engineering contractor in Victoria, or in Australia for that matter, and built a lot of things, like railways and bridges, and father designed some. The firm got the contract for Prince's Bridge, the third on the site, and father may have had something to do with the final drawings; he certainly discussed them with Professor Kernot, his old teacher. Young as he was, father had a responsible job in a large and growing firm as chief estimator and confidential engineering adviser to David Munro and he certainly had business on the site works for the bridge. Monash visited the site with him and this turned his interest towards engineering.

In the 1884 examination results Monash passed his second-year arts with brilliance and also the additional subject of Surveying for Engineers. In that same year he was one of the most energetic of the small committee

which established the *University Gazette*, which became quite an important journal and lasted for decades. Pencil notes in a bound volume of
the early numbers show that father and Monash did a large proportion
of the writing–and both wrote well. Monash was also a capable musician
and there is family mention of his being interested in drawing, though
we have no samples of his work.

At the end of the next year when he finished his arts course, father
got him a job with David Munro as his assistant, while he did his engineering course part-time. Whilst together there, they discussed going
into partnership as consulting engineers.

The start of the great depression of the 1890s brought down Munro.
There was a bank loan of about half a million pounds; the bank itself
was shaky, and it took over the firm. Contracts were abruptly closed
and no new contracts were made; the assets–quarries, sawmills and ships
were sold at panic prices on a falling market. Although the bank kept
father on for a while, eventually he too had to go and he went with
three months' salary and set up as a consultant.

Monash had left the firm and was the engineer for a firm building
the Outer Circle railway. Although only in his very early twenties, he
carried out the work with real competence. He had no time to attend
lectures so he completed his course using father's notes and textbooks–
and he topped the honours list and won a scholarship.

Despite the bad times, father got married. Mother was eighteen and
prided herself on her cooking and Monash was their first dinner guest.
She served roast pork, and Monash ate it like a Christian. Mother could
not be expected to know anything about Jewish dietary laws.

Father wrote of a much later visit:

One evening, shortly after the birth of my first son, John Monash
visited us. He took a keen interest in the baby, and knelt beside the
cradle looking at the snowy haired, rosy cheeked baby. 'By Jove, Jim',
he said, 'I would give anything to have a son like that'. Shortly after
this, he himself was married. But he never had a son.

Monash kept an interest in the elder brothers but seemed to be closest
to Keith and there still exist the notes he wrote to him in France across
the barriers of military rank.

In the 1890s things were becoming steadily worse in Melbourne.
Banks were failing and the most substantial firms were going bankrupt.
Work was hard to get and there was real hardship–far worse than in
the later depression around 1930. People left for other places and the
population dropped to below that of Sydney.

Father's consulting work just jogged along–after all, there was
nothing else for him to do until he managed to get a sure salary as
Director of the School of Mines at Daylesford. Then he went back to

the University as a temporary lecturer in the absence of a man gone overseas, and he had to shed some of his consulting work so he pushed it to Monash.

The difference in temperament between the two men was shown in an incident about this time. Monash was a member of the German Club, for after all, his father had been born a German subject, and he wanted to keep up his German, and the Club was a jolly sort of place and very popular. He took father along as his guest. We were always a little embarrassed by father's love of reciting; to us it did not seem the sort of thing a mature engineer should do. That evening he recited 'Little Yacob Strauss', a mawkish piece about an old German immigrant's love for his lively little boy and spoken in the most amusing broken English; it later wrecked my dramatic career at the Sunday-school concert. When he finished his recitation there was a dead silence. Monash would never have been so clumsy.

The only major new engineering works were those for the sewerage of Melbourne and father took shelter with the Board of Works. It was here that he met his other close friend, Uncle Chris Kussmaul. His older friend, Monash, got a job with the Harbour Trust.

There was casual work to be picked up. With the shortage of money, disputes on contracts were frequent and both men acted as arbitrators and Monash was particularly enterprising. His arts degree left him only two years of part-time study to obtain his law degree, and he was very successful in court, here and in other States.

Then father had good luck. The Emu Bay Railway was being built across the wild country of the north-west of Tasmania. The bridges designed in London just could not be built in that heavily timbered country with its steep river valleys and rivers running in sudden floods and all to be done in cold driving rain. Monash designed one of the bridges and father did the others, very light steel trestles of considerable height above the water, and they attracted some notice overseas. In 1907 his paper 'Some Bridges on the West Coast of Tasmania' got him the Telford Premium of the Institute of Engineers, London, and few Australians have ever got that. John Monash was later noticed by the Institution; they gave him a good obituary in 1933.

Then father was offered the job of reviving a sick mine and it was this that brought the family to live in Tasmania. He did well and was a figure to be reckoned with in both mining and bridge building.

John Monash had weathered the financial storm and flourished. He had kept up his interest in the Volunteers and was known as Colonel Monash and was on the University Council. He was an enterprising man and acquired the local rights for the Monier Reinforced Concrete system in 1900. The bridge over the Yarra at Anderson Street was the first concrete bridge in the State and Keith remembers going with father to discuss it with Monash, the designer. His firm also built the dome of the Public Library, the biggest dome in concrete at that date. Although the design was the result of a competition, Monash must have had an important influence as he was the only man in the State with a full grasp of the new method. A funny thing he built was a little two-storey house at Mentone, all in reinforced concrete, roof and all, and the appearance suggests that the design came from France.

If there had been no war Monash and father probably would have had similar careers, both as engineers of repute in Melbourne. The war gave Monash the chance to use his genius and organizing ability on a world scale. 'The most resourceful general in the whole British Army', Lloyd George wrote of him. The war left father deeply in debt and with a wrecked career. The few jobs he picked up on his old reputation did not amount to much.

It was November and the war was three months old and we had done nothing great and glorious, not our side. The best thing they could scrape up in France had been the Retreat from Mons, and this did not sound as splendid as all that. Of course we Australians had captured German New Guinea, and apart from Austrian territory captured by the Russians, this was the only territorial gain, but after all, it had not been a particularly stirring conquest.

Glorious news. The *Argus* of 11 November:

LAST OF THE EMDEN

SHELLED BY H.M.A.S. SYDNEY

ENGAGEMENT IN INDIAN OCEAN

RAIDING CRUISER COMPLETE WRECK

And the news was confirmed. The ship which had been sunk by the Russians and captured by the British had now been sunk by us. We would have to wait four years for any news as splendid. It was our H.M.A.S. *Sydney* of His Majesty's Australian Navy, a navy only a few years old and only there because the Labor government wanted it instead of a subsidy for naval defence paid to the British. They had not sunk the *Emden*; we had.

We had deeply resented the *Emden*; she had been doing what we expected of the Royal Navy, she had been brilliantly successful at our expense. More disconcerting, she had behaved with the utmost chivalry to the crews of the captured ships, and we did not like it; we did not expect Germans to behave like that. Two days later, the Admiralty directed that the honours of war should be accorded to the captain and officers and they were not to be deprived of their swords. This chivalry seemed out of place; the past wars had been civilized affairs but this one was against the uncivilized Germans and the Admiralty should have known better. Worse still, a group in Perth wanted to entertain the captain at dinner and our papers made loud protests.

And although the *Emden* was sunk, she had the last laugh. Some of the crew who were ashore on Cocos Island got away in a ketch, right under the nose of the *Sydney*. But they could not get far with the Royal Navy in command of the seas and that ketch kept being captured and sunk. It got clear away to a Turkish port and the crew got home and were all issued with Iron Crosses.

The end of the year was coming, the end of the year which was to have seen Germany smashed. We Australians had done quite well, and now there were 20 000 of our troops in Egypt. We would have to wait a little longer for the promises of August to be fulfilled.

The Russians were not in Berlin or Vienna and the Germans had not been thrown out of France and Belgium. Joffre, the French commander, said that 'The Allies' coming victory was a mathematical certainty', but he may have been counting on the Russians to win on the Eastern front.

The *Argus* of 23 November:

> It seems that the Allies are compassing no overwhelming victory against the Germans on the Western front, but are content with making their position in France and Belgium secure – their strategy appears to be generally planned to prevent the Germans using troops against the Russians, to whom they must look for the more decisive movement in the war. The Eastern campaign has so far developed with practically uniform success for the Russian arms.

Yet our map on the breakfast room wall was unconvincing.

The Eastern Front

The Russians needed just a little more time. On 27 November: RUSSIA
TRIUMPHS. GREATEST VICTORY OF THE WAR. The next day: GERMANY
IS THREATENED WITH CRUSHING DISASTER. The *Argus* quoted the London *Times*: 'The Russians do not hesitate to say that German generalship
has broken down, and that German strategy is so bookish everywhere
it has failed to survive'. It was odd that the Germans seemed pleased

with themselves and were making a fuss of Hindenburg and wearing buttons with his portrait on them, for the Russians were sure and confident. On Christmas Eve General Sukhomlinoff, the Russian Minister for War, said 'all information which the Germans gave regarding a so-called brilliant victory in Poland was sheer invention'.

How could we know that the British Cabinet had a secret report from the British military attaché in St Petersburg telling of 'an alarming shortage of ammunition, generals with no previous experience of command of fronts, 800,000 reservists ready to go to the front, but with no rifles to equip them'; of 'panic retirements from the front line, and neglect of arms and ammunition'?

And Lord Roberts, the hero of the Boer War had died. He had gone to France to encourage everybody there and it had been too much for him, for he was an old man. He was a loss; he had been a sort of mascot, a chirpy little fellow, a foil to the massive and taciturn Lord Kitchener.

And there was more talk of the disloyal Sinn Fein in Ireland and Sir Roger Casement had been in Germany trying to recruit a force of Irish war-prisoners to fight against England. Summing it all up, things were good, but not nearly as good as we had expected.

But there was still enjoyment in the war. Lawside had always been very patriotic, but never as patriotic as on its 1914 break-up.

The first sign was that we all had to bring along a Union Jack. This was all right, as I already had one in quite good condition, but then we all had to wear a wide red, white and blue ribbon and pay Miss McAllister sixpence for our pieces. Mother was being very careful of family funds and was reluctant but I got mine in the end.

We children sat in the front seats of the Presbyterian Sunday school, just as we always had done, with our parents behind us, and groups marched on to the low stage and sang songs. This year they were all patriotic songs and we waved our Union Jacks and there was one item when the three biggest girls carried on three really big Union Jacks provided by the school.

There was 'Rule Britannia'; this was standard procedure, but we had other more popular ones. We boys sang 'Soldiers of the King' as a completely male chorus. This was the first time that the boys as a group had done anything important at the break-up. We now had an importance because there was a war and we were males—the oldest of us just nine.

Then came the grand finale. The whole school on the stage, Union Jacks and all, and the three big ones of the senior girls, which they waved in time with the music.

Hurrah for the red, white and blue,
Then hurrah for the red, white and blue;
And so shall they wave proudly for ever,
The glorious red, white and blue.

—or words to that effect.

The first year of the war was going out in glory at Lawside Kindergarten, Armadale.

1915

9
The War Continues

The first Sunday of 1915 and the Jones boys thundered into church in their neat uniforms, but we were not impressed. Already some of the young fellows had come to church in clumsy khaki, not nearly so impressive as the Joneses, but somehow, they looked better; they came once or twice and then were seen no more. They had gone overseas and we expected that the Joneses would be off soon.

Most of the fun had gone out of the war; it had lost its novelty, like the Jones boys. The Rosenfelts moved out of my life and went to Sydney and I only saw Max once again, years later. Pretty little Marie disappeared forever but their Standard car survived. It had become part of the family and when it got too old for service, it was retired to a big shed at the back of their house on the North Shore, where it was joined by other Standards when they, too, went into retirement.

The Rosenfelts had gone, and if that was not enough, Lilah was leaving. To all of us younger ones she had been mother's deputy. If we wanted permission to do something and mother was not there, we asked Lilah. For seventeen years she had moved about with the family and was more one with it than the elder brothers who spent most of the year away at boarding school.

We all went down to the boat to see her off. It was quite a little steamer; Lilah was travelling steerage and her place was right in the bows with curving walls. She was off to California to marry her admirer of twenty years ago who had been forced out of Melbourne by the depression. Now he was in California and could support a wife. Off she went.

Mother and Lilah exchanged letters every couple of weeks and then we got the news. Lilah had a daughter, not at all bad after that long wait.

Lilah's place was taken by Nellie; she was a friend of Lilah's but it

The family in 1915: (back) Ronnie, Owen, Keith, Athol, Ralph; (front) Phyllis, Mother, Father, Brian, Neil

must have been a tolerant friendship. Lilah was plump and jolly, Nellie was bony and miserable. She too, was Salvation Army but she was strict; she was like the extreme Scots and Northern Irish at church who disapproved of most things. The kitchen was no longer a warm refuge, it was a place to be avoided.

Nellie stayed for about two years and then moved on. The load of housework had decreased and we could make do with something less efficient. A girl from the Salvation Army Home was cheap but unreliable. Elsie was a nice generous one who was good fun; she left before her stipulated time of probation to open up a laundry with a friend, and mother connived. Another one was very presentable but got roaring drunk one night and had to be removed screaming and her room was full of empty brandy bottles. Young girls were quite cheap but needed training in elementary things. The cheapest of all was someone with some handicap. Towards the end of the war we got the cheapest on the market, a nice Englishwoman in her thirties who had been careless enough to have a child but no husband.

After Christmas 1914 I met a Belgian and spoke to him. Ronnie had taken me camping near Frankston and one evening we went to visit the Bathursts, who lived in Dandenong Road and had a holiday house on the beach at Frankston. A pleasant still evening and we were sitting on the sand and there was Mr Van der Keelan; not only was he a Belgian, but he was the Belgian consul, and I spoke to him for quite a time. None of my friends had ever seen a Belgian, let alone ever talked to one.

We had hoped that the war would be over by now but it was going steadily on. There had been no great victory at sea; the British fleet was sheltering from submarines, but even so the submarines were sinking odd ships and others were blowing themselves up. The Russians were not yet in Berlin, in fact they were further from it than when they started, but they were doing well against the Austrians and the Turks. But that part of the war did not seem quite real; we were beginning to think that the real war was in France.

The papers published accounts of Christmas at the front and the Germans had not been bestial at all; both sides had been nice to each other and sung carols and given each other presents, but it seemed that these were not the real Germans, the Prussians, but only Saxons, Bavarians and Wurttembergers.

Both sides were now besieging each other from trenches, and although they looked to be only thin lines on our map, neither side seemed able to break through. Now it was possible to walk all those hundreds of miles from the Belgian coast to the Swiss Alps without putting head above ground. Trench warfare had become standard.

Warfare was changing. At the end of January we read OFFICERS OF INFANTRY ARE NO LONGER TO CARRY SWORDS. They were to carry pistols and rifles, just like ordinary men. I suppose swords were not very good for fighting in the trenches.

Then the war came to Australia, right into the heart of the country, to the remote mining town of Broken Hill, hundreds of miles from anywhere else. It came on an ice-cream cart.

It was a beautiful day for the New Year holiday and at ten o'clock a picnic train of open trucks set off. When they were about two miles out of town there were sudden shots and in the trucks people started dropping with wounds and terror.

Beside the line stood an ice-cream cart flying the Turkish flag, an eighteen-inch red square with a white crescent and star stitched on it; alongside were two elderly gentlemen potting away with rifles and they got in twenty or thirty shots before the train got out of range.

At the next station someone rang up the Broken Hill police and they roused the rifle clubs and what military there was and hundreds swarmed out to battle. The two enemy had taken up position in a quartz outcrop, stopping on the way to call at a house and shoot the man who opened the door.

For nearly three hours our forces shot at the enemy but by one o'clock there was no answering fire. Poor old Mulla Abdulla, a butcher, and Gool Mahomed, an ice-cream vendor, lay shot full of holes and only one of them was still breathing. They had scored four killed and seven wounded.

TURKS ATTACK TRAIN

BROKEN   HILL   SENSATION

FOUR   PERSONS   KILLED

SEVEN   OTHERS   WOUNDED

POLICE SHOOT MURDERERS

A mob went to the German Club in Delamore Street, set it alight and hoisted the Australian flag over the ruins; then along came the military to guard it with fixed bayonets. The mob moved off to destroy the Afghan camp outside the town, for they too were foreigners.

Then the war in Europe was resumed after the Christmas break and it felt good to know the tide was sweeping us on to victory. The Russians were carrying us along and winning victory after victory. They told us that the German attacks were now half-hearted, badly concerted and showed a lack of impetuosity, and that the condition of the Germans taken as prisoners was pitiable.

The Germans were in a bad way, for the French official estimate was that they had suffered three million casualties out of the six million men who had started the war not so very long ago. They must be feeling sorry that they had started it, for now they were calling up middle-aged and elderly men. We were gaining in strength. Britain's New Army was in the making and there were 35 000 Canadians in France.

The German offensive in France was at a 'complete stop'. The Germans seemed to be as wasteful of human lives as we and the French were; they were so short of officers that all we needed was patience and they would be beaten. They must be feeling desperate for they were acting viciously. Zeppelins were raiding the east coast of England, and there was 'trustworthy evidence' that they were being guided by the headlights of motor-cars driven by German spies.

We were energetic about our Germans and new regulations were issued at the end of January. 'All able-bodied Germans between the ages of 18 and 50 were to be arrested and interned; no German was allowed to own pigeons, motor cars, a motor boat, a yacht or aircraft, a camera, a map or any fire-arm, nor more than 3 gallons of petrol'. They were not permitted to 'frequent hotels or other licensed premises, nor any place of public amusement'. Aunty Dora was not now allowed to go to the pictures with us.

We already hated the Germans and now we were officially encouraged to do so. 14 January 1915: KIPLING TO WRITE WAR SONGS, 'something better than "Tipperary"'. We knew what Kipling thought about the Germans.

Rudyard Kipling, with his wonderfully catchy phrases, was the most popular writer in England. He wrote for the middle class, and this was the first middle-class war in our history. In previous wars we had supported the armies of the upper and lower classes; now they were reinforcing us. The upper class read books but made no great parade of their capacity; the lower class had recently learned to read newspapers, but not books. Books were written for the middle class. Kipling was particularly popular with Australians for he had been complimentary about our troops in the Boer War and had visited us and even made references to our countryside in his jingles. He voiced our opinions and did much to shape them.

His most successful early stories had been fantasies of the Empire at its greatest, all the better for not being restricted by pedantic knowledge of the Indian jungle and other backgrounds. To him the English were above criticism, the Irish and Scots were quaint, the French were ridiculous, Russians were barbarous and Americans were crude. As the war approached he changed his views and concentrated on dislike and distrust of the Germans. We accepted his views.

In 1911 in 'The Horse Marines' he had been appreciative of a French naval petty-officer who was one of a party going to Portsmouth where a French cruiser lay with the British fleet. (A few years earlier that cruiser would not have been there and Kipling would not have been nice about a Frenchman.) On the way they ran into army night-manoeuvres and were held up by a group of Boy Scouts acting as army auxiliaries. Boy Scouts were new and we had not realized their potential military value in the coming war.

In 1913 in his 'Edge of the Morning', a plane containing two German spies made a forced landing in Kent. It was as recently as 1909 that Blériot had flown twenty miles across the Channel, but aviation had improved since then. In Kipling's poem the plane had flown from Germany, crossed the Channel and got twenty-three miles inland and was still expected to fly back to Germany. The plane was soundless and we gained an inkling of the capacity of German spies. The spies were killed in justifiable homicide by an aristocratic house-party, which included a Law Lord, a viscount, and an uncouth but nice American— what made him particularly nice was that although he had fought for the Boers, he now had a reverence for the English and the late Queen Victoria. They were quite justified in their killings, for the spies had set out with bundles of personal letters which established their nationality, and an album of photographs of British forts, which established the reason for their mission.

In 1914, before our propaganda had been properly organized and we were still talking about the 'Germans', Kipling wrote 'The Hun is at the Gate'; this was before the French had invented 'Boche' for them.

In 1915 in his story 'Mary Postgate', a prim old-maid saw a child who had been killed by a bomb from a German plane. When she returned to her house she found a badly injured German airman in anguish in the garden; his hair was so closely cropped that she could see the 'disgusting pinky skin beneath'. He moaned for help. She went about her affairs patiently in the garden near him until she heard him die, then she went inside and had a 'luxurious hot bath'. Kipling wrote that for us.

About this time he wrote 'The Beginnings': the time when the English began to hate the Germans.

> Their voices were even and low,
> Their eyes were level and straight.
> There was neither sign nor show,
> When the English began to hate.

The Germans responded:

> We will never forgo our hate,
> We have all but a single hate,
> We love as one, we hate as one,
> We have one foe and one alone —
>   England.

But the German Catholic press deplored the hatred of England: 'It was un-Christian, immoral and unworthy of the German nation'. Funny that the Germans should hate us.

We could retaliate. The *Age* of 6 February reported an incident in South Australia, probably in the Barossa Valley.

> Major Logan and men from the Citizen Forces arrived this morning and immediately began raiding the business premises and houses of Australian Germans living here. [By 1915 most of them must have been third generation born in Australia.] All traffic into and out of the town was blocked by sentries who interrogated all who arrived and left the town. Major Logan inspected a score and more of places, not only of naturalised Germans but also of Australian-born residents. Major Logan states that he found nothing whatever on which action could be taken. He expected to find nothing, but certain information of an indefinite character had been given to the Military Authorities.

Our Irish Australians were pleased about things. The *Hygeia* took 1500 of the United Irish League on a picnic down the Bay. Dr N. M. O'Donnell, their president, reminded them that Home Rule was now the law of the land and that 'the blood of England, of Ireland and of Scotland had flowed in one stream on the plains of France', and the mix-up of the war with Catholics and Protestants in the ranks on both sides meant that sectarian difficulties 'were done away with forever'.

On 6 January Keith went into the army; it was the infantry, because he had got tired of waiting to be called up for the Engineers. Although he had been commissioned in the Citizen Forces he went in as a private; in May he became a second lieutenant.

It was something to have a brother in the army. He had a uniform and all uniforms were splendid, even the Boy Scouts'; they looked like infantile soldiers with their wide-brimmed hats with dints in the crown like the New Zealanders; they wore khaki shirts and shorts and even their long sticks looked like rifles.

The Boy Scouts were a new thing which would bring out the best in boys and make them manly; they marched about the place in straggling groups and attended patriotic meetings in a vaguely official capacity in a row at the very front. They could wear their uniforms quite often and their numbers shot up as a result. Alan Gibbs and I thought they were priggish, but still, they had uniforms.

I climbed over the back fence and down into the Pykes' garden one Saturday morning and boasted to Mrs Pyke about the patriotism of our family. Keith was in the real army, the elder brothers were in the Citizen Forces or the Senior Cadets; even Neil was in the Junior Cadets and I thought of joining the Boy Scouts. She may have been impressed at the time, but neither Alan Gibbs nor I ever got round to it.

Keith Lewis

On Keith's first weekend leave, it seemed right to have a family photograph taken. Keith changed into his old civilian clothes and we all went to the photographer in Chapel Street. This was the second formal family photograph – the first had been taken by a travelling photographer at Lottah, but it was regarded as an interim affair, for the family had not yet stabilized its numbers. In that photograph I was the baby in mother's arms, but there would be another who did not last long. Now the number was settled at eight. The family of 1914 was well-dressed and comfortable. We would never again have such tidy clothes and we would never all be together again. The war would blow us apart.

The next important photograph was taken in May; it was of Keith as a second lieutenant, the lowest sort of officer, but impressive enough. The two shoulder straps on his Sam Browne belt looked like a pair of braces; that style was going out of fashion and being replaced by a single diagonal strap. The photograph was so important that it was put beside the old one of Major Monash on grandmother's table. Monash was now a full colonel in charge of the second batch of Australian troops which was to go overseas soon.

On 29 March the University was embarrassed. Professor Wallace of the English department returned unexpectedly.

In December 1914 the Council had considered a letter he had written from England. He had asked for leave of absence so that he could enlist; he was being markedly patriotic for he was forty-two. The University's reply was both patriotic and generous. It granted him leave on half-pay and agreed to pay his insurance premiums. It appointed Archibald Strong, lecturer, as Acting Professor with a loading of £300, thus doubling his salary. As a professor's salary was £1000 the University made a profit from its patriotism and improved its teaching.

In those days professors were expected to lecture and the University had two whose lectures could not be understood – Laby of Physics, then called Natural Philosophy, was incomprehensible; Wallace of English spoke such broad Scots that he could not be interpreted. Julie Hickford attended his early lectures in 1913 but gave up attendance and passed because of her reading. Strong was a lucid lecturer.

Wallace explained that the University's reply had come too late for him to get a place in his old regiment; he said that he had sent a cable, but if he had, it had not been received. So he was back in his old job and Strong was back on his £300 a year.

Wallace did get into the army in 1917 and Strong did become Acting Professor and was brilliant and popular.

10
Armadale State School

Now the war hit me and I was indignant. I had expected to be more privileged than my brothers and to go straight on to Wesley with no break at the State School, which the others had had. It was all very well father having no income but it meant that I had to face the humiliation of going to the Armadale State School when my friends were going to public schools; only Alan Gibbs would share my humiliation.

Mother takes me along on Monday morning, over the railway bridge at the Armadale station, beside the picture theatre, across High Street into a part of Armadale I do not know.

There it is: the State School. Two buildings at either end of a sort of prison compound. We enter at the side gate into the asphalted space with crowds of big boys and girls running about; rough they are and use shocking language – we can hear it already.

Yes, Mr Hill's office is in the big building, an immense forbidding building, a cruel building. The years since have shrunk it and it has mellowed; it now looks cosy and friendly. Mr Hill's office is on the left at the top of the stairs. We pass through a corridor crammed with nervous children and a few mothers; in to Mr Hill, pepper-coloured and peppery he looks, no wasting time. 'Yes, I think he can manage Fourth Grade, first door on the left and Miss Quin will look after him. Has he got a school-paper? No? There is time to get one at the little shop on the side of the lane.'

Back to the first door on the left; there mother leaves me, this is Monday and she must go home to the washing and Mrs Leach. A long wide room ahead. Miss Quin does not look a bad sort, a bit severe; beside her is Miss Farr, who is just about Phyllis's age, and she looks nice. 'Name? sit in the front seats with the other new ones.' Behind us are the old hands who have come up from the Third Grade and they look quite friendly, as if they would like to talk to us afterwards.

Some are about my age but most are older; they have no air of superiority and seem to welcome new recruits into their army. Better than I thought.

There is a lot of messing about; many of the children have not got their school-papers yet, they are retaining their Monday penny hopefully. That school-paper will be our sole textbook. We do not have history books and geography books as we did at Lawside; the school-paper has it all at the cost of a penny every second Monday. It is quite good reading, pictures and poetry and one thing and another.

We study history, even if we have no history book; it is all in the school-paper. This is a new sort of history. The explorers of Australia, we had never heard about them, although Burke and Wills had set off from Melbourne. There is Scottish history: Robert Bruce looking at the persistent spider and being inspired; Wallace, whose head was chopped off by the English; Bannockburn where the English were trounced, and to balance it, the tragedy of Flodden Field; the Fair Maid of Perth sacrificing herself to save her king. This is the only Scottish history I will ever be taught, and I learnt this much only because it was the custom to import the Director of Education from Scotland. We were never taught any Irish history. We did not know that Catholic schools taught it and the 'Great Oppression', but then they did not teach English history.

There is a ten-minute break and we go out to the crowded playground. We must keep to our end. The other end is reserved for the Third Grade and those even younger, but we are the youngest from the big building and are careful not to get in the way of the older grades. Quite a number of the old-stagers go out of the way to talk to us: 'Where do you live and what does your father do?'

We go into our room again and a couple of boys give trouble. 'Come out you two.' Miss Quin goes to her desk and brings out a thick leather strap. Each licks his hand. 'Now hold out your hand', and Miss Quin holds it in her left hand and brings down the strap with her right; each boy yells in his turn. 'Back to your seats.'

Public punishment is new and looks unpleasant. We gradually learn that Miss Quin will use the strap much more than Miss Farr. She, when she gives the strap, does not hold your hand and you are able to drop your hand just as the strap hits it.

Before the break we had all shared the lesson. Now a curtain is pulled across the big room and Miss Quin has the lot near the window, they are the bigger and duller ones. Miss Farr has the lot near the door, they are not so big and are brighter and their clothes are neater. They are more conformist. I am selected for Miss Farr's lot. We like her. She may not be able to strap as well as Miss Quin and she may not strap

The Armadale State School: grade room on left; then Mr Hill's office; junior school right foreground

so often, but we respect her and keep reasonably good order. But that first morning is a strain.

The bell rings, just like a church bell, and we go home for lunch. We from the Fourth Grade cross the station bridge in a straggling group and we sense that we are the aristocrats. Most of us live to the south; few live to the east, for there the houses are smug and most children go to private schools. No child comes from the grand houses to the north; those from the west are toughs.

We are the aristocrats. There are enough of us to form a faction and we dress more neatly than those westerners, and this is very important to the girls. The three greatest girl-aristocrats allow me to go with them. We cross the station bridge and go up Armadale Street. So does Bert Morland, and he is the top boy-aristocrat. He dresses neatly, not that this is a virtue in a boy, but he is top aristocrat because he can clean up every other boy in the class and some are older and much bigger than he is. He is amiable, not particularly big but compact, and gives one the feeling that, if roused, he will come in hard.

School seems much better in the afternoon. Even the numbers seem less overwhelming, although our Fourth Grade has more than three times the number of the whole of Lawside. In that host there are recogniz-able individuals who are already friends who will take your side against the world. We had thought of those state-school children as a rough lot, but now they don't seem rough. They seem mature and responsible, ready to protect and help. By the end of the first week our Fourth Grade is a group.

Our week has three great occasions. On Monday morning there is saluting the flag, we join with the whole school in that. On Wednesday morning we have 'Lidgy' – religious instruction. On Friday afternoon there is class singing.

On Monday morning we assemble in our different grades, from the First to the Eighth. Each grade marches to the flagpole and forms up. We do something patriotic and we sing something and the flag is raised in a sort of ball which breaks open when it hits the pulley at the top. Sometimes it doesn't break open and has to be pulled down and raised as a flag. It is the Australian flag, the wrong one with a red ground, but we sing to it just the same.

Monday morning is not the best time for a moving ceremony because everyone is feeling fresh after the weekend and Mr Hill is often cross with us. One Monday morning I was late, the only time it had ever happened; I was hopelessly late and very frightened. The parade was over, the flagpole was standing lonely with its flag and the playground was empty. I went up the stair and into the corridor and found it crowded with the Fourth Grade all waiting to go in turn into Mr Hill's office for the strap – I think the girls were exempt, but they suffered in some other way. I was able to go along to our room and sit there whilst the others drifted back snivelling. Fourth Grade had done something discreditable at the flag raising and only about three latecomers escaped. That was luck.

Wednesday morning, 'Lidgy'. The roll was called in our Fourth Grade room and we moved off to share our religion with groups from other grades. As there was no official religion and religion was desirable, there were optional groups – three, I think.

My group was the biggest and we went to the Fifth Grade room. Some volunteer visitor taught us, usually a mature lady; mother often taught. Sometimes we had a minister of some sort, Methodist or Presby-terian, I suppose. We had a Bible story; it was just like Sunday school, but the academic standard was lower and some seemed not to know or care about it. But it was fun and a change from other days. There was a fair bit of playing-up and an official teacher made occasional appear-ances to restore order.

I suppose the Church of England had its own group; the Catholics certainly had, and they were taught by a priest. There was no Catholic school near so there were quite a few of them and we thought them rather curious.

Religion entered into our daily lives: we heard the upper grades often calling on God or Jesus, but we in the Fourth Grade never did. Religion was lucky. Nuns walked about in pairs and it was very lucky to pass between them. Most of us felt that the rudeness did not justify the luck, but funnily enough, it was the Catholics who were most aggressive.

White horses were very lucky and to be the first to see one had very good luck. You called out, 'First luck, white horse', and whilst you were saying it you were licking your forefinger to make the sign of the cross on the sole of your boot, and you counted 'One, two three . . .'; if you got up to ten uninterrupted, the luck was all yours.

Class singing was the last thing on Friday and it was the whole of the Fourth Grade, with no curtain subdividing us.

We knew the songs—the war had as yet given us no new ones—and everybody knew the words. There was the kookaburra song, and in the first stanza we could use all the shocking words which we would never use at any other time, well, not we of the Fourth Grade. They were the old essential Anglo-Saxon words which have no modern equivalent but have been relegated to become the worst language of all, the four-letter words which we did not use then nor have since, but we sang them loudly in the class-singing, all of us did.

> Kookaburra, Kookaburra, [Cook you bugger, Cook you bugger,]
> S[h]its in an old gum tree
> Until a lizard passes,
> Rustling through the gr[arses].

The only song which had any application to the war was 'When Johnny Comes Marching Home Again'. Quite a few of us had relations at the war. When Johnny came marching home 'the men would cheer and the boys would shout', but what we sang about what the women would do was an anatomical impossibility, and we already knew it, but we liked to use the word in chorus.

We were learning something of comparative anatomy, we eight-and nine-year-olds. At Lawside there had been some inkling—the separate lavatories were a clue. The Third Grade seemed to know quite a bit, but not nearly as much as we did. Now we knew that the physical differences between boys and girls were denoted in the worst of the bad language which we had learned; that those words were 'rude' and referred to rude things, things which were very interesting but were obscene. It would be degrading to satisfy our curiosity or that of the girls. We would take violent action if a girl tried to look at us in an unguarded moment and the girls were just as secretive, but there was an occasional freak.

'Aw, do you know what she did? They went behind the lavatories after school and she pulled down her drawers and let him *look*.'

Those two had tasted of the fruit of the tree of the knowledge of good and evil, and we were dismayed. He was a bounder; we might envy him but we did not approve. That nine-year-old was a Scarlet Woman. The top girls of the Fourth Grade shunned her. She had wantonly revealed their common secret. What she had done would be remembered against her through all her years at the Armadale State School and into the years beyond. Later, any curious boy would expect to investigate her without any preliminary courtesies.

We gathered that our physical differences were more than just curiosities, they were essential to what the grown-ups did between themselves. Funny, you could not imagine sensible grown-up people doing anything so absurd, but it seemed they did; it was not only absurd, it was so ridiculous as to justify the very worst word of our new vocabulary.

State School was mature and competitive and male-dominated. We might fear Miss Quin, but she feared Mr Hill. In class it was the boys who settled things, they were in a majority; State School was reckoned to be too rough for potential ladies of the middle-class.

It was certainly violent and competitive and position depended on fighting. Fighting was different from scuffling—there had been interrupted scuffles at Lawside. Scuffling was an instantaneous retaliation; two boys might wrestle and scuffle on the ground, but the result did not affect their position in the hierarchy. This was settled by fights.

A fight was a studied and deliberate affair. Its origin might be ambition or a misunderstood gesture—a kick on the backside was only a gesture, but it might be too hard and would then generate bad feeling; or there might be long-standing animosity, so it had to be a fight.

The rules and procedures were as rigid as the laws of chivalry and had universal support. The two principals and their friends would settle the preliminaries. If the matter was not a serious one, the playground might be selected as the site, with the possibility of intervention by a teacher but the certainty of an audience. Serious fights were held in the lane.

Each combatant had a couple of friends as a mobile base, and it began. There was no fuss about taking off jerseys or jackets, no shaping up like artificial professional boxers, just pile in. No hitting below the level of the navel, and if one went down, no hitting until he got up.

Aggression was what won most fights. The one who went in more eagerly, and took a couple on the way in, could keep hammering away once he was there – this was where Bert Morland was so good. Although he was smaller than most he was solid and very quick. He did look like a fox-terrier.

The usual end was a blood nose. Black eyes were too slow in coming up but half an hour later the winner might look worse than the loser. Sometimes one would call it off and own defeat and it was settled – no shaking hands but a forgetfulness of what had started it all.

Scuffles might have involved a lot of people but fights were personal duels, except for the most noteworthy fight of 1915, a playground fight with a packed audience. It was a family affair between two pairs of brothers, a feud between the Ring brothers, sons of the local fuel merchant, and sons of a minister. There had never been a fight like it in living memory. It was not a particularly vicious fight, but interesting in that there was no knowing who would be hitting whom next. The Ring brothers won.

The girls at Lawside were lady-like and had never fought. The girls at the Armadale State School did and they were ridiculous. There were no preliminary arrangements: some sudden offence and they were clawing and scratching at each other, then one got the other's hair but it meant that hers was within reach and they were both tugging and squealing. Invariably, in walked Miss Quin and the girls got the strap, and serve them right for being so impetuous.

For the first few days school had felt precarious but soon it had an air of confident cosiness. Our Fourth Grade was a group which took no liberties with the Fifth Grade and we looked down on the Third Grade. Alan Gibbs was there but during school hours there could be no contact between us.

The Fourth Grade stood united against the teachers who strapped us, but we collapsed before the dreaded and omnipotent Mr Hill. We stood united against the adults of the outer world and we attacked the weakest of them.

It was a mechanical duty to yell at them: a Chinese greengrocer's cart demanded something about 'Ching Chong Chinaman'. We would improvise yells against those who could not take counter-action: a drunk man was vulnerable and there was a dirty old demented woman who hobbled about the streets near the school; she was fair game.

At Lawside we had looked down on the common children who played games in the street, and socially inferior games at that. Then we would not think of playing marbles; now we found it very enjoyable. Even lower was hopscotch and it turned out to be a pleasant social occasion, the only game we shared with the girls.

The streets were fun and it took a long time to get home after school came out at four o'clock. Much more interesting things happened in the streets than in some other boy's garden after kindergarten.

Those inferior State School boys used to 'whip-behind' carts, get a ride on the back; others seeing would call out 'Whip behind!' and the driver would lash his whip to the rear. Now we 'whipped-behind' and we found it good.

The two best types of cart were a light lorry and a baker's cart. The light lorry, used for delivering heavy goods like firewood, was an open platform on four wheels pulled by a medium-weight horse. If you could get to the back of the lorry unseen, you could hang down with knees bent to clear the road and you were almost invisible to the driver and almost out of range of his whip. Better still was the baker's cart, a sort of little cabin on four light wheels pulled by a light brisk horse. The cabin had a door at the back for the baker to take out his bread; under the door was suspended an iron step which the baker mounted to reach inside the cabin. That step provided a comfortable seat. You were quite invisible but in easy range of the whip when someone called, 'Whip behind!' The baker's cart went faster and was more exciting.

Much faster even than the baker's cart were the new electric trams in High Street. No one had thought of whipping-behind them, but Alan Gibbs and I did. We got on to the ledge outside the rear cabin at Orrong Road and off went the tram, frighteningly fast, too fast for me. Alan kept his place and got off at the next stop to come back and pick me up. I had fallen, been dragged along and skinned my knees and hands, and worse, broken one of my very new front teeth, an expensive disability I was to carry through life. We went back to Alan's house where his eleven-year-old sister was the only one at home; she bandaged me up very neatly and telephoned home for a brother to collect me.

We eight- and nine-year-olds of the Fourth Grade were no longer children and now had military obligations. We drilled.

The twelve-year-olds of the grades higher than ours had legal obligations under the Defence Act; they were Junior Cadets and would be prosecuted if they missed their official drills. I suppose it was easier to arrange drill by grades rather than by age of individuals and the Fourth Grade was the youngest involved.

On Wednesday afternoons we boys really drilled, much more seriously than on the Monday morning march to the flag-saluting; we drilled for half-an-hour and a fat Instructional Sergeant from the Defence Department came to supervise us. We drilled in platoons of our grades and 'Gussy', the young male teacher of Third Grade, was our commanding officer.

The boys were let out of class whilst the girls stayed on. Down the stone steps to the schoolyard we went and milled about, all the boys from the Fourth Grade to the Eighth. Then Gussy blew his whistle.

Two officious boys immediately ran up and stood at attention in front of him; they were the markers. The rest reluctantly formed lines beside them and then started the longest half-hour there ever was: marching and wheeling around that playground, standing at ease, standing at attention, marching and wheeling until the school bell rang four o'clock.

One Wednesday David Speedie and I talked things over. David was the bigger and simpler of the Scottish Speedie twins; Ronald Speedie was brighter and more conventional, he was getting on very well. David and I reasoned that as there was no roll call at drill, two would not be missed. We came out of the Fourth Grade at half-past three; when we came to the stone stairs we didn't go down them, but climbed over the fence alongside. We were free, and played in the street out of sight of the school.

We did it again the next Wednesday. 'You'll cop it', the others said, but we didn't. Next Wednesday a whole lot of the others followed us, so many that I was worried; this would be noticed. So I climbed back into the school yard. When Gussy blew his whistle, Ronald Speedie and I ran and briskly stood at attention in front of him. 'That is very good, boys. You can go.' So Ronald and I were excused drill.

It was certain to happen and it happened. Next morning Mr Hill, sandy-haired and fierce, came into the Fourth Grade and stood in the centre in front of the class. 'Come out all the boys who missed drill.' Twenty or so sheepish boys stood and walked to the front. I had no great wish for a beating from Mr Hill, but just as the sheep were moving off to slaughter I became afraid that I might be found out and that would be even worse, and so I reluctantly stood up. The sufferers and those who were safe called 'Gussy said he could go, sir.' 'Sit down my boy, sit down.' I was able to sit in comfort for the rest of the day because of the fellowship of the Fourth Grade.

Then it became unpatriotic for us to miss drill; the war was real and we eight-year-olds should be ready to take our place when the time came. Our war had not burst on us, it was fizzling along like the flame of the damp wick of a cracker; it was just possible that it would fizzle long enough to set off a splendid bang.

We of the Fourth Grade were interested and told each other the news; quite a number of us came from homes which had a morning paper. At Lawside that paper was the *Argus*, at the Armadale State School it was more commonly the *Age*, but there was no great difference in the war news. Most of us came to school knowing what the headlines had been. We were all waiting for something big, far bigger than the Boer War when little groups from each State had been allowed to go and join in the affairs of their betters. Now our troops were the Australian army and we could sense that we were living at a crucial period.

Our 20 000 men had not gone to England and France after all; they had been landed in Egypt, and that was not so silly now that Turkey was on Germany's side. It was interesting that they should be in the Bible lands and soon we had pictures of them in front of the pyramids.

Our troops were splendid men, we believed. But then on 20 January we saw the headlines: A LEAVEN OF WASTERS. WEEDING OUT THE UNDESIRABLES. This was a shock, but after all, we supposed that some were not up to representing us in our first appearance in the greatest drama of history.

The Turks made a muddled attack on the Suez Canal and it was AUSTRALIANS IN ACTION. ENGINEERS COOL UNDER FIRE. Our men had heard shots fired and it did not seem to have worried them and none was hit. So the Turks had shot at, or at least near, our own men. It seemed that the A.I.F. might get mixed up with the Turks and we had a quickened interest in what was going to happen.

On 15 February: FUTURE OF CONSTANTINOPLE. TO BE HANDED OVER TO RUSSIA. Funny that, a lot of us knew that the Crimean War had been fought by Britain and France to keep Russia away from there, but now it seemed that as Russia was going to win our war, she should be given something really big.

On 23 February: THE DARDANELLES. RIDICULOUS TURKISH REPORT. Those Turks said that the British battleships had fired 600 shells at the forts and had managed to kill only one man and injure another. This really was silly, because we knew that earlier efforts had badly damaged the forts and landing parties had gone ashore and made more damage.

On 6 March: 'General d'Amande it is said, is to command an Allied expeditionary force which is to land in Turkey and the first detachments of his troops had arrived off the Dardanelles'.

Then CONSTANTINOPLE MAY FALL WITHIN THREE WEEKS' TIME. On 9 March: TURKEY'S DOOM APPROACHES. On 10 March: AUSTRALIANS MAY GO TO THE DARDANELLES. The *Age*, quoting the Berlin Socialist paper *Vorwarts*, predicted that 'the Australian troops in Egypt will be utilised in connection with land operations against the Turks'. If we in Australia really did not know what the A.I.F. would do, at least the Germans, and through them the Turks, had a very fair idea. It now looked as if the Australians in Egypt would be given a place in the victory parade to Constantinople.

On 12 March the *Age* column 'Notes on the War' said 'if Mr Lloyd George persuaded his colleagues [of the British Cabinet] to consent to operations against the Dardanelles, then he deserves full credit for a very astute move'. Lloyd George got credit for a lot of unusual things because of his support by the Northcliffe press, but none because of Gallipoli. Later he got some credit for opposing it in Cabinet.

Gallipoli would temporarily wreck the career of Churchill. He had originally proposed a naval effort supported by the troops of Greece and Bulgaria, but the Russians would 'in no circumstances allow Greek forces to participate'. He demanded that a record be made of his 'formal disclaimer of any responsibility if a disaster occurred because of insufficiency of troops'.

On that very day, 12 March, decisions were made which would profoundly affect us, but, of course, we did not know about them. It had been decided to send troops to the Dardanelles, but not what to do with them. It was thought possible that the navy would get through, and if troops were used, they might only be for holding the land behind. Or there might be a predominantly military expedition, and for this the commander was appointed: one of those British generals who had advised us on our defence plans. He was important to us but we never seemed to hear much about him; the criticism was, that neither did his troops. General Sir Ian Hamilton was to take charge of a great expedition with no clear aims, no preparation, and only the vaguest idea of the conditions to be met.

The expedition had two guidebooks to Western Turkey and an out-of-date manual of the Turkish army. The British vice-consul at Chanak had recorded local conditions and the British military attaché to Turkey had made a survey of the straits and of the actual and possible gun positions in 1914; neither was ever used. Admiral Lympus, who had headed the British naval mission to Turkey, had advised on the naval defences of the Dardanelles. He was not consulted.

On 22 March: THREE BATTLESHIPS LOST. BOMBARDMENT CONTINUES. GREAT FORTS IN FLAMES. THE LOST BATTLESHIPS. OLD AND SLOW. The *Herald* of the afternoon of the same day: ON TO CONSTANTINOPLE. HAVING REPLACED LOST BATTLESHIPS. ALLIES RENEW EFFORTS IN DARDANELLES.

Those ships that were lost on 18 March were obsolete and there had been no tremendous loss of life–70 British and 639 French; more were lost every day in France and no fuss was made about it. More modern ships were ready to go forward; if necessary, more men and more ships would be lost, but the straits would be forced.

A hundred miles away in Constantinople the 19th must have been an anxious day. Would it be today that the great ships would appear in the Bosporus? If they did, the city would be cut in half; not only the city, but the armies and the nation would be divided by the British-controlled Bosporus. All the munition factories along the shore would go up in the first salvo. There would be riots and the pro-German government of the Young Turks might be displaced by the conservative pro-British party; the Christians were a sizeable minority, Greeks and Armenians, and they would run loose through the city. No landing parties would be necessary; it would just happen.

In the Dardanelles the Turks stood to their guns; it was all they could do, for the ammunition was almost spent and there was no hope of more. They stood waiting all day through the 19th and through the 20th.

It seemed too good to be true. Perhaps the warships were not coming, perhaps the Turks had won a victory—it was a long time since they had.

The weeks passed and it was clear that there had been a very great victory: the empire which had been falling to pieces, the 'Sick Man of Europe', had defeated the greatest armament of the world. Constantinople would remain. On the hills overlooking the Dardanelles still stands the Turkish monument, just big letters in white: 'Mart 18. 1915'. As the English had defeated the Spanish Armada, so the Turks had defeated the British Navy. Now would be a fitting time to get rid of troublesome minorities like the Armenians, for now there was no nation in Europe able to make a fuss. Russian exports would remain bottled up—all her wheat crop and two-thirds of her exports had gone through the Dardanelles. As the Baltic was also closed to her, no munitions could be sent to her ill-equipped armies.

But unlike the Spanish Armada, the enemy was still in a position to land troops and the Allies gave notice that they intended to do so. Goods were assembled and marked 'for the Constantinople expedition'. In our papers: DARDANELLES. COMBINED ATTACK PREPARING. 'The Allies can land three armies on the shores of the Peninsula. We may expect the Allies to attempt to capture the hills opposite Chanak Kalissa, thus enabling the fleets to steadily proceed with the work of clearing the Straits'. This had been published in the London *Times*. It was precisely what the Allies attempted six weeks later and the Turks may have appreciated the preliminary advice.

We sensed that our men would get mixed up with the Dardanelles and the Turks. We became less interested in what was happening in Europe and rather worried that the war would be over before they could do anything, for 'one of the officers of high command on General

French's staff' said that the war would be over by June, if not before.

Things were now going very well in Europe, particularly with the Russians. First thing in January, we read: GREAT RUSSIAN VICTORY. GERMANS IN FULL RETREAT. Then on 24 February there was BERLIN STATEMENT, claiming the capture of seven generals, 100 000 men and 150 guns, but this was only a temporary disappointment. It seemed quite proper to read that SLAV RULER SEEKS CONSTANTINOPLE. BRITAIN FAVOURS ASPIRATIONS. After all, they had already almost earned the place.

They kept going, those Russians. On 8 March: CRUSHING BLOWS. RUSSIA'S MIGHTY ARM. ENEMY HURLED BACK, and VON HINDENBURG'S FAILURE. SLAVS SWEEP ON. GERMAN SOIL APPROACHED.

Yes, things were going well. On 13 March: TURNING POINT PASSED. OPINION OF JAPANESE GENERALS 'PEACE WITHIN SIX MONTHS'.

And there was no doubt about the Russian success against the Austrians; they had been on Austrian soil for months but had been held up by the great fortress town of Przemyśl. It fell at the end of March and they captured 117 000 prisoners. They later did a re-count bringing the figure up to 700 000, though this seemed rather doubtful, even to us. But it was a real triumph and there was nothing to bar the way into Hungary. WILL AUSTRIA SUE FOR PEACE? Those funny Slav names were now to be taken seriously.

We were doing just as well in France. On 15 March: THE BRITISH SUCCESSFUL. MUCH ENTHUSIASM IN FRANCE. BATTLE OF NEUVE CHAPELLE. BRILLIANT FEAT OF ARMS. CONSIDERABLE GAIN OF GROUND. On the 18th: BATTLE OF SAINT ELOI. ANOTHER BRITISH VICTORY. On the 19th it was VICTORY AS USUAL; on the 27th the King named a filly, 'Neuve Chapelle, after the great victory'. So at last we were having a happy and successful war, although there had been 12 000 casualties—the number grew later. We swept on and captured Hill 60, 'after a fierce struggle during which many lives were lost' but it was the KEY TO FLANDERS. VALUE OF BRITISH CAPTURE. We did not know then that the Germans had recaptured it and that we would have to do it all over again years later.

The King congratulated General French; Haig's nose was out of joint as he had not been given the credit although he was responsible for it all.

On 16 April: NEUVE CHAPELLE. COSTLY BRITISH GAIN. A GENERAL BLUNDERED. The poor devils who survived the battle remembered it as a muddled massacre and we could see no gain on the map on the breakfast-room wall.

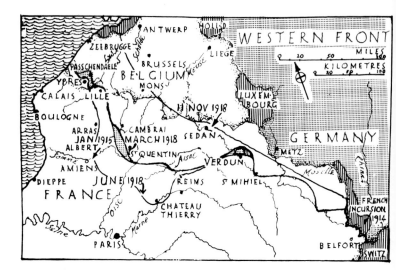

The Western Front

In August 1914 the Allies expected to be in Berlin by Christmas; by then they had got as far as the line on the map across north-western France. Three years of fighting and millions killed took them about ten kilometres nearer in two places. Ypres, the bulge on the extreme left of the line, cost 100 000 British lives and left a tortured patch of land and a dispirited army to face the German attacks of early 1918. The Somme bulge was just as costly in lives but it gave its place names to the streets and homes of post-war Australia—Bullecourt, St Quentin, Armentières, Albert and even Villers-Bretonneux. The southernmost bulge near Verdun only regained some lost land and cost a million lives, more French than German, and left little of the old French armies to face their disasters of 1917. In a matter of weeks in early 1918 the Germans pushed the line back as far as sixty kilometres and once again threatened Paris.

At the end of April the Germans used poison gas as a weapon, an atrocity in a year crammed with atrocities. It was a risky thing to do for, if gas warfare continued, we had the advantage with the westerly prevailing winds in our favour. The French panicked and their line melted, but the Germans had not enough men to exploit their success and the Canadians stood fast on the flank.

We used gas against the Germans in September as a preliminary to the great attack at Loos. The gas company was officered by academics from the University of London and the troops expected them to make a muddle, but in fact it was headquarters who made the muddle. There was not a breath of wind. A message was sent to headquarters that gas could not be used. The reply was that it was 'to be discharged at all costs'.

The gas drifted out and filled our trenches and our men did not know whether to go back to avoid it or forward to the attack. Some went forward and to jolly things up, someone kicked a football forward. The interesting thing was that it was not a rugger ball, but a soccer ball: this was a tiny indication that the men who were not gentlemen had been recognized as important in the war. The same idea was used later quite often and a lot of men were killed at football.

On 28 September: ALLIES' SUCCESSES. GREAT GAINS IN WEST 16,000 UNWOUNDED PRISONERS. BERLIN ADMITS REVERSES. 'The Allies' offensive has achieved success unprecedented since the Battle of the Marne'. On 30 September: THE GREAT ATTACK. ALLIES STILL ADVANCING. On 1 October: ADVANCE OF ALLIES. HUGE GERMAN LOSSES. EXCEED 120,000 MEN. But on 7 October: LOOS BATTLEFIELD. WARNING TO PUBLIC 'STILL FAR TO GO'.

Loos had been abandoned after eleven days and 60 000 casualties. General French reported it as 'a most successful attack under the brilliant leadership of General Sir Douglas Haig'. This was not good enough for Haig. He thought French was gaining kudos for his effort and wrote that 'it is unmanly to take credit which belongs to others'.

The *Official History* records Loos as 'the useless slaughter of infantry'; the survivors remember it as 'a bloody balls-up'.

Although we were doing so well, there was a feeling in London that we should have done better. On 19 May: THE BRITISH FORCES. SUPPLY OF AMMUNITION. IS THERE A SHORTAGE? 'There was a statement in several newspapers, apparently inspired by the military, that the British Army was fatally short of ammunition. This conflicts with Mr Lloyd George's statement of 22 April that the production of high explosive had placed the Government beyond anxiety'.

On 24 May the Liberal *Manchester Guardian* and the Northcliffe papers, the *Daily Mail* and the *Evening News*, complained that Kitchener had refused to supply the army with high-explosive shells. All other papers unanimously denounced the attacks and the *Pall Mall Gazette* stated that the Chancellor of the Exchequer, Lloyd George, was responsible for the trouble. On 26 May Lloyd George was appointed as Minister for Munitions.

Here in Australia we were looking for British leadership. Asquith, the British Prime Minister, seemed to be a quiet but effective leader, but he lacked glamour. We looked to the bright men. Carson, the leader of the Irish Protestants was bright enough, but he had a lot of things against him. Churchill we had known for years as energetic and forceful. Lloyd George was an unstable radical—after all, he had cut the naval vote just before the war as he said that there was no chance of a war with Germany.

The Germans had Hindenburg, and we could not help respecting him. We had Kitchener, but now Northcliffe was attacking him and building up Lloyd George so that his stature increased right throughout the war, until Northcliffe pulled the chair away from under him.

But if the war against the Germans was not going as fast as we hoped, at least the war against alcohol was being won. The sale of absinthe was perpetually banned in France, so both the French and the Russians were setting us a good example. In England Lloyd George was 'still inclined to enforce prohibition'.

On 30 March a South Australian referendum supported 6 o'clock closing for hotels with 74 166 votes, a clear majority over all the other times set out on the voting papers. The Labor Conference also advocated 6 o'clock closing. In Ballarat Father Lockington gave an address and after it 2000 knelt and repeated the pledge. The staff of the University had set an example when they pledged at a meeting to abstain from alcohol except under medical advice, and a lot of people followed them. It was an economical, if unpleasant way, of supporting the war effort. The Victorian government fixed trading hours from 9 a.m. until 9.30 p.m.

But drink was not beaten, even if it was in retreat: Senator Pearce may have closed the wet canteens in the camps, but unofficial canteens established themselves within walking distance, and worse, they had ' "harpies", degraded women, who now sought to degrade our young men'. The Presbyterian, the Rev. Professor Rentoul, said so.

In Melbourne men in uniform could count on getting free drinks and they were lying about all over the place. Archbishop Carr suggested re-opening the wet canteens.

The British blockade of Germany seemed to be hurting. The Germans said that the blockading of food supplies was against the rules of war and that view was shared by the European nations, but Britain controlled the seas and had not signed any convention. Germany seemed beaten and helpless.

Then at the beginning of February the Germans said that they would blockade England by sinking all ships trading with her by means of submarines. This seemed ridiculous, for at the beginning of the war Germany had only twenty-eight submarines as against the thirty-six British, and of those only ten were sea-going, very slow vessels carrying only two torpedoes; the other submarines were only suitable for harbour defence.

BLOCKADING BY BLUFF. FOE'S THREAT AMUSES. THREATENED ACTION MERE BLUFF. SMALL LOSSES EXPECTED. A fortnight later it was THE BOGUS BLOCKADE. 'NOBODY THE WORSE'.

In the first three weeks of the blockade, of the 3500 ships using English ports, only seven had been torpedoed. One of these was the S.S. *Harpalian*. The chief engineer was saying grace at lunch: 'For what we are about to receive, the Lord make us truly thankful'. A tremendous bang and she had received her torpedo.

As the weeks went by there seemed to be references to submarines sinking ships, and although we were not given the score, that German blockade seemed to be more effective than we had expected.

On 5 June: SUBMARINE A WEEK. 'ENEMY'S FEAT REMARKABLE'. These submarines seemed to be much better than the old ones and could travel hundreds of miles. As the Germans held the Belgian ports, they were able to start near the main shipping lanes.

The war seemed to be closing in on us now that there were 20 000 of our men overseas ready to go into battle, more on the way, and still more waiting to be sent – Keith amongst them.

Last year the war had seemed to be fun, a high-spirited adventure. Now it looked ominous. Our men might be safe in Egypt, but whatever they did there, sooner or later they would come up against our real enemies, the Germans, once they had settled the Turks. Then it would be no fancy-dress parade, but a wholly Christian effort to right the wrongs of the world. No matter how mendacious were the stories we accepted, nor how credulous we were, we believed that our young men were called to sacrifice themselves for the good of others.

Someone had said that 3000 men a month would be needed to make good the wastage of our force overseas; in March 9000 men joined up, but after that the numbers dropped.

Recruiting became a happy and popular activity for those who would always be safe, and although there seemed to be no immediate need for men, men were called for. Miss Beatrice Day recited 'You' at the Melbourne Picture Theatre, before the King's message appeared on the screen with the portrait of the King himself. The piece ended with:

> We want a Hundred Thousand Men
> And the first they want is YOU.

In Britain there had been talk of 'The First Hundred Thousand' and we took it up here. Every Monday our papers published the score of enlistments over the past week as the numbers climbed towards that hundred thousand.

Ingenious schemes were used to tempt men into the army and pressure built up as the year went on.

Only the larger cities had enlistment centres, and in November a group at Gilgandra decided to march the 320 miles to Sydney and gather others on the way. Quite a pleasant excursion it turned out to be, girls kissing them in the little places they passed through, mayoral receptions and turkey dinners. The group of thirty which had started had grown to 263 by the time it reached Sydney. There were eight of those marches, mainly in New South Wales but, for some reason, they stopped within three months.

Young fellows who had never imagined going into the army began to feel that it was inevitable, for the public told them that it was shameful to stay. Particular groups felt more strongly than others. The squatters of the Western District rushed in early; they were horsemen and good ones; they went into the Light Horse and were wiped out on Gallipoli or survived through the Palestine campaign, and both got tremendous credit.

All our friends claimed to be middle class, and enlistment was accepted as a middle-class duty. Most people claimed an affiliation with some church or another; all churches ruled that enlistment was a religious obligation. The six public schools and their imitators, the suburban grammar schools, established enlistment as obligatory on leaving school. The University was strongly pro-war, so much so that student politics swung to the extreme right and it was a freak student who would express Labor sympathies or avoid enlistment.

The family was caught in its surroundings: middle class, university, public school and conventionally Presbyterian, it would have been difficult to break out.

Keith would soon be on his way to the war, and although there was not yet any great pressure to enlist, both Athol and Ralph felt that they should join at the proper time. Athol was in the final year of his law course; he was delicate and army life would be rough and he was hoping to marry his Elsie. He would not rush in and perhaps the war would be over before he was needed. Ralph was in the last year of his geology course and now it looked to him as though his engineering course at the University would have to be deferred. He was the quietest and most introvert of the brothers, very gentle, with a hatred of violence, but now was feeling ashamed that he had not enlisted.

Owen, nearly nineteen, was the youngest of the four and a devout Christian, the most devout of the family. He too hated violence. Keith could be expected to cheerfully hold his own in any mix-up, but the other three had escaped all physical rough-and-tumble and none would happily rush into adventure.

Owen was in residence at Queen's College at the University on a scholarship and was in his second year of engineering, having done brilliantly in his first year, and at school. He could not enlist without the consent of his parents; father was away on one of his rare trips of the war years and Owen wrote to him:

> Queen's College
> Carlton
> April 27th 1915

Dear Father,

I have made up my mind to enlist and am writing to get your consent as, although I am sure you will grant it, yet I would not like to go without it.

This matter has been worrying me for several months but has at last reached a climax and I feel I must go.

It is hard to explain exactly what is impelling me to go but there is something allied to conscience which bids me go.

A factor which will make it much pleasanter to go is that Malcolm Stirling one of my sincerest friends is also going. And to have the company of one such as he is in such a crisis would be a great help. Especially when I am beginning to enjoy my work, as I have never enjoyed it before; however I think that if I did not go now I shall always regret it.

I believe in a hereafter and if following the will of my conscience I enter it sooner than under ordinary circumstances I do not think that anyone should regret it.

Those things that hurt most however, are not the laying aside of a promising course or of a life which I enjoy very much, but the sorrow which I know I shall cause both Mother and you. Also the fact that what has been spent on my education, at the cost of many comforts you have not been able to have, may perhaps be wasted.

What comes home to me a great deal is, that I am abiding here in comfort while others perhaps having people dependent on them are fighting my battles and giving their lives for me.

Death must come to us all sooner or later and there is no way so noble of leaving than that in which you 'Lay down your life for your friends'.

You must not think that I am making a hasty decision. The decision has been arrived at after long hours of meditation.

I have not told mother yet but I thought you would make things easier.

Would you please wire an answer as now that I have definitely made up my mind I do not like waiting. I shall go and get medically examined tomorrow.

> Your loving son,
> Owen

Owen's letter to his father

Queen's College
"Carlton
April 27th 1915.

Dear Father,

I have made up my mind
to enlist and am writing to get your
consent so, although I would rather you
will grant it, yet I would not like
to go without it.

The matter has been
worrying me for several years
but has at last reached a climax

but there is something which is
closely allied to conscience which
bids me go.

. . . of facts which will
make it much pleasanter to go now, is
that Malcolm Stirling one of my
surest friends is also going. And
to have the company of one such as
he is in such a crisis would be a
great help.   I will admit that I
find it very hard to lay
aside my University course

2

especially when I am just beginning
to enjoy my work, as there never
enjoyed it before; however it is
that if I do go some help
always regret it. I believe in a hereafter.

And if following the will of my
conscience leads it sooner than even
my circumstances I do not
think that anyone should regret it.
These things that hurt me
however are not the beginning

the sorrows which I know shall
come both Mother and you. Also the
fact that what I have been spent on
my education, at the cost of many
comforts you have not been able to
have, may hereafter be wasted.

What comes home to me a
great deal is, that them abiding here
in comfort while others' boys, having
having people dependent on them are
lifting my bottles and giving them

Death must come to me at

3.

ever a late and there is no way
a couple of leaving them that in
which you lay down your life
for your friends.

You must not think
that I am making a hasty decision.
The decision has been arrived
at after long hours of meditation
I have not talk Mother
yet, but I thought that you remember
make things easier.

If would you please
wire an answer so soon that I
have definitely made up my mind.
I don't like waiting. Shall go and
get medically examined to-morrow.

your loving own
Owen.

Owen's friend, Malcolm Stirling, enlisted in May and was to be killed in France in October of the next year.

Father did not do as Owen asked. He would give his consent when Owen finished his year at the University. So Owen stayed on and again topped the examination list, but he was impatient for the time to pass.

We feared for him. His letter seemed to show a foreknowledge of death, but we did not talk about it to each other. Years later in World War II I knew three men who thought they would be killed. They seemed quite certain about it and it did not seem to worry them; they were all killed. I suppose that they and Owen could have made some attempt to dodge what was coming to them, but if they had succeeded, they would not have thought much of themselves later.

No body of troops which have ever been assembled could have been as morally divided as those which left Australia early in the war. Many of those who rushed to join in the first hysteria had felt a deep moral compulsion and the proportion of such men increased as the war went on. Next year at Wesley I would learn one of the new war songs:

> Young Galahad has gone to fight
> In countries o'er the sea,
> For King and Empire, God and Right
> And Truth and Liberty,
> Nor ever went a nobler soul
> Nor e'er a truer heart.

And this was not a ridiculous exaggeration. They had the same high calling as had Sir Galahad, and like him, were 'pure'. They had never known the love of a woman and many never would; they were puritanical in the best sense of the word. They did not drink and most did not smoke; they were at one extreme. At the other were those who went in because they were out of work and the pay was very good. A uniform would give them prestige and a lot of free beer. Their morals were non-existent; they were the larrikins of the Melbourne 'pushes', anti-police, anti-authority and anti-discipline. They followed a pattern of rebellion against the ridiculous excesses of the military system. Some made superb soldiers in action, many made deplorable soldiers out of action.

In Egypt their conduct was violent and often vicious. It might be funny to oust a tram-driver and take over the tram, but it was irresponsible to throw the driver and conductor off while it was moving, or to assault a minor official, or to scatter the goods of a street stall, or to knock over the baskets of the orange hawkers.

Admittedly the Egyptians were the first foreigners these young men had met in bulk and they found them incredibly sordid; it is not every country where a policeman offers to take you home to his twelve-year-old sister or to escort you to a display given by a woman and a donkey. Of course the most notorious areas were out of bounds, but this was part of discipline and was to be ignored. It was not surprising that those larrikins got into trouble.

Training in Egypt was tedious and trouble started. The Wassa district of Cairo, quite near Shepheard's Hotel, was a sordid prostitutes' quarter, and not many places could be more sordid than an Egyptian brothel, drunks vomiting on the stairs, bugs and lice everywhere and the women rotten with venereal diseases.

A story spread that someone had been stabbed in the Wassa district. A mob gathered outside a brothel, threw the women and the stand-over men outside and then the furniture, which they set alight. The British military police came along on their horses and shot off their revolvers; the fire-brigade turned up and the soldiers cut the hoses or turned them on the firemen. It was a rather cheerful battle, the first of the A.I.F. in the war.

There was a second and smaller Battle of the Wassa and then an Australian garrison was installed. Its commander was awarded the first Australian battle-honour of the war–'Wassa Armstrong', commanding officer of the Wassa. I met Major Armstrong later in Melbourne when he was a building contractor.

Australians were a very isolated and self-centred people before the war. We did quite a lot of travelling by ship, but that was only between the State capitals; few could afford the fare or the time to go to England–it took at least five weeks–and England was the only country we knew anything about. We were getting a lot of news from Ireland but we knew little about the place, or about Scotland.

Then Egypt became well known to us; in a matter of months we had learned more about Egypt than we knew of Western Australia. Of course we had known something of ancient Egypt because of going to church and Sunday school and a lot of our Bibles had pictures of Egyptian things in the back. But now 20 000 of our young chaps were there and more were on the way; there would be 100 000 of them there before the year was out.

They wrote letters home and they were passed around amongst the family friends. What they said about Egypt became part of our fixed beliefs.

New words came in, and oddly enough, they were, and are, used only by males. 'Buckshee' meant something gratis; 'imshi' meant 'get out fast'. 'Bint', meaning a girl, replaced 'tart'. In those days 'tart' had no derogatory meaning, it meant simply a girl, and a respectable one:

a man's fiancée was his tart. It was possibly a diminutive of sweetheart.

It was just about this time when the A.I.F. were waiting in Egypt that father had a bitter disappointment. He was turned down for a sure job after his long period of idleness.

It had been decided to form the Australian Mining Corps and he was called to the Defence Department for an interview and all seemed to be going well and there was only the medical examination to be passed; it had got as far as that, then he was rejected.

He had been almost blind in one eye since boyhood but it had been no great hindrance in his mining work. He thought that perhaps his rejection may have been because of his association with Monash, for there was an anti-Monash faction in the Defence Department.

Edgeworth David, Professor of Geology at Sydney, was accepted by the army and went overseas as a major in charge of technical work at headquarters. He was five years older than father; he was a recognized authority on geology and had been to the most unlikely places, such as Antarctica, and few had better qualifications. He ended up as Chief Geologist to the British Army and increased his reputation. Father was more experienced in actual mining and there would have been room for both – they had already worked together and got on well with each other.

Edgeworth David did not spend his time at headquarters, for Ralph saw him in the tunnels under Messines Ridge and thought it was a funny place for a professor.

Two tunnelling companies were formed in Australia. Keith transferred to one after his sick leave in Australia and Ralph joined the same one later as a reinforcement, but most came directly from the Australian mines and had some difficulty in adjusting to military discipline.

One elderly lieutenant was offered the managership of a gold mine just before they were due to sail and petitioned the Minister for Defence for a discharge, but was refused. He tried to get his discharge by playing up and getting drunk on every possible occasion and eventually got it at base in France by running foul of the very proper British officers. It was a 'disgraceful discharge'.

11
Gallipoli

The *Argus* of 16 April: PLIGHT OF TURKEY. LEFT ALONE BY ALLY. GERMANY DECLINES AID. SEPARATE PEACE POSSIBLE. On 24 April: TURKISH TROOPS MASSING.

Then it was real. The *Herald*, 29 April: 'ADVANCE ADVANCE AUSTRALIA'. COMMONWEALTH EXPEDITIONARY FORCE SUCCESSFULLY LANDS IN TURKEY.

It was true. The *Argus* of the 30th:

AUSTRALIANS IN ACTION

FIGHTING AGAINST TURKS

CONDUCT COMMENDED

SPLENDID GALLANTRY SHOWN

Early in the morning of 20 April the landings had been made. Five separate British landings on Cape Helles on the tip of the Gallipoli Peninsula, the Australian and New Zealand landing along the coast about six miles to the north, and a French landing on the opposite Asian shore. Two of the British landings were aborted and the French left Asia and came in beside the British on their left flank, where they were to remain for the rest of the campaign.

There was certainly a muddle in giving us the news of our great national adventure—no information, but only telegraphs of congratulations from the British government and the King, and official War Office news that the Australians were on Gallipoli.

On 8 May we got the first description from a British war-correspondent, Ashmead-Bartlett. The Turks had been hurled back by

The Dardanelles

splendid bayonet charges and there had been no finer feat in the war than the storming of the heights. That gave us the picture, lines of men charging forward with fixed bayonets with astonishing heroism. The dispatch was ordered to be read in all Victorian schools, and, I suppose, it was read to us at the Armadale State School.

That picture imagined by a remote war-correspondent was fixed in our minds and was never replaced when the real facts filtered back to us. The fantasy became history.

The Australians and New Zealanders—the Anzac Corps—had landed in the wrong place. Some little unknown man in the navy had blundered in the dark and the troops were put ashore on a narrow beach backed by steep broken hills, and not on the flat land a mile away.

The first lot got ashore without a shot being fired at them and they climbed up the steep hills with fixed bayonets; it is said that there were only 500 Turks in the vicinity, but they fought as they fell back and the later landings were mauled. In the rough country it was impossible to keep formation and little enthusiastic groups pushed ahead independently. It was Captain Lalor's lot that got to the top of the ridge and saw the waters of the Dardanelles ahead of them below. If they had stayed and been joined by the rest, the battle of Gallipoli would have been won. It was only a glimpse; three months later some New Zealanders would have the same glimpse but would not survive to tell about it.

The outnumbered Turks were reinforced; our forward groups were pushed back or eliminated and the line was stabilized a mile and a half inland. There it was to stay for the rest of the year, overlooked by the Turks on higher ground and with artillery control over the whole area. In a day or two we were told that 8000 Turks had been captured, but it was not true. Very few prisoners were taken on either side on Gallipoli. It was a very rough war.

But it was very splendid and we read about it with pride. We were in the big war and we had been noticed. The Secretary of State for the Colonies approved; there had been splendid gallantry and a magnificent achievement. Once again crowds waited outside newspaper offices for more news.

The British landings at Cape Helles had worse luck and many men were lost. One landing was abandoned because the men got tired of it and the general was not interested in it and did not know what was happening. There was a much better chance of pushing ahead there but no one seems to have felt any urgency. The force at Cape Helles settled down in quite a small area of land and the Turks brought up men and kept it that way, but we were not really very interested. Our landing became known as Anzac, after the corps of that name, and we assumed that it was entirely our affair; but there was some exchange and the Australians made a very respectable charge at Cape Helles and the British and Indians joined in at times on Anzac. The war in France no longer seemed important to us. Our little bit of Turkey was what mattered.

On 1 May our papers printed advice from Allied headquarters on Tenedos that a British force was established across the narrowest part of the peninsula and that the Turkish garrisons were cut off. This was just what we wanted and expected–it was a pity that the news was not confirmed.

We were pleased and so were the Italians; Turkey would be out of the war and all the Balkans would declare against Germany. On 3 May: ALLIES' OFFER TO ITALY. SUPERIOR TO ANYTHING GERMANY CAN OFFER. Italy must hurry if she was to expect any pickings. She declared war on Austria, and Austria was in a bad way with the Russians hammering her to the north; maybe the Russians had just lost Libau on the Baltic, but the Grand Duke Nicholas was confident and predicted 'A glorious end'.

So Italy was now one more gallant ally and we would have to listen to her national anthem. We felt rather awkward about it; we had had time enough to adjust our thinking and were now able to approve of France and Russia, but Italy was hard to swallow. Her desertion of her old allies was too fast for us. Italians had been figures of fun, little men with big moustaches, organ-grinders with monkeys on their shoulders, not very martial figures at all. Now we were told that they were great fighters who 'delighted in the bayonet'. Soon the stories from the Italian front were as remarkable as those from the Russian, and I suppose we believed both. During the capture of Montenegro–either the state or a mountain, but we were not told which–a Sicilian named Dimarco, after a fierce struggle on the edge of a precipice, lassoed and took prisoner an Austrian major-general. King Victor Emmanuel decorated him with a gold medal. We could picture the general in his shining riding-boots and dangling medals being hoisted up to ignominious captivity.

Italy was to be rewarded for deserting its very old alliance with Germany and Austria and there was to be no nonsense about the rights of minorities. Italy was to be given the solidly German areas on the southern slopes of the Alps; these would be added to the solidly Greek Dodecanese Islands she had already bagged from Turkey. She was also to get the solidly Slav lands beside the Adriatic, but someone had been careless and forgotten that they had already been promised to Serbia.

The Italians attacked the Austrians with a superiority of three to one. They got nowhere and did not even divert the Austrians from their fight to the north. It had been splendid when the Russians captured Przemyśl in March; now the Austrians recaptured it and went on to take Lemberg. It looked as if the Italians had come in too soon. We heard little about them until their disgraceful defeat at Caporetto in 1917 when troops had to be sent from the Western Front to hold them together; there was talk of the Australians being sent.

In fact Italy was not an asset but she was paid the promised price with the exception of what had also been promised to Serbia; there was to be bickering about that.

We got another *Herald* map to put up on the breakfast-room wall beside the one of the European fronts—Gallipoli with the Straits of the Dardanelles. Anzac was to the top, and in the bottom right-hand corner you could see where Troy was supposed to be.

It was on a vastly bigger scale than the other map, if you thought about it, for really there was not very much land involved; but the pins moved forward just as slowly as they did on the map of France.

But we were doing all right on Gallipoli. VICTORIOUS ALLIES PRESSING FORWARD, but this was the French and British. They had captured the village of Krithia and we were not greatly moved, but then they said that there had been an admirable Australian charge, and we had thought all our men had been away at their own war to the north.

A British submarine had gone right through the Dardanelles into the Bosporus and sunk two Turkish gunboats and a big Turkish transport. Then our Australian submarine tried the same thing and got sunk and the crew was captured. This was our second one gone; the other had disappeared off New Guinea.

Then there was bad news. Our Australian, Major-General Bridges, was shot by a Turkish sniper; this was disaster.

Walking home for lunch from the Armadale State School we discussed the matter. I was something of an authority, for my brother Keith was now on his way to Gallipoli and I expected to be listened to, but Cliff Brown was a much greater authority and silenced me. His father was actually on Gallipoli, Corporal—or perhaps Lance-Corporal—Brown. Cliff let us know that now General Bridges had gone, his father was likely to be put in charge; we now treated Cliff Brown with great respect.

We were flattered by what the British said about the Australians. We had got good notices in the Boer War from people as eminent as Kipling; now people almost as eminent said even more flattering things and recorded them in their books later.

John Masefield wrote that they were 'the finest body of young men ever brought together in modern times—they looked like kings in old poems'.

Compton Mackenzie wrote:

> The splendid appearance of these Australian troops had become a commonplace of war-correspondent journalism, but a splendid appearance had seemed to introduce somehow an atmosphere of the parade-ground; such litheness and powerful grace did not suggest the parade-ground; their beauty, for it really was heroic, should have been celebrated in hexameters, not headlines. There was not one of those glorious young men who might not himself have been Ajax or Diomedes, Achilles or Hector. Their almost complete nudity, their tallness and majestic simplicity of line, their rose-brown flesh burnt by the sun and purged of all grossness by the ordeal through which they were passing, all these united to create something as near to absolute beauty as I shall ever hope to see in the world.

Much later Duff Cooper wrote of them on the Somme, 'their high courage and their high spirits remained indomitable'. When a battalion began an action with 900 men, he said, it ended up with 1300 owing to the addition of volunteers from the units which had been ordered to retire for a rest. 'A tendency to under-estimate dangers was their only failing'.

That British correspondent, Ashmead-Bartlett, consistently praised them. Here he is on 6 August: THE UNCONVENTIONAL ARMY. AUSTRALIANS ON GALLIPOLI. SHIRTLESS AND BOOTLESS. 'GREAT BIG-LIMBED ATHLETES'. We were tickled by that. War had previously been a matter of men in uncomfortable scarlet jackets with high necks, but this was a new sort of war and our men were dressing for it as they would for a job in the bush. We had invented a new and more efficient uniform.

The British troops on Helles, in the few pictures we saw of them, wore buttoned-up uniforms and clumsy sun-helmets, not the sort of thing to wear when physical exertion was required. Ours wore their broad-brimmed hats or, more commonly, peaked caps—rather different from the old British pattern in that they had no wire-stiffener for the cloth and were soft and floppy. They went out of fashion later.

We already knew that our men were very casual about saluting officers. We approved when they did not salute quite important British ones and there was even approval for it in England in the jokes which appeared in the papers. We were establishing our own traditions.

The photographs of Gallipoli showed the steep eroded ridges covered with miserable scrub. How could troops charge up those sheer hills? We knew that our men slept in burrows scraped out of the hillside, safe from bullets and shrapnel. We knew that they went down to the beach to swim, and ducked when the shrapnel burst above them.

General Birdwood went swimming with them and we liked him for that; it made him seem warm and human and very different from the gorgeous generals with their cocked hats and white roosters' tails. Our Birdwood was a man and you could make jokes about his name. He was more popular here at home than on Anzac, but he was popular enough. He tried hard to fraternize but he did not talk easily and had an air of condescension. 'Birdie's bull' was how his conversation was described; that was a very early use of 'bull' in common speech.

There were so many successes printed in our papers that it was imposs-ible to recognize the really important ones. One which passed almost unnoticed was on 18 May. Anzac was regarded by the Turks as more dangerous to them than Cape Helles and they had double the number of troops there; now was the time to take the offensive and drive down to the sea and eliminate Anzac.

The Turkish attack was expected. It turned out to be more wasteful of life than any other on Gallipoli and comparable with the most stupid attacks by the French or British on the Western Front.

In the early morning the first Turks got out of their trenches, lined up and were shot down; another lot lined up and were shot down, and another. No-man's-land was covered with bodies and only a few Turks got far enough to die in our trenches. Afterwards 3000 lay dead and there were another 10 000 casualties out of the 40 000 or so in the attack. There was pity for those hopelessly brave men and for those lying in pain between the lines. We lost only 168 killed and 468 wounded.

An armistice was arranged for burial of the dead, and the two sides met each other as men in shared danger. We got no idea of what happened from our papers but we could sense a change in attitude.

At the landing we had known that the Turks were savages. We remem-bered the stories of a few years earlier when they had massacred the Armenians; they were then the 'unspeakable Turks'.

From now on the Turk was recognized as a fellow-sufferer in cruel circumstances. Now we knew him as 'Johnny Turk' or 'Abdul', and he was a 'fair fighter', 'not a bad chap' and 'a real gentleman'. We heard that our prisoners were well treated and there were not many in the savage fighting. The heroics had gone out, and the lust for killing.

Killing would start again when there was an attack, but in the mean-time it was a matter of sitting it out. Life settled down and the Turks could safely leave their trenches to gather firewood, hang out washing or relieve themselves, until a new unit arrived which did not know the conventions, and shot at them.

There was no propaganda to stir up hatred and the attitude lasted out the campaign and into the years beyond. Each side liked and respected the other. Twenty-six years later the neutral Turks were very hospitable to those Australians who escaped to Turkey from Crete. They should have interned them; instead they fed them up and sent them south to rejoin the others in Syria.

Things seemed quiet on Gallipoli but Birdwood made a plan to start things going again. The troops were to break through at Lone Pine and capture and hold the ridge, so cutting the Turkish lines in two. Hamilton approved the plan; but General Walker, who was to be responsible, protested strongly, as all previous attempts by either side on a narrow front had ended in disaster. He was told to get on with it.

Then the political wind in London changed and three divisions of the New Army were to be sent out—about as many men as at the first landings. Walker's attack was postponed until their arrival, and in the meantime, the plan grew.

In addition two columns would break out in the night from the north of Anzac and push up the undefended gullies right up to the undefended top of Sari Bair; if either group took and held the high ground, all Turkish movement by land or sea would be controlled.

That gave us three chances, but there was to be a fourth and biggest. The three New Army divisions would land at Suvla Bay, even further north, and make their own way up to Sari Bair; they would have to move fast whilst the Turks were busy elsewhere.

The New Army divisions were formed into a corps under a new general and Hamilton had a lot to do with his selection. Stopforth was a nice chap, like Hamilton, but unlike Hamilton in that he had had absolutely no experience of commanding troops in action. He had been an aide-de-camp and then military secretary to Buller in South Africa and had accompanied him home to England after his bungles. He was sixty-one and in poor health; he had retired in 1909, but he still had seniority. He was rushed out to the Dardanelles, arriving just four weeks before his green troops went into action. Looking back across the years, it does not seem to have been a suitable appointment in serious war.

On 6 August it all started. The diversionary attack at Cape Helles was a bloody failure.

There was a surprising success at Lone Pine; it was perhaps the only successful attack by either side on the narrow fronts of Gallipoli. General Walker might not have liked the idea but he did his best and planned well. Tunnels were dug behind the lines for the approach of following troops. More tunnels were dug under no-man's-land; they were broken open and the Anzacs were on the Turks before they knew what was happening. The front lines were overrun and there was a real gain of land, but it fell just short of complete success. There were still a few trenches and a few men in the way; the Turks fought back hard and kept fighting for a couple of days.

We read about in on 12 August: ON GALLIPOLI. SEVERE FIGHTING. AUSTRALIANS GAIN GROUND. On the 14th: ENEMY'S WEAK SPOT. FOUND BY ALLIES. AUSTRALIANS 'CARRIED THE DAY'.

And whilst this was happening off went the two columns on their night attack. The nearer column of New Zealanders swept through a few surprised Turks and got to the ridge. The summit, their objective, was a thousand yards ahead and there were no Turks in the way. The commander called a halt to wait for reinforcements. The only reinforcements which arrived were Turkish, and when the final advance was attempted, the summit was unattainable.

The outermost column left four hours late and got lost in the steep gullies; it suffered minor casualties from snipers in the dark, enough to destroy confidence. When daylight came it was far from the ridge and exposed to rifle fire from the higher ground. Monash, the leader, did not do well; he was an excellent planner and tactician but does not seem to have been a great leader in close combat.

On their ridge the New Zealanders held on until they were relieved by the British and only seventy of the original 760 went back. The Turks attacked and the ridge was lost. Further along a group of Gurkhas and British were also forced back. That was the nearest we came to winning on Gallipoli.

History is probably right in giving the credit for the Turkish success to one man, Mustafa Kemal, later 'Ataturk', the founder and architect of modern Turkey. As a divisional commander he was ahead of his men when the Australians were almost on the ridge on the first day of landing, and he was actually seen by our men. In this later attack he was there again and was responsible for bringing up reinforcements. It would be a very remarkable British general who was ever seen by the enemy.

Whilst the battle for the ridges was going on, there were other attacks from the old lines. Now it was our turn for the terrible loss which the Turks had suffered in their narrow frontal attacks.

The attack at Quinn's Post was abandoned in failure; at Pope's some gains were made but lost again; but it was at the Nek where there was tragedy. We read about it on 28 August: LIGHT HORSE SUFFERS. TWO REGIMENTS WIPED OUT. Next day it was 'SHEER HEROISM'. AUSTRALIAN LIGHT HORSE ATTEMPTS THE IMPOSSIBLE. SOLDIERS FIGHT OVER BODIES THREE DEEP.

The 8th Light Horse (Victorian) and the 10th (Western Australian) had been dismounted and were fighting as infantry in their first engagement, crowded into a narrow front. It was obviously hopeless from the start. 'Boys, you have ten minutes to live', their commanding officer told them, and he was right.

The first wave was shot down on the parapet; the second got into no-man's-land and one man reached the trenches and disappeared; the third wave was stopped short—and there was a fourth attack.

Of one unit of 550 only forty-seven answered their names later. In an area the size of a tennis court 234 lay dead or dying. The Charge of the Light Brigade may have been more stupid than those attacks, but it was a Sunday-school picnic compared with them.

Our church got its first death of the war: one of the three Borthwick boys, Keith, a lieutenant in the 10th Light Horse; of the eighteen officers he was not one of the two who survived.

Mother's connections, the Coles and Blacks of Camperdown, caught it. Two of the Blacks were killed; I think our distant cousin, Isabel Bennet was engaged to a Cole. She lost her fiancé, father and brother. Mother asked her to stay with us to cheer her up, but she remained pretty miserable. The 8th and 10th Light Horse really had been wiped out.

Whilst men were dying in thousands on the hills, a mile away could be seen the men at Suvla Bay landing, sauntering about on the beach, swimming, drilling and brewing tea.

25 August: SURPRISING THE TURKS. GREAT FORCE LANDED AT SUVLA. 'MOST BRILLIANT FEAT OF WAR'.

The first landings were made without any casualties. Later ones suffered only minor losses, for they were made from bullet-proof landing-craft, built for a fool scheme of Lord Fisher of the Admiralty for a landing in the Baltic, which had not been made available for the original landings.

There were only a handful of Turks to resist at Suvla, and 20 000 men were put ashore. They looked at two little hills on the coastal plain and someone thought of occupying them, and after a while, they did get one of them. As for a dash through the empty country up to the heights, well, it was much better to stay by the shore.

Suvla ended up as just one more coastal shelf with the Turks commanding it from the higher ground. By the end of the year the 'MOST BRILLIANT FEAT OF WAR' had become THE SUVLA BAY FAILURE.

That turned out to be the end of Gallipoli. With the hot summer weather it was a disgusting place with scattered unburied bodies and swarms of bloated flies; disillusionment took the place of fervour and sickness and anxiety impaired morale.

For over three months those of the initial landings had no relief from the foul and crowded conditions and were going down with sickness in droves.

German submarines were in the Mediterranean. Bulgaria was in the war – not on our side, as we had confidently expected, but on the German. The Russians had been promised Constantinople and the Greeks had wanted it; now, it was said, the Turks had promised it to the Bulgarians.

Troops were diverted from the Dardanelles to Salonika to go inland to check the Bulgars, but they were too late to do any good, and there they sat, waiting for something to turn up.

Gallipoli settled into a stalemate. We had nearly won twice and both times it had been 'a near-run thing', but we had no Wellington to run it. The Turks had.

12
The War at Home

The bright promises of the earlier months had faded. We were beginning to doubt the continuous Russian victories; the victories in France now seemed just as doubtful. Of course we knew that a lot of Germans had been killed in the fighting, but we had no way of knowing that our losses were almost double their number.

Lord Kitchener was still a towering figure to us, but unlike the German, Hindenburg, he had not been supported by victories. Lord Northcliffe again attacked him in his papers and personally wrote a nasty article, but the public was not prepared to let him go and the *Daily Mail* was burnt on the floor of the London stock exchange.

But the blame should fall on somebody. Lord Haldane, the Minister for War, got the sack; he had built up the army before the war but he was reckoned to be pro-German because had had studied in Germany and knew more about that country than any other politician.

In Australia recruiting was now a serious preoccupation. We got the 100 000 men which had been talked about for so long, but it was not enough in the opinion of Billy Hughes, the new Prime Minister. He ordered a war census in September: every man between the ages of eighteen and sixty had to state his job, whether he had foreign parents and under what terms he was willing to enlist. The census was not popular.

We regarded the Irish as disloyal and disreputable. In our view John Wren, a real guttersnipe, was the worst of them. He had made a fortune by running an illegal totalizator and was said to have got along by bribing a wide variety of people. But John Wren enlisted and expected that his example would encourage others to follow him. John Wren, a good Catholic, aged forty-three, had enlisted and there were a lot of good Protestants ten years younger who had shown no such enthusiasm. It gave us something to think about. Wren was a shameless man, puckish and cheeky, but of all people, he was the personal friend of the austere Dr Mannix, whose views on the war were very different. Wren remained very patriotic throughout the war and included soldiers with the Catholic Church in his charitable gifts.

We still had hopes of Gallipoli and our Anzacs, but we could not appreciate how bad things were. The misty photographs could not show the flies and the stinks and we could not make out that the lumps on the parapets were the bodies of our men.

Our pride in Gallipoli had become a sour sort of pride. In the early days if some vague third cousin had been killed, a woman would wear a black bow and a man a black armband, and people would gently ask about the bereavement. 'My cousin has been killed on Gallipoli.' Now black appeared only for first cousins; even fathers and brothers often got no black at all. The war was an anxiety rather than an excitement and there was not much fun in it.

We still sang 'God Save the King' after church and now we added an extra verse, a parody of the original, but it had more meaning. It had been published in May:

> God save our splendid men
> Send them safe home again
> God save our men.
> Keep them victorious
> Patient and chivalrous
> They are so dear to us,
> God save our men.

There were enough young chaps from the church on Gallipoli or on the way there to make it a heartfelt prayer on Sunday mornings.

We felt that, on the whole, things were still going well for Australia. The disaster of Suvla Bay was hidden from us and it seemed that all those names in the casualty lists were there for some good reason. We had added a new name to the map of the world. 'Anzac' was now a place-name.

Anzac had been the first great venture of the new Commonwealth of Australia and gave it a meaning that was very creditable indeed. We, who were so far from Europe where the big things happened, were actually fighting in Europe, if in a remote part, and we had already gained a place in world history.

In the Victorian parliament Mr Warde asked the Premier to consult with the other premiers, suggesting an annual commemoration of the landing on 25 April, Anzac Day, the real Australia Day – and so it was, it was the day when we became Australians.

Anzac could be the name for the new capital, but Sir George Reid did not think it a good idea and we were disappointed.

Although we had got our 100 000 men, recruiting had been an erratic affair. At first it had been a matter of selecting from the surplus number of applicants; now there was a strain to get enough and the papers whipped up interest by publishing weekly and monthly totals. It had been 10 225 in January, but only 6250 in April. There was a record 36 575 in July, and it was not only Gallipoli which had brought the rise, it was also the *Lusitania*.

It seemed that the Germans were doing better with their blockade of England than our papers said, and that they were sinking ships around the English coast. In the *Argus* of 5 May was MYSTERIOUS WARNINGS. GERMAN SCARE FAILS. It seems that telegrams had been sent to fifty wealthy Americans who had boarded the *Lusitania*—the biggest ship afloat—warning that the liner would be torpedoed, and some of them decided not to sail in her.

The *Lusitania* was torpedoed and 1447 people were drowned. This was by far the greatest atrocity of the war and it firmly established that the Germans were utterly bestial. There was an outcry in all English-speaking countries. The Germans' claims that the ship was armed and carrying munitions were unconvincing; so was their argument that the sinking was the only possible response to the blockade of food for Germany, which the Germans said was immoral and illegal. As far as we were concerned, all Germans were damned and it was the duty of every man to go and kill a lot of them.

The sinking of the *Lusitania* prompted riots in England and the looting of German-owned shops all over the country. Looting became so attractive that foreign-owned and British shops were looted as well. German-born members of the London stock exchange were man-handled and thrown out.

Not content with sinking the *Lusitania* the Germans actually crucified Canadians: an officer on 10 May, two privates on 17 May, and a sergeant at some unspecified date. They did it later in the war, too, and it was only Canadians that suffered. The reports said that they might have been dead first, but it was not a nice thing to do and verged on blasphemy.

We did our best here. Senator Pearce, Minister for Defence, ordered the closing of all Teuton clubs, and women wrote to the papers saying things like, 'it is inconceivable that any self-respecting woman can enter the doors of a German tradesman's shop'.

And that Senator Pearce had shut up Mr Wallach. Mr Wallach had been born in Germany but had been a British subject since 1898 and was married to an Australian woman who had two brothers on Gallipoli.

He had never been a member of any German club, but he was manager of the Australian Metal Company, and perhaps Senator Pearce still thought that someone was selling our metals to Germany.

Wallach appealed to the Victorian Supreme Court for release under Habeas Corpus and the Minister was forced to appear as a witness. He had interned Wallach as he believed he was 'disaffected and disloyal'; he had been told so, but he refused to say what the evidence was or who had told him. Wallach was discharged; the Chief Justice held that it was abhorrent to British justice that a man could be locked away without any disclosed reason. Half an hour later Wallach was again arrested; whilst the case was being heard a new warrant was being prepared under a new law.

Wallach appealed to the Australian High Court but he had been forestalled. A War Precautions Bill had been passed 'in view of the decision of the Victorian Supreme Court in the Franz Wallach case'. His appeal was disallowed, but the Bench could not be accused of patriotic hysteria. Of the judges Isaac Isaacs was Jewish and Higgins and Gavan-Duffy were both sons of Irish Nationalists; it was purely the matter of the new law.

There were plenty of disloyal and disaffected persons about the place making quite a noise, but they were not interned: none of them had been born in Germany. Some people got terms of imprisonment for opposing enlistment, yet British subjects of German origin who had said or done nothing disloyal were kept shut up until the war was over.

The University Council continued its fight against Germans, started in the previous year. At a meeting of Council Dr Leeper moved 'that the services of unnaturalised citizens of any enemy country be dispensed with as soon as possible'. He did not get quite what he wanted: they were to be allowed to remain until their term of engagement was up–and that was at the end of the year. Only three voted against his motion: the Vice-Chancellor, Dr McFarland, born in Ireland; Professor Masson, born in Scotland; and Dr Bride, who wanted something stronger.

It was the Conservatorium of Music which was most suspect. 'Australian' wrote to the *Argus*:

I am not a musical man–far from it–but I desire to write about this matter because I am a father. The Conservatorium's musical staff seems to be teeming with the German element. Now, have not parents of the girls who are taught by these Germans any sense of responsibility towards their children? A musical child, of all children, is the most impressionable. The very fact of its being taught by a German, especially if he is a clever German, must influence that child's mind in favour of that German, and the child, at a time with its mind duly impressed, may be induced to resent anything of a derogatory kind being said of a German, and the first seeds of disaster to the child's career may be sown.

'Australian' was shooting at old Scharf; some minds must have already been influenced, for thirty students wrote to the papers in his defence, saying that they had never heard him say anything unpatriotic or improper in their hearing.

Dr von Dechend, lecturer in German, was to go too. He had survived for a year after he had established that Dr Leeper's attack on him had had absolutely no justification, but now his time was up.

The students were not as patriotic as the University Council and they grumbled; they would rather be taught by a German of good reputation than an Englishman unknown to them. They appealed that at least von Dechend should be allowed to conduct the final honours examination of his students in the following March. Council deferred action on the request.

But the students did patriotic things; they organized a procession in aid of Red Cross funds, and the girls had a centre where they made shirts and pyjamas and gathered piles of knitted socks. Some of the girls demanded that all the men should enlist, although there would not be a dozen who did not plan to enlist at the proper time.

The girls entered the Common Room – they had been rare visitors previously – and hung recruiting posters on the walls and defied the males by sitting in a row on the big sofa and going on with their war knitting. Then they became uneasy; they looked around; they left in a hurry. Behind them on the wall was a poster they had put up: 'Boys, come over here, you're wanted'.

Melbourne was not alone amongst the Australian universities in fighting local Germans. It received a letter from the University of Adelaide asking if it had any proposal for the removal of aliens from the university roll of graduates, and another from the University of Queensland dealing with the award of scholarships to the children of aliens and in relation to electoral privileges of naturalized persons of enemy origin. Both were referred to the Professorial Board, as being primarily of educational concern.

The Board was not as anti-German as the Council and replied that the University had taken no action about cancelling its degrees awarded to enemy aliens and had no power to do so. To the University of Queensland it replied that the University did not propose to order civil disabilities beyond those imposed by the law of the land and that naturalization was no business of the universities. Council accepted the Professorial Board's answers, but Dr Leeper moved a motion against the last clauses.

The Council was gracious enough to approve of a new diploma being made out to a Mr Field to replace the original issued to Mr Feildchenfeld.

The University Council persisted in its patriotism; it had got rid of the Germans in the Conservatorium but there was a German piano there, a Beckstein grand. It had to be expelled, and it was. It was replaced by a Steinway which was regarded as American; although the firm had started in New York, its export trade was handled from Hamburg.

The war on German pianos went on outside the University. The *Herald* printed PATRIOTISM OF A POTT'S POINT HOSTESS. She had sent invitations to a 'smashing' instead of the usual 'music'. When the guests were assembled maids served around hammers and the guests piled into the piano and smashed it up in less than a quarter of an hour—ivory keys lying about, and the strings coiled up like barbed-wire entanglements.

The distant war was real and savage and our own people were being killed, but at home it was still exciting and romantic.

The map on the breakfast-room wall showed the lines of trenches which stretched those hundreds of miles from the Belgian coast to the Swiss frontier.

There were trenches on Gallipoli too, and that made them particularly interesting. We learned a new vocabulary: the 'parapet' was the defensive bank of earth in front of the trench and there was a rear parapet to mask the silhouette of anyone looking over the parapet. There was a 'fire step', where you stood to shoot above the safe level of the trench and, of course, there were sandbags to keep the walls of the trench in place. A 'periscope' was an arrangement of two mirrors so that observation was possible from the safety of the trench. A 'dug-out' was an artificial cave as a refuge from bullets.

Boys played trenches. Few had enough land at home for sets of trenches, but we had. There was the stable-yard, where they would have been rather in the way, but no one ever used the back lane and the soil was soft and sandy. Our trenches stretched across the ten-foot width and were fifteen feet apart. Neil's trench was next to the stable-yard and the slope gave him an advantage in height over mine, but they were convincing trenches with everything which trenches should have.

We did not use the Daisy air-gun in the trenches; we fought with hand-grenades made of soil wrapped in newspaper and to get one between the eyes was quite something. Our dug-outs were of light construction, just an opening from the trench roofed with sticks and newspaper to hold up the soil above. Alan Gibbs and others came round on Saturday mornings for the battles.

Then we had to fill in our trenches. Father came around to see what we were up to and fell through the roof of my dug-out. It was not a great loss as the fun had been in digging them rather than fighting from them.

At the end of July we had a Cake and Fancy Fair at the Armadale State School, but it was rather disappointing, for we of the Fourth Grade were not asked to help and were not encouraged to come along. We raised £231 1s 7d for the new military hospital at Caulfield. It could have been more: on the Monday after the fair I found threepence on the ground and wasn't sure whether it was not the property of the hospital, but the lady in the cottage at the corner of the playground—she was the caretaker—said that it would be quite proper for me to keep it.

The hospital was only a mile or two away and we felt that we were close to the war with those nurses there. One of them was Nurse Campbell, some sort of vague relation of Mother's. She often came to have tea and once went to the pictures with us. I was very proud to walk across the bridge at the Armadale station with a nurse alongside; perhaps it was not quite as grand as I had expected, for Nurse Campbell wore a voluminous grey flannel uniform, not the dazzling white of the Red Cross nurses in the pictures of nurses comforting wounded men. Still, it was something.

The Red Cross nurse was part of our new faith. The war was a new religion and our dual godhead had been the soldier and sailor; now, as in many religions, we added a female. The Red Cross nurse looked religious. She wore a white wimple, like a nun—not that we approved of nuns, but at least they were religious—and she dressed in pure white with a big red cross on her chest. She did not have breasts, she was sexless just as she should be, pure and chaste. Hers was the cool comforting hand on the brow of the wounded soldier lying in no-man's-land and there were coloured postcards showing her doing it. She was fearless and close to the dangers of war and we read about it in the *Argus*.

The *Argus* reprinted from the London *Spectator* a letter from a nursing sister at the Dardanelles:

> The Red Cross St Bernard's dogs are a great help in finding the wounded. It is remarkable how the animals know the dead from those who are only unconscious. When they find a living man they give a low mournful howl to fetch us. Sometimes we cannot find where the man had been found. If we do not go the dog comes in carrying the man's cap, by which means we know whether he is British or Turk. Then they lead us to the spot.

I suppose we believed all that just as much as we believed in the great victories of the Russians.

Saturday afternoon at the pictures; ten minutes of pictures of the
war, long grey lines of men in uniform jerking along, then a special
feature.

The lights went up and there was a toothy baritone in a fancy-dress
uniform and he sang 'The Rose of No Man's Land'.

> There's a rose that blows
> In no man's land
> And it's wonderful to see.
> Though it's sprayed with tears
> It will live for years
> In my garden of memory.
> It's the work of the Master's hand
> In the war's great curse
> Stands the Red Cross nurse,
> She's the rose of No Man's Land.

This was intensely moving and the most sacred thing we have ever heard;
so sacred that we would not dare to parody it. It was months before
a later version was sung by the blasphemous.

> There's a nose that blows
> On my old man
> And it's wonderful to see.
> Though it's sprayed with beers
> It's the work of the barmaid's hand . . .

Then the Germans deliberately shot an English nurse; sinking the *Lusitania* had been their biggest atrocity so far, but this was unbelievable
and utterly horrible; they shot Nurse Cavell.

We had got used to them raping Belgian girls, even upper-class ones;
we knew that they had chopped off the arms of little boys and girls;
but now they had callously shot a woman and a nurse at that.

The Belgians had been assassinating Germans and we had been pleased
when some important ones had been killed, but the Germans did not
like it and took counter-actions.

Miss Edith Cavell, the 50-year-old matron of a clinic in Brussels, had
been one of a group smuggling escaped Allied soldiers across the border
into Holland. The group was caught and Miss Cavell and another were
sentenced to death. Even if the shooting had been justified, it was a
profound blunder. Even the Kaiser was shocked and the whole world
was outraged.

She was immediately beatified. Her years were stripped from her and
Matron Cavell became a virginal Red Cross nurse standing defiantly
in front of her executioners. She still stands in white marble at pedestrian

level in Trafalgar Square, and high above her Nelson turns his back
on the woman who displaced him as the most heroic of the English
nation. No one forgave the Germans.

The Germans said that the French had already shot two women, but
the French explained that they had not been nice women nor Red Cross
nurses.

We tried to think that our soldiers were as immaculate as our nurses,
but we had hidden doubts. We were still proud of anyone wearing khaki,
and a uniform meant free beer from an appreciative community. We
did not talk about it, but there were a lot of men in uniform lying
in the gutters of Melbourne. Perhaps some of them were not genuine
soldiers; at the end of August there were 700 deserters adrift in Victoria,
and of course Melbourne had most of them. The civil and military police
did their best, but the public supported the men in uniform, as they
did each other. Even so, one successful raid collected 300 bogus soldiers.

Then it could not be hidden. There was a riot in the centre of the
city near the town hall.

The police had tried to arrest a man wearing the colour patches of
a returned soldier. It turned out that he was bogus, but everybody joined
in attempting to release him. Swanston Street was blocked to all traffic
until half-past one in the morning and the theatre-goers had to make
a long detour around the battle. If the man was fit enough to get mixed
up in a fight, why was he at home? Was he a hero?

We now had doubts. There was a special camp at Langwarrin, thirty
miles out, with 370 men in it, and none had been on Gallipoli. The
papers did not tell us what they were doing there, but the word went
round. They had a 'certain disease', but we of the Fourth Grade had
not the faintest idea why they should get this special treatment. It seems
that they were not pure Christian soldiers. These were men who had
picked up something called venereal disease in Egypt and had been sent
home in disgrace, and we had thought they were heroes. The new term,
V.D., puzzled us. Those officers who had served fifteen years in the
volunteers had been awarded the Volunteers' Decoration, and many,
like Colonel Monash, had V.D. after their names. Was that the same
thing?

The Progress Association of Mornington objected to the public being
forced to share the railway station conveniences with the men from
Langwarrin, for everybody knew that lavatory seats spread the disease.

But only a minority of soldiers disgraced themselves. There was something noble about those who had given up their hopes and broken their
careers by doing what their community had asked of them. Now the
community was trying to force men into the army by social blackmail.

The man who stayed at home was a 'shirker and a coward', said Bishop Stephen to his Church of England congregation in Hobart, and his was not a lonely voice in the churches. A man who was a shirker and a coward could achieve salvation by enlisting and becoming a hero in one day.

Hatred of the Germans was voiced from many pulpits. The German Catholic press had deplored the hatred of England; now one of our churches gave a lonely response. The General Assembly of the Presbyterian Church officially 'deprecated the spirit of hate in regard to the enemy in the present war', which, it said, 'seemed to be taking possession of some people' and a pastoral letter was sent to be read in all churches. Many in the Armadale Presbyterian church persisted in their hatred.

The long casualty lists from Gallipoli were depressing, but there were more pathetic casualties here at home. Those men who had decided to risk death in battle died ingloriously here. An epidemic of meningitis hit the camps and in one day there were five deaths and seventy new cases.

It was depressing. We had not got far on Gallipoli; the victories in France can't have been as big as all that, or the line on our map would have moved forward. Now we learned that the capture of Hill 60, the 'key to Flanders', had been transient; the Germans had got it back but the news had been suppressed for months. Most dubious of all were the Russian victories.

RUSSIAN MORALE AND STRATEGY SUPERIOR TO THE GERMANS. But there was nothing to show for it. The *Melbourne University Magazine* could be less discreet than the daily press and it suggested that 'the Russian strategy seems to be to lure the Germans to Manchuria and there join the Japanese in inflicting a crushing defeat on the invader'.

The Russians were heading that way. WARSAW SAFE. It fell to the Germans a week later, and then Vilna fell also.

The Poles, who had been going to get civil rights under the Russians in 1914, were now to be reunited as a kingdom again with an Austrian Archduke as king. Lithuania, a country which we had not heard about, was also to be reunited, with a younger son of the Kaiser as its king. We were supposed to be fighting the Germans to give freedom to the world, and here they were giving freedom to two nations.

Those Russians and their victories; some stories from Russia were just as dubious. At the end of August there was an account of a 'unique duel in the air'. A Russian plane had been attacked by three albatrosses and had managed to kill one of the birds and drive the other two away. Yet, if you thought about it, there were no albatrosses in the northern hemisphere. There was a German plane called an Albatross, just as there was another called a 'Taube'—a dove. The British ambassador to France had a story that the Pope, who was reckoned to be pro-German, had seen his first aeroplane, a 'Taube', and thought it was the Holy Spirit.

It was this year that we were given evidence of the horrible way the Germans were fighting. The proof could be seen in the museum in Melbourne. Going to Melbourne on a Saturday morning was a serious matter: the fare was fivepence by train and there was quite a walk at the other end. As my regular income was now threepence a week, this was of grave importance. At the entrance to the Museum and Library a glass case with a display of German things—a saw-edged bayonet, there it was: 'the most abominable weapon known to civilized warfare. These bayonets tear the flesh and splinter bones, making recovery almost hopeless'. We had never considered how much more comfortable it was to have a straight-edged bayonet stuck into you. The Germans were making the war really nasty. Their explanation was that the Pioneers had to do a lot of quick building and their bayonets could not only serve as saws for wood but could also be stuck on a rifle in an emergency. That explanation was just not good enough.

German spies had been quiet recently, but still, you had to be careful. Things were dangerous in Sydney; within a few minutes' walk of the Houses of Parliament was a German chemist's shop with the notice 'By Special Appointment to the Governor-General'. This shop was dispensing medicines, despite the fact that 'the Germans were poisoning our soldiers on the battle-field and had sowed the seeds of typhus to the Servian troops'. They would use any devilish device, those Germans.

The window of a German barber's shop was smashed in the Melbourne suburb of Moreland; the shop next door was lucky to escape, for it was kept by Mr Dess, a Dane, and Danes were almost as bad. One of the Dess boys was in the army and a younger one in the mercantile marine and had already been torpedoed, but this was no protection. Then Mr Dess's son-in-law, Green, won the V.C. on Gallipoli, so his picture was put up and the window became the safest in Melbourne.

A draftsman at Newport had been seen sketching troop transports as they sailed down the Yarra. He would not have been able to draw many, for all the ones we knew about had sailed from Port Melbourne, but still, it was not a nice thing to do.

On Gallipoli an Australian captain of German descent had been detected sniping our officers and it roused indignation in federal parliament and an investigation was ordered; otherwise, there was little news from Gallipoli.

We had time to look about us in Australia. We were getting tired of all those people in uniform who would not go overseas—like the

Jones brothers at our church. There were worries that the best jobs would be filled by the stay-at-homes and it would be hard for the troops when they returned.

In September in both Melbourne and Sydney, returned men met and formed an association 'to keep green the memory of fallen comrades, to help deserving comrades, to help one another in the battle of life'. So was born the Returned Soldiers' Association, which did all it set out to do and more. As more were invalided out of the army its numbers grew, and it had the fervent support of the rest of the community.

The young idealists and reformers were precisely the ones who had rushed to enlist, but those who returned found that Labor, the party of reform, had changed in their absence. It had stood for self-sufficiency in defence and had promoted compulsory military training, but now it opposed many of the policies which the Returned Soldiers thought essential for a vigorous war effort and it had a wing of Irish and trade unionists who were actively hostile to the war. The Returned Soldiers became a party of reform, but of right-wing reform.

Things did not look too good in the countries near Gallipoli. In May when Italy had done her sums she had included our expected victory in the total and felt she could not afford to stay out and miss the chance of looting her old treaty partners. When Gallipoli did not look quite so good for us, Bulgaria had done her sums and got a different answer; our expected ally was now one more enemy. That made it awkward for the Serbs on their eastern border, and they were fully occupied with the Austrians to the north.

Of course Russia was bound to come across the Black Sea to her help, but the Russians did not arrive. Of course we would come to their aid from the south through friendly Greece, but Greece had done her sums again and was no longer friendly. After all, she had got a kick in the teeth when Russia had vetoed her offer of help in the capture of Constantinople.

All that the British and French could do was to seize Salonika, despite Greek protests, and strike north, but they did not strike hard or fast. Serbia was in a bad way, but we would settle with Bulgaria after our victory on Gallipoli.

Gallipoli was quiet; perhaps both sides were licking their wounds, but it looked as if we had really won and would know about it soon.

On 9 September there was a report from Athens that the surrender of a large Turkish force was imminent—it had been surrounded. This could mean that we had pushed right across the peninsula from Anzac and cut off the Turkish armies.

We were itching for victory and expecting it. The little country town of St Arnaud heard of the total defeat of the Turks and put in an afternoon of celebration. We were one of the very few families in Melbourne which believed it had really happened. Our cousin, Archie Sharpe, was mixed up in mining and had got the news from London, but it could not be released yet for security reasons. We waited until the next day before we told others, and we kept on waiting.

But we did not expect to have to wait long. Turkey was on the verge of collapse and was burning the coastal towns before retreating into Anatolia; the Turks had told the Kaiser they could not continue without German aid.

We were not the only ones expecting a quick victory. America was the centre of the world's wheat trade and there was a sudden big drop in the Chicago Wheat Pit in anticipation of the bottled-up Russian supplies reaching the world through the Dardanelles.

The war in France looked very promising. The only reason our earlier victories had not been bigger was that we did not have enough shells. In October Lloyd George gave us the good news, we had 100 times more shells than a year ago and he had done it all. He had been appointed Minister for Munitions in May and in five months he had made our armies invincible. In those intervening five months he had built factories, recruited and trained thousands of workers and brought them to full production, or so he claimed. He claimed a far greater miracle than the Angels of Mons, and it had no sounder basis, but his claim was never disputed. He was now the 'Welsh Wizard' and he seemed to be more than a mere man; perhaps he was a superman who would lead us to splendid success.

In spite of the extra ammunition, the year was ending badly. At the end of September Loos had been a 'success unprecedented since the Battle of the Marne' under the 'brilliant leadership of General Sir Douglas Haig', in Sir John French's words; it was now becoming accepted as just one more disaster.

Lloyd George mistrusted Haig and held that his complacency was sending thousands to their deaths, but had no hope of replacing him. Haig was solidly seated on the military machine, the King at his side and Lord Northcliffe's full weight of influence pushing him forward; Lloyd George also depended on Northcliffe.

Haig in his turn attacked French; he and Sir William Robertson, Chief of the General Staff, decided that it was time for French to go. Haig approached Lord Esher, Asquith and members of Cabinet, and wrote to the King. He won his first victory and ousted French in November.

In Australia we accepted the change in our leadership without enthusiasm. Haig never inspired us, he looked to be a wax-work figure beside our great Kitchener. Our indifference became active dislike as time went on, until Haig extinguished his reputation completely when he published his papers after the war. In England the feeling against him was not as marked as here.

So there was no victory in France after all and no victory at Gallipoli; now the Serbians were hopelessly beaten and their capital was captured and they were in full retreat.

They were getting worried in England; if there was a German triumph in the Balkans–and there had been–then Germany would be able to join forces with Turkey. In fact trains were running between Berlin and Constantinople within six weeks, and Germany could effectively help the Turks against us at the Dardanelles. And there was soon no Serbia left for all those men in Salonika to assist; all they could do was to sit on the coast. No wonder they were worried in England and asked questions.

Our *Argus* quoted the *Times* which said that 'something was amiss' and criticized the conduct of the war; the Gallipoli campaign was 'a costly experiment'. Lord Milner proposed withdrawal from the Dardanelles as the task was hopeless. The general, Sir Ian Hamilton, was to return to England and would be succeeded by General Monro; our General Birdwood would be in temporary command.

It looked as if Hamilton was in trouble, and we had rather liked him. He was an amiable chatty sort of man who wrote ornate literary essays as his communiqués–funny that he could spare the time. Someone had to take the blame for the blunders.

There was little news from Gallipoli but our papers were reprinting London articles. THE DARDENELLES BLUNDERS. 'After the Suvla Bay landings hours were wasted when minutes were precious.' Certainly there had been no impetuous rush to the almost undefended height of Sari Bair whilst thousands were dying in feint attacks from Anzac to hold down Turkish reinforcements. 'The passion for drill was indulged to the utmost. Trenches were dug in useless positions and night marches were muddled . . . The British reinforcements failed to hold the heights of Sari Bair, which one tenth of the number of Anzac troops had held previously'.

The English were now saying what our own men had said in their letters home about the British New Army. Our beliefs had been established by those letters; now they were confirmed by the English press. Our troops were comparable with the regulars and far better than the pathetic untried new British troops. What had been written confidentially about English generalship was in print in the English papers.

We still revered Kitchener and had no reason for doubting him, but some English did, and he was again attacked violently in Commons. Our Australian, Arthur Lynch, said that he had made a series of blunders, and 'his blunders would stand out like the Rock of Gibraltar in the realms of Blunderdom'. There were whispers of his resignation, but they were officially denied. In fact he had left London and was on an important mission to the Middle East and this looked as if he might call in at Salonika and Gallipoli.

To us Kitchener towered above those English generals who had muddled everything they touched on Gallipoli. We could see no blame attached to him, but the British were desperate and even hysterical and they had the Northcliffe press to excite them. But just as Hindenburg was the war-god to the German, so Kitchener was still ours in Australia. He had no victories to his name, as Hindenburg had, but we felt that it was not his fault.

Keith's weekly letters started coming from Anzac and they gave us a family interest. We showed them to our friends and the aunts copied them to show to their friends. Then Keith's name was on the casualty list. It was not the very worst, but bad enough; he was dangerously ill.

A couple of weeks went by without letters and then we got one from Malta. He was in hospital there with enteric fever but was now on the mend and it looked as if he were safe and would recover. The lists showed that many had died of fever.

In October the reprints from the London papers showed a markedly pessimistic attitude towards the situation in the Dardanelles. Troops should be withdrawn to help the Serbs; the situation was grave; the task was hopeless; it had been a costly experiment; there had been blunders but our prestige would not suffer if the enterprise stopped.

We did not like it. Anzac was our enterprise. It was now our history and people in London were saying that we should be stopped when we might be just on the point of winning at last.

Early in October the *Argus* printed the news of Rudyard Kipling's son being killed in France; we were sorry about that, for Kipling was our greatest writer and had given us the conviction that England was right in whatever she did and that her army was magnificent. Young Kipling had been very dull—it was feared that he would not have been able to pass even the army entrance exam—and he was of poor physique, but he had insisted on enlisting at the age of seventeen and Lord Roberts had got him a commission in the Irish Guards.

A couple of days later two young Melbourne chaps merited a paragraph on their deaths on Gallipoli. Corporal Burns was well into his twenties;

he had been to Scotch College and was a graduate of the University and was already an established journalist. He had written 'For England', the best bit of war verse from Australia. His father was a prominent Presbyterian minister, but Burns died as a mere corporal.

Private E. R. Grimwade was a member of a very solid family and his uncle was Brigadier-General Grimwade. He had been at Melbourne Grammar and had finished his third year of medicine at the University, but he died as a private.

It all seemed nonsense. That callow young Kipling had been given charge of the welfare and lives of men far more responsible than himself, and it seemed to us that this was not the way to make an effective fighting force. The two Melbourne men were years older and it looked as though they could have become reliable officers in time, but both had been cut down before they were given the chance. Our army had a lot like them and it might be that it was wasteful of its human material.

We did not like this continuing English talk of Gallipoli being abandoned. Surely we should be consulted on a thing so significant to Australia. They were still arguing about it in London and the British Cabinet had not accepted General Monro's suggestion of withdrawal; some papers in Britain were pressing for withdrawal and others were saying that there would be none; the Turks were reported as saying that the British would not withdraw. Kitchener would report on the position and we had faith in him. On 21 December: ANZAC EVACUATED. INSIGNIFICANT CASUALTIES. That was crushing news and we were shocked.

In the aunts' papers was a copy of Monash's letter to his wife describing it all.

Anzac
Gallipoli
Dec 12th 1915

Like a thunderbolt from a clear sky has come the stupendous and paralyzing news that, after all, the Allied War Council has decided that the best and wisest course is to evacuate the Peninsular, and secret orders to carry out that operation have just reached us here . . . This operation of withdrawal is going to be every bit as critical and dangerous an enterprise as the first landing . . .

Dec. 13th. The move has already commenced. Tonight the whole of my 15th Batt. and about 100 of odds and ends are being taken off in barges.

Dec. 14th. About 600 of 14th Brigade with all their impediments got safely away last night – although there was a half moon . . .

Dec. 15th. It is curious and interesting to watch the machine unwind itself . . . The supply of fresh meat and bread stopped a couple of days ago, and as reserves of these are being used up, we are going back steadily to an emergency diet of hard biscuits and bully beef . . . Although the move is still officially a secret, the men would be fools indeed if they have not already guessed what is in the wind. Yet . . . all ranks go about their day's works as if we were to stay here till the end of the war.

Dec. 15th. Later—It was decided that I am *Not* to go away in advance, at which I am very glad, because I want to be the last man of the Brigade to leave . . . we have established a casualty clearing station to accommodate 1,200 patients with a full staff of doctors, dressers and hospital gear . . . The medical officers and personnel in charge, will of course, have to stay, too.

Dec. 16th . . . The total strength of Anzac has in the last four days been reduced from 45,000 to 20,000 and we shall continue to hold the lines against at least 170,000 Turks (10 Divisions) and on the very last day we shall have only 10,000.

Dec. 17th. In view of the steadiness of the barometer and the operation of re-embarkation tomorrow and Sunday . . . General Birdwood himself came over from Imbros . . . He went along my whole line . . . and expressed the hope that many would come through alive, 1,600 will have left—on the last night I take the remaining 825. These I have divided into three echelons or groups, the first 400, the second 255, the last of all 170 moving respectively at 6 p.m., 10 p.m. and 2 a.m. The last 170 or 'die-hards' have been chosen from the most gallant and capable men in the Brigade. Even these will not all leave the trenches in a bunch but a few of the most daring men, who are good athletes, will remain in the front and keep up a fire for another 10 minutes . . . I am myself going, as ordered, with the first group of the last 170.

Dec. 18th. Everything is going smoothly. The enemy is exceptionally quiet . . . We have worked out a very clever device for firing off a rifle automatically at any predetermined time after the device is started. It is done by allowing a tin to slowly fill with water until it over-balances, falls and jerks a string which fires the rifle . . . the enemy will think we are still in the trenches after we have got a mile away.

Midnight. The last party of the first night has embarked safely . . . everything is normal, just the usual sniping and occasional bombs and bursts of machine gun fire. I think, now, I had better try and get a couple of hours sleep, as everything seems normal and not more than the usual noise for this time of night.

Dec. 19th. 1915 Noon. The last day on Gallipoli. Last night's move passed off smoothly and without incident . . . The weather today is absolutely perfect for our purpose—perfectly calm air and sea, cloudy

and foggy and dull, with a very light misty drizzle, so that everything
in the distance is dim and blurred.

8 p.m. Everything is going swimmingly without a hitch ... at the
present moment there are not more than 5000 troops in the whole of
Anzac.

Dec. 20th. 4 a.m. The last hours on Gallipoli were tense and exciting
in the extreme. About 9 of my last patrol came in and reported that
they could plainly hear the Turks digging and putting wire out in Hack-
ney Wick and Green Knoll. This meant so far they suspected nothing.
The last hours passed most warily. Every crack of a rifle, every burst
of rifle fire, every bomb explosion might have been a general attack
all along the line. By 10 o'clock our final numbers—1500 spread along
a front of over 8 miles. As it was, the final withdrawal commenced
at 1.35 then the balance of the machine guns and 30 men came out,
and at 1.45 another 60, and at 1.55 a.m. my last man left his foremost
position, leaving only the automatic devices working ... Down dozens
of little gullies leading back from the front lines, came little groups
of six to a dozen men, the last in every case an officer, closing the gulley
with a previously prepared frame of barbed wire or lighting a fuse which
an hour later would fire a mine which would wreck a sap or a tunnel
which the enemy could follow. All these little columns of men kept
joining up, like so many rivulets which flow into the main stream and
so at last they coalesced into four continuous lines ... There was no
check, no halting, no haste or running, just a steady, silent tramp in
single file without lights or smoking—every yard brought us nearer to
safety ... each line marched like so many ghostly figures in the dim
light in single file on to the allotted jetty, the sound of marching feet
having been deadened by laying a floor of sandbags, and so into motor
barges (beetles we call them) each holding 400 on to these Generals,
staff officers, gunners and privates all packed up promiscuously and
quietly... 'Let's go all over'. 'Right away' was the last order and slowly
we moved out ... It was a brilliant conception, brilliantly organised
and brilliantly executed and will, I am sure, rank as the greatest joke
in the whole range of military history ... Arrived at last on the little
transport the strain being over, the reaction came in wild and hilarious
greetings, mutual felicitations and hearty handshakes all round ... I
got a bunk in the pantryman's cabin but found myself quite unable
to sleep so decided to write down my impressions while they are still
fresh. It is now 6.30 a.m. and we are just dropping in the outer anchorage
of Udros [Mudros?] Harbour and a new day is breaking.

John Monash

It was defeat. We tried to think that the evacuation had been a victory,
just as the British had claimed that the Retreat from Mons had been

one, but inside ourselves we knew it was defeat. We had thought that we were doing very well and another push would topple the Turks out of the war. If we could only make another attempt things would prosper. There would be no more bungles by inert generals and callow troops, an advance of a mile or two and the straits would be cleared. But now we felt let down; the only land we would hold on Gallipoli would be those thousands of graves.

The Light Horse which had died so uselessly and gallantly may have come from the Western District of Victoria and from Western Australia, but they lay in Australian graves. Those graves were the foundation of the new nation of Australia.

It had been a bad year. Father took out the four drawing pins and took down the map of Gallipoli. It had not been there long enough to leave a trace on the wallpaper. Anzac had been a bright meteor and the sky was now dark.

ANZAC   EVACUATED

Insignificant Casualties.

TROOPS GO TO "ANOTHER SPHERE"

In that dark year the lights had been doused, one after another. Whilst Gallipoli was being fought there had been a splendid success against the Turks in Mesopotamia. Two days after Turkey came into the war a force from India had landed at the mouth of the Tigris and pushed victoriously upstream to capture Kut-el-Amara. We were treating the Turks as they deserved; it was all so easy as to be almost funny. The Slav place-names had been comical enough but the Arabic ones were even better. We made up some for ourselves—'Beer-in-Bottle'. We may have stuck on Gallipoli but that splendid advance was something to set against it. We were almost at Baghdad. Then on 8 December: BRITISH

RETIRE WITHOUT LOSS. They had retreated back to Kut and there they were besieged. The year had been a dead loss there. (In April next, Kut would surrender and 9000 of our men would be marched off into captivity. Twenty-four thousand casualties would be suffered in a relief attempt by troops drawn from France.)

Our new ally, Italy, had done absolutely nothing. Our older ally, Serbia, had been obliterated and only a pathetic remnant of her armies had escaped across the winter mountains. They would wait in Salonika with all the other troops, doing nothing. The Germans said that Salonika was just a big internment camp, but it had a lot of our side in it.

Our remaining wall map was discouraging. The French and British pins had not moved forward and the Russian ones had tumbled back. The black German pins now formed a line from the Baltic to the Mediterranean.

1916

13
Enlistment

It was 1916 and the first Sunday of the New Year. The Jones boys again marched into church, perhaps not as loudly as in the past. They were still two sergeants and a warrant-officer, third class, of the Instructional Corps, but their tailored uniforms looked theatrical. They had the air of hack actors who had been on the stage too long. Once they had looked like real soldiers to us; now we felt that the real soldiers were the boys we knew who had walked on briefly in their baggy uniforms and made their exit, and might not appear again.

Quite a few had gone from the congregation and there was some talk of putting their names up on an honour board. That sort of board was getting quite common in schools, churches and workplaces. It showed that we were proud of those who had enlisted, and it would encourage others to do so. There were even a few personal memorials: the first had been at the Richmond State School where a big photograph was put up of an old pupil who was killed on the *Sydney* in its fight with the *Emden*.

We were beginning to feel ourselves to be as good as, or better than the British and we were already differentiating between the English, Scottish and Irish. The extravagant praise of the bravery and physique of the Australians on Gallipoli had enhanced our self-esteem.

We were a minority group and felt kinship with other minorities. We thought that the Irish divisions on Gallipoli were better than most and that the Scots were even better – and so did the Scots. Even Englishmen with very remote affiliations with Scotland would try to join the London Scottish, who were sure that they were better than any other Territorial unit; we agreed with them. We got on particularly well with the Scots in both wars.

The English did their best but they found it difficult to adjust to a new sort of war in which the lower classes were important, and were, in some cases, very decent sorts of people who should be encouraged. Wars had previously been for cricket and 'rugger' players, the upper classes; the lower classes played soccer.

In Lord Northcliffe's *At the War* he sets out why the English soldier was superior to the German, who

> had never played individual games; football, which develops individuality, has only been introduced into Germany in comparatively recent times. . . Our soldiers are individual. They embark on little individual enterprises. The German is not so clever at these devices. He was never taught them before the war, and his whole training from childhood upwards has been to obey, and to obey in numbers.

Yet the German officers, who had not played cricket, and their men, who had not played soccer, had not done badly against the sportsmen of England. Indeed, in our victories at Loos and Neuve Chapelle, they had done rather better than we had realized at the time. The individual initiative of the English at Suvla Bay had not been obvious.

But the Germans were not sportsmen. An Englishman would not hit a man when he was down, and when he himself fell, he called 'Play up, play up, and play the game'.

But on 6 January a remarkable item passed the censor: SUBMARINE MURDERERS. SHOT BY BRITISH SEAMEN. GERMAN CHARGES ON INHUMANITY. SIR EDWARD GREY'S OFFER. We did not approve of submarines sinking passenger boats and people getting drowned, but it did not seem like playing the game to shoot the submarine crews. The Germans appealed to the world.

A German submarine had stopped the *Niconian* and allowed the crew to leave before a party boarded her to set charges to sink her. Up came a vessel flying the U.S. flag, the *Barralong*, and suddenly opened fire with guns previously hidden. The submarine began to sink. Some submarine crew clung to the ropes of the *Niconian* until they were killed by cannon and rifle fire from the *Barralong*. The submarine commander in the water raised his hand in surrender and was killed by a shot in the neck. Four of the submarine's crew who had boarded the *Niconian* were shot in cold blood. The commander of the *Barralong* had orders that no one was to mention the incident, but six Americans of the *Barralong* crew swore affidavits and the news reached Germany and the world.

To us this seemed like an atrocity, and up until now, all atrocities had been German. Northcliffe's *Daily Mail* said it was 'retribution for pirates' and that 'everyone knows that British naval humanity will emerge unscathed from the investigation'.

In Australia we knew that it was a dirty war and that all the dirt came from Germany, but this shooting of helpless men by our side really did not sound to be sporting. We felt that it was a pity that the censor let us know about it and were relieved that our papers carried no more news of the incident.

We kept on about the Germans here. International patent law was suspended and German patents were sold by the government. The aspirin patent was one: it became Australia's Nicholas 'Aspro' and brought a quick fortune to the Prahran chemists who bought it. They were two brothers who had been to Wesley, and 'Aspro' money later rebuilt the school.

Enemy trade-names were suppressed, and the names of all persons of enemy origin, whether naturalized or not, were struck off the lists of shareholders – they had been 'stealing and plundering private property'. Even more drastic was that land ownership was forbidden them.

Fifteen employees of the Victorian Brewery were sacked, although some of them had worked there for twenty years. One lot of Senior Cadets refused to parade because the grandfather of their lieutenant had been a German.

In January *The Anzac Book* came out – a pity it had not been in time for Christmas and a greater pity that Anzac was finished. Some of it was of about the same standard as a school magazine and some of it of very high quality. There were some good drawings and some good verse, some pathetic and some comic.

I made water-colour copies of two of the pictures and took them to school and got some credit. One was of a fat Turk getting a bang on the side of the head and 'Apricot Again', a skinny fierce ginger man, fierce, for the English apricot jam on ration was really bad, and we did not think much of the best of English factory jam.

The Anzac Book was presentable, but it was like any obituary. We put our copy on the wickerwork fitting in the corner of the drawing room with the things that Keith had sent home.

The troops from Gallipoli, the 1st and 2nd Divisions, returned to Egypt and half of each was drafted into two new divisions, the 4th and 5th, and so each division had the same proportion of experienced men and a common tradition shared with the untried reinforcements. The 3rd Division was still in Australia but transfers were made to it when it got to England. The Anzac tradition was common to the whole force. It was a firm tradition, quite as strong as the regimental traditions of the British army with its funny caps and buttons.

It had become clear in 1915 that the war would require more than the normal output of medical graduates. Medical students who had survived Gallipoli were recalled from Egypt to complete their courses. Medicine was something that women could usefully do for the war, and amongst those who did were Julie Hickford and Mary Lyle, the daughter of Professor Lyle, who both transferred from science–both did remarkably well in their new course.

Some medical students still in camp in Australia were sent back to university in time to complete the year which they had abandoned in August 1914, but it was in 1916 that the returned soldier students from Gallipoli set the pattern of university sentiment. They were very patriotic and very antagonistic to some fellow students–the 'War Babies'.

Of all the courses only medicine prevented enlistment. There was a suspicion that some eighteen-year-olds were doing medicine not because they wanted to, but because they or their parents had selected a course which would keep them safe. The feeling against the 'War Babies' lasted out the war.

The first stampede into the army was over. Now most young chaps went in regretfully because they and their friends thought that it was the right thing to do.

There was no great rush about it; at work a man would give a week or two's notice that he was going to enlist and his mates would collect for a present for him–just like getting married. Then just before he left they would have a meeting to say goodbye and good luck and he would be given his present.

It was always a wrist-watch. Before the war they had been regarded as flashy modern things, but now they were just the thing for the war. They were quite big, with black faces and numerals in phosphorus paint that could be read at night in the trenches. They were a new male status symbol.

The old pocket-watch with its chain across the waistcoat had been as masculine as a rooster's comb, but it was now archaic. In those baggy khaki jackets with the big pockets, a pocket-watch would be hard to find; no chain was permitted for pulling it out, you just could not drape a chain across a uniform. The war caused the death of pocket-watches.

At the church we would probably have a small social for particular friends who were leaving, and some other smaller present might be given. The new fountain pens were quite expensive but suitable for writing letters home. They were black cylinders with rubber intestines which held the ink and let it out when needed, and at other times. The pen fitted into a top pocket but it might get smashed in rifle training and a lot of pockets had blue ink stains. A cheaper present was one of the new safety razors; it never would cut as well as the old cumbersome cut-throats, but it was easier to carry and a new blade would revive it. Or we might give a tube of toothpaste. The army issued round, flat tins of gritty pink paste, but a tube was better and tasted better and could be shared without qualms.

The year 1916 was the peak year for khaki socks. Every woman was knitting them; it was about all she could do for the war.

The people of Australia—that is, our sort of people—demanded that every young man should enlist, and every young man was reminded of it in conversation, by the newspapers, and by Lord Kitchener. We were not just distant devotees of that war-god; he had dwelt amongst us in 1910 and told us how to defend our country and that we would need 60 000 men to do it and that we ought to train them compulsorily. Every male from the age of twelve to twenty was now doing his hours of military training each week.

Enlistment was accepted as an honourable and inevitable duty, even by the gentlest and the most unwilling; they felt bound to go and when they did enlist they immediately regained their self-esteem.

At the Armadale Presbyterian church there had been a trickle in 1914 growing into a steady stream by early 1915, and now two most unlikely soldiers felt called.

Innes Gunn was a friend of our family and as blind as a bat. He wore great thick glasses, but by learning the letters of the eye-test by heart, he slipped in. He was so blind that he could not tell one end of a rifle from another, let alone aim one. He ended up as a stretcher-bearer with an infantry battalion. About the same time just as unlikely a soldier joined up—our Senior Church Elder. He must have been a remarkable man to be Senior Elder for he was still in his thirties. James MacRoberts was a cautious, gentle man with a pretty and gentle wife. He was the last man to want to kill another, but he felt that he was bound to go and went into a service unit.

The war really caught my family in the New Year of 1916. The recruiting office opened after the holidays and Owen went along on 3 January taking father's consent with him.

Ralph joined up on the 6th. Athol waited until 28 February. He was delicate and very unsuitable for the army and now he was engaged to his Elsie.

Ralph and Owen went into the intake camp in the Domain, just off St Kilda Road near the city. They marched about the place near the Botanic Gardens and Ralph felt that he could now be seen on the streets without feeling ashamed.

We came to visit them on Saturday afternoon. There was a high barbed-wire fence with a gate guarded by a uniformed sentry with a rifle and fixed bayonet; very martial he looked, but the brothers didn't.

When we met them they were in sloppy two-piece blue dunagaree suits with floppy white cloth hats—the sort that cricketers wore. We went to their tent—Ralph and Owen were in the same one. It was circular with a central pole. There they slept like the spokes of a wheel with their feet towards the central pole. They slept on waterproof ground sheets and palliasses stuffed with straw, just like big chaff bags. We gave them jam and cakes from Friday's baking and talked awkwardly until half-past five.

When Athol went in he was sent off to a camp on the race-course at Geelong. Although it was much further away, Athol got home on leave just as often as the others.

In a couple of weeks the three of them moved to Broadmeadows camp, about eight miles out in rolling country beyond the suburbs, and things became more military. They were all issued with khaki uniforms and they were all doing their basic infantry training. The tents were in neat rows and they were rectangular, like the two we had at home for our camping trips, but these were much bigger. It seems that we had adopted the English bell-tent as an army tradition but found that the local rectangular tent was more serviceable. Athol did not sleep in one of these, but in a big marquee with a crowd of others. Marquees went out of fashion before long.

There was a hospital there, rows of low galvanized-iron sheds under the pine trees near a big old house, which had been the centre of the estate. I got to know them well later, for Broadmeadows was still a camp for the Citizen Force of my time and we slept in those huts. One of them, or its twin, was moved to the University after 1918 to become the first school of architecture, and a recreation hut became the Students' Union.

The Defence Act and its compulsory military training was being of some use. Instructors were available from the Instructional Corps—like the Jones boys—and training-officers were available from those who had already got their commissions in the Citizen Force. But already there was criticism—these were young chaps on good pay living comfortably here and training better men to go overseas, and they were blocking promotion.

Most of the intake had had some training and gone to the annual compulsory camps, so there was little novelty or friction. Rifles were available, for they had been called in from the Citizen Force depots. They were real rifles, quite good and modern. More were being made in New South Wales where an ordnance factory had been established under the Defence Scheme. They were the standard short British Lee-

Enfield and we would use them in our turn in our training and in the next war, and they would still be good. Those early rifles had one thing which was later omitted: a wind gauge. It was rather delicate on an otherwise sturdy rifle and not much use at less than a thousand yards – and at a thousand yards you were lucky to come anywhere near a hit.

Visiting Broadmeadows was quite a business and we seldom went there. It meant a change of trains in Melbourne and a dusty mile along the road to the camp. We walked that mile: the big two-horse drags charged a shilling. But the boys often got weekend leave and we were very proud when a couple of them came to church with us in their uniforms. Soon they were corporals and sergeants; temporary rank, of course, which they would lose when they went to their final units.

Twice on his leaves Owen took Neil and me to the theatre – the real theatre, Shakespeare; it was much better than the only other time I had been, when it was to a silly pantomime.

We went into town and walked up to the Princess Theatre. Owen bought three tickets from a window on the pavement and then there was a wait in a crowd at the door. The door opened and in we rushed, up a stone stair between green-painted brick walls, up and a quick turn round and up again, up and turn, up and turn. We were puffing when we got to the top. There we were, at the very top of a great dim space with rows of seats sloping steeply below us; down we rushed and got to the very front.

We had time to fill in; Neil went all the way down again and got a pass-out check and bought a newspaper parcel of potato chips; the seats below began to fill with well-dressed people and the lights brightened. Owen did not laugh at me this time, not until it was all over. I wanted to see the people below and pushed my head between the top of the ledge and a rail above it and couldn't get it back. Other people laughed, but Owen waited until I struggled clear before he did; of course Neil laughed.

The lights dimmed and the curtains lighted up and parted. Bright and splendid, a sort of garden. It was magic each time the curtains opened: a palace; a forest with brown and yellow leaves on the ground and a little stream, an English sort of forest. The play was *As You Like It*.

It had a real story, not like the pantomime. There were two girls, about the same age as Phyllis and her friends: Rosalind, rather pert and talking too much; Celia, blonde and plump, she was my favourite and she looked like Norah Crawford, a friend of Phyllis. They talked in an old-fashioned sort of way, just like the Bible, and this made it sound very genuine. They dressed up as men for part of the time with long stockings on their long legs, but this did not matter because we knew they were really girls, even if the men on the stage did not.

The second time, *Twelfth Night*, was not so gripping, but Sir Toby Belch had a comic name and he and Malvolio were really funny, much funnier than the clowns in the pantomime. It was good to have Owen sitting between us and we were proud to be beside a brother in uniform, and a corporal at that.

The curtains closed and it was a soft awakening after a happy dream. Down those long stairs we went and into the quiet street. We walked down the Collins Street hill with just a late cable-tram glimmering as it glided up the hill and the clip-clop of the horse of a four-wheeler cab on its last trip of the day. Flinders Street station and a lot of people waiting on platform 5 for our train. 'That fair young chap looks young to be in uniform.' 'Yes, he is my brother, Owen, and he has just taken Neil and me to the theatre.'

On 21 February Keith came home. He may have been pretty sick in Malta, but the sea trip had done him good and he looked well, but a bit thinner than when he went away less than a year before. He was lucky to get over enteric fever so well, for quite a few died of it. He was lucky, too, for he had been transferred to the Engineers from the 22nd Infantry Battalion; it got cut up badly in France before 1916 was very old.

It was something to walk along the street beside a soldier, but it would have been very much better to walk along with a returned soldier— one who had been on Gallipoli. But it did not work out that way. Keith was on leave and wore his old civilian clothes. When he was coming out from Melbourne on Saturday morning, a young woman on the train gave him a white feather. His refusal to wear uniform was not the only disappointment; he had no stories of the gallantry and glory of war. Yes, he had seen Turks but he had not shot any. He had a good chance when one got out of his trench a hundred yards away, but he had got out to relieve himself and Keith had regarded him as out of season.

He brought things back. We already had a photo of him on a camel in front of the pyramids. Now he gave us things from Egypt, silk cloths which mother put under the vases in the drawing room, and of course, that picture of a sunset with the pyramids and palm trees in front. He gave me a little wooden camel, and a picture of a milkman in Malta milking his goats at the door of a house, and a big silver crown-piece, five shillings. We had no coins as big in Australia. It only roused passing interest at school and a High Street shop gave me five shillings for it.

We had just one Sunday when the four of them all managed weekend leave together. The whole family went to church, just like the old days, and mother was proud of her four sons in uniform, all with rank of some sort from lieutenant down to two corporals.

Athol Lewis

Ralph was a temporary corporal, but as he had passed his officer's training course quite easily, he would almost certainly become a lieutenant after he had been in France for a while. He had done his course in Sydney, where our old neighbours, the Rosenfelts, had adopted him. When he went overseas, they sent him parcels regularly. Not all enemy aliens were bad.

Athol was a sergeant in the infantry, but he was company clerk and did not think it much of a way of fighting a war. He transferred to the artillery and lost his stripes and it took months to get them back. As a gunner, he had leather leggings, far more impressive than the puttees of the others, and he wore riding breeches which flared out splendidly above the knees.

More than that, he had been taught to ride, although he was the worst natural horseman of the whole lot of us. He told us of long conversations he had with his horse and what the horse said about him was not flattering. He nearly got into trouble: at Maribyrnong the day for the artillery began with a blank round fired from a field-gun captured from the Boers and somebody had put a loaf of bread in the barrel and it had brought down a tent.

Owen came top of the N.C.O.s course for the Engineers and was offered a commission as an instructor. This would have meant his staying in Australia, for he had a long time to go before he reached twenty-three, the minimum age for a commission in the A.I.F.

After a couple of weeks at home Keith joined the three others at Broadmeadows. He was transferred into the new 2nd Tunnelling Company and embarked with them.

It was a secret departure; with all those submarines waiting for troopships ten thousand miles away, of course all troop movements had to be secret.

The transports were ready at Port Melbourne and it was obvious that they would be leaving soon. A fuss at camp and somebody would get a message to Melbourne and a crowd would turn up for the 'secret' departure. Mrs Shepherd lent her car to the family and Neil and I were allowed to miss school and we all piled in. We saw Keith and Ralph off but missed Owen. When Athol went, Elsie's father took us in his Country Roads Board car. It was a big ship with rows of faces along the rails and it was hard to pick out Athol, but Mr Calder got some photographs. Then we bought rolls of paper streamers from the boys with trays and we threw them up to the ship. As the ship pulled out, the rolls were unwound and the streamers got longer and longer until they were so long that the wind broke them. The last one broke and the faces became too small to recognize and we all went home.

The family had broken up. The four eldest brothers were away. Ronnie was in residence at the University on a scholarship at Queen's College, where he had taken over Owen's old room. There was just Phyllis, Neil and me at home and the big house was too big for us.

The family fortunes were better, for all four brothers had allotted some of their military pay to mother; she had had Keith's over the past year but now the others allotted three shillings a day each, the maximum permitted out of the basic five shillings. The amount would be increased when they got more pay on promotion.

It was just as well, for there seemed to be even less work for father to pick up. We didn't have enough to keep us as we expected to be kept, and we had empty rooms. We could not take in boarders, but we could take in friends as paying guests.

We took in Sylvia, not as a boarder, of course, but to help her father. Mr Black was some distant relative of mother's and was an architect; he had trouble with his wife and was getting a divorce. We did not hold with divorce, but it was kind to help him and it paid.

Sylvia was a charming golden-haired girl of nine – just my age – with entrancing dimples when she smiled. It was a pity that she only stayed six months, she made home seem more natural. She had first bath on Saturday night and when Neil and I got into the same water, she looked through the crack in the door at us. She was as interested in us as we were in her. Her father used to bring old architectural drawings on Whatman's paper on his Friday visits, and I could paint on the back of them.

14

The School at War

In the *Wesley College Songbook* was a song entitled 'To the School at War'. The words had been published in the *Times* of 19 December 1914; they were written by the Rev. C. A. Alington, then headmaster of Shrewsbury School, who in 1916 was appointed headmaster of Eton. The Wesley headmaster, Mr Adamson, had written a tune for it. The last verse ran:

> And you, our brothers, who for all our praying,
> To this dear school of ours come back no more,
> Who lie, our country's debt of honour paying —
> And not in vain — upon the Belgian shores,
> Till that great day when at the Throne in Heaven
> The books are opened and the Judgement set:
> Your lives for honour and for England given,
> The School will not forget.

My life changed when I was sent to Wesley College Preparatory School; Owen agreed to pay the fees out of his military pay. He thought I would have a better chance if I went to Wesley younger than he and the others had gone. Of course I was sorry to abandon my established position at the Armadale State School as I would have to start all over again, but it was the price to be paid for joining one of the six public schools.

Wesley, a pleasant enough grey building with two stumpy towers at its ends — that was my Wesley. Since my time that building has been indecently assaulted and now stands shameless in American academic architecture, more shoddy than anything illustrated in the advertisement pages of technical journals. Its dingy dignity has been stripped and pallid antiseptics substituted.

It looked across a sports field to St Kilda Road, a splendid wide road with avenues of trees dividing its magnificent width and more trees beside the footpaths on both sides. Like the boulevards of Paris, they

Wesley College, as it was, from St Kilda Road

said, the grandest road in the southern hemisphere. It started at the St Kilda junction, where the tower of the Junction Hotel looked down its central width to the city and through the city to where the Carlton Brewery closed the imposing vista. It ran between rows of solid mansions in big grounds, past the sombre Victoria Barracks, past parks dotted with statues of kings, governors and one of Robert Burns, right up to the city. It crossed Prince's Bridge into the city, St Paul's Cathedral on one side and Young and Jackson's hotel on the other.

Down the wide central division silently drifted the cable trams through a cloud of dust and horse-droppings blown by the hot north winds. Noiselessly they ran, never fast, never slow, just at their fixed speed, the speed of a cable running under a slot between the rails. The cable was pulled by great wheels driven by steam engines in power-houses – there was one near Melbourne Grammar, nearer to the city than Wesley.

The tram was in two parts; the dummy in front did all the work while the rear cabin was just pulled along. The dummy was completely open; in the middle stood the grip-man who worked the lever which grasped the cable, and flanking him were two rows of seats facing side-ways from the tram almost at road level. If you missed a tram, you could chase after it and jump on to the near-side seats. If you were careless in getting off you might find yourself under the nose of a horse on one side, or in front of another cable tram on the other.

The best seats on the dummy were the two pairs in the very front, divided by a narrow gap for the grip-man to get his place. There you could sit and watch the city get silently closer. The worst seats were the pair at the other end which looked back into the cabin car trundling along behind. Only mature people travelled in the cabin, all the lively ones were on the dummy.

They were gentle trams. At the end of the school year going in to speech night at the Auditorium, it was usual to try to ride on the roof and nobody seemed to mind very much; at University Commencement, when the students had the run of the city on a Saturday morning, the wits would pull out the pin and when the policeman on point duty moved on the traffic, the dummy would leap forward leaving the cabin stranded. At times of national rejoicing a group would lift both dummy and cabin from the terminus in Elizabeth Street and carry them across to the line in Flinders Street, and there was nothing for it but for the Coburg tram to grip the cable and set off for Clifton Hill; that was interesting, for it had a different colour scheme from the Clifton Hill trams.

Cable trams served only the old parts of Melbourne, and Armadale was a middle-aged suburb. When we took a tram it was an electric one down High Street to go shopping in Chapel Street on Friday night. I can just remember the older horse-buses which went down Dandenong Road, little things seating a crowded eight; you entered at the back, and pushed forward and put the fare in a box behind the driver in the dim light of a kerosene lamp.

It was always an important occasion when we went beyond the range of our electric tram and rode on a cable tram—as when going to the Zoo. We went by train to Flinders Street, and crossed the road to a cable tram waiting at the end of Elizabeth Street; of course we got on to the dummy, even mother, for this was an occasion. Through town, past the University to a big road junction, where we got off and crossed the road to a really funny sort of tram, a horse tram; it was just like a cabin from a cable tram. It was pulled by a heavy slow horse and meandered through Royal Park to the Zoo. It would have been just as quick to walk and it cost a penny, but the horse tram was a part of a visit to the Zoo.

With our cheap scholars' tram tickets, it worked out a penny cheaper to go into town by tram, rather than train. The electric tram terminus was where High Street, Prahran, butted into St Kilda Road. We walked across to the side section of the road, which was reserved for motor-cars, and across the middle of the wide central horse-section to wait in the rain until a cable tram drifted along. Every now and then someone crossing the road was knocked down by one of those new motor-cars.

It was the same electric tram to Wesley; we got on in High Street at the corner of Kooyong Road, where the trams in each direction

A cable tram

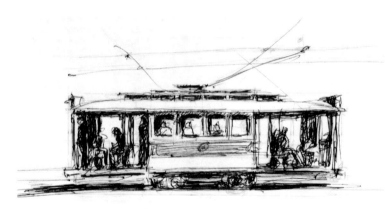

The courteous sort of electric tram

stopped for a while and the conductors got out and turned a key in a box under a clock, one on each side of the road. There were two sorts of electric trams. The older ones were quite small, just a single bogey of four wheels with a central cabin balanced over it and two cross-seats at each end for smokers. As the little tram went along balanced on its central wheels it swayed up and down, rather like royalty bowing to the people it passed in the street.

The bigger new trams had two bogeys with cabins at each end separated by seats for smokers running across the full width of the tram. When the conductor moved from one end of the tram to the other, he had to edge along the footboard on the outside of the tram and every now and then he was scraped off by passing traffic. For eight years trams were part of life at Wesley.

On the first morning I set out with Neil, along to the tram stop in High Street, and it was exciting to go to school by tram. We waited on our home-side of High Street and on the opposite side were two groups of girls going in the opposite direction; most of them had already had a train journey and got out at the Armadale station. One lot was going to a convent school near the Malvern town hall and we would never have any interest in them. The other group was going much further, to Korowa Girls' School. For years they were just curiosities but eventually they became very interesting indeed. My Jean was one of them.

Past Chapel Street the tram took us, and I had not been past it often before. Then all the purple caps got off at Punt Road, the stop before the terminus at St Kilda Road, and I felt naked without a cap.

Neil delivered me to the Preparatory School. It had nothing of the grandeur of the Big School about it, just a red-brick huddle like an untidy house set hard on the fence of unimpressive Punt Road—a poor thing compared to the Armadale State School. I joined a group of lost-looking new boys who had just been abandoned by their fathers.

We new boys were sorted out; most of us went to Middle I, a form of thirty boys in which we new ones amounted to half. The old-stagers expected us to treat them as aristocrats, and with some reason.

They had an assured social position established by past years at the Prep; they had the superiority of age, they were all a couple of years older than us; they had financial power, they were obviously more afflu-ent than us new boys.

Mother had been obliged to go the expense of fitting me out in the Prep uniform: grey shorts, grey socks and jersey with little purple and gold stripes around the extremities. The aristocrats all wore little two-piece grey suits as a permitted variation from the prescribed uniform. I would never get one of those little suits in my four years at the Prep.

That morning my new satchel had been empty except for the lunch which Phyllis had cut, a specimen of eight years of lunches. Two rounds of sandwiches, one with jam, the other with something else, perhaps cold meat or the new spread Marmite, a piece of cake and a bit of fruit. We ate our lunches on the steps of the sports pavilion facing the playing field. The aristocrats had a hot lunch in the Prep boarding house on the other side of Punt Road.

There was a lot of coming and going on that first day; we were issued with our school books and a purple cap and a little gilt lion for mother to sew on the front of it. That lion had a number impressed on it which was recorded against our names. It seems that the older boys were giving

Wesley College Preparatory School

Wesley lions to the girls at Central Park on Sunday afternoons, and that number might make it possible to trace the boy who had let down his school.

We were given a form signed by the school for cheap tram tickets, the only thing not on the bill as an extra at the end of term. After school we took a tram right up to the Malvern town hall, well beyond Kooyong Road, then a walk along Glenferrie Road and round a corner to the tram depot, where the form and four shillings bought a linen-backed strip with numbers down each side; on each trip the conductor would punch out the highest surviving number.

Next morning in my purple cap the public could recognize that I was a member of an important group. We could have real lessons today; for yesterday had been just a scramble, running about and getting things. Miss Connor already knew some of our names and we were part of her Middle I. A kindly lady, Miss Connor, but of negative importance in our man's school. No woman was allowed to teach boys older than us, but we were kind to her from the height of our male superiority.

We got our new names. I was Lewis II – Neil was in the Big School. At Lawside I had been 'Brian Lewis'; now it felt very masculine and mature to be just 'Lewis'. We met our companions who were to become our friends; two of them, Mickey Cohen and McCallum II, were to rise through the school alongside me for eight years.

Mickey was not Cohen's real name, but he was over-weight and worthy of a nickname, which could be used on informal occasions. McCallum II, like me, had a brother in the Big School, and like me, had even older brothers who had passed beyond the school. His father was a dis-tinguished Methodist minister, all of whose seven children had their birthdays in the first week of October, perhaps the result of some annual midsummer Methodist orgy.

We were put into our places by the ten- and eleven-year-olds, the old-stagers who had moved up from Middle II. Their Sultan was Brockhoff II. That might sound to be a German name and therefore disgraceful, but it really wasn't. Brockhoff's biscuits were so widely advertised that the name was part of our cultural heritage, just as no one would suggest that the Woinarskis, prominent in law and medicine, were anything but Australian, and even Monash, if you thought about it, might be a foreign name. But the Brockhoffs were wealthy and we did not suggest that they might be German. Brockhoff II was a kindly Sultan.

His Grand Vizier was Robert Bruce; Wobert Bwuce, he pronounced it. He was close to the Sultan and reported to him on any important matters he came across in the day-to-day affairs of the sultanate. He selected culprits for punishment, but sometimes the Sultan graciously spared them.

On the second day began the terrors of being a new boy. The terror of the tram passing the Prahran State School and the nine o'clock bell already ringing and you would probably be late and face an unknown punishment; then at school, the terror of unknown and inexplicable things. At the Armadale State School it had been a rough yet rapid merging into a group with common enemies; now the enemies were the old-stagers in our group. They had a code of conduct which we could not understand and which seemed to have no logic, except that money was important. There was nothing we new boys could do to ingratiate ourselves; we came from families with no money to spare. My threepence a week was not abnormally little, but very paltry compared to the five shillings of the aristocrats.

Those few of us who had come from state schools were in the lowest caste and it would take a long time before our unfortunate background was forgotten. Jack Turner made a prodigious blunder. He joined his old friends selling *Heralds* outside the St Kilda station, purple cap and all; he was seen and his conduct was reported to the Sultan. He was not forgiven during his four years at Prep. The Big School was far more tolerant. It had the 'Twenty', a special class for winners of scholarships from state schools; despite its name there were about thirty of them, and some of them became quite good at games.

Two weeks after we were there, Bwuce found that Osborne, a new boy from a very intelligent family—his father was a professor at Ormond College at the University and his mother wrote books—he found that Osborne had no lining in his pants and shouted his shame with glee.

It was so ridiculous that anyone should be so poor, that it was worth reporting to the lower form, and Bwuce and his friends rushed into Middle II and shouted 'Osborne has no lining in his pants'.

Up stood Syd Abrahams: 'I've got no lining in my pants and I bet you haven't either.' Of course they had not; nor had we, but we had been too miserable to defend our companion. It was more than sixty years ago but I still feel respect for Abrahams and shame for myself.

'The happiest days of your life.' No days since have been so miserable. Miserable with the fear of punishment inflicted by your fellows older that yourself for unconscious sins, as part of the team-spirit nurtured by the dread and distant Head.

If it was something notoriously evil, like not voluntarily attending a school cricket match on Saturday, it was reasonable to expect the consequences, but an unknown cabal would rule on other matters and the sinner would be ducked. We had our little duckings in the Prep, but we rushed to share in the really imposing duckings of the Big School.

A mob would gather at lunch-time and the culprit would be hustled to the Back Turf, where hundreds would shout happily and viciously as he was up-ended into the barrel. No master could interfere, for all authority rested in the Head. A ducking entailed a lasting loss of caste.

I was luckier than most new boys in gaining a safe position during my second term, and although fighting could not gain a sure social position, I got my safety through it.

The Prep were playing Melbourne Grammar Prep at football. We were allowed to use the grandeur of the Front Turf. The field had been shortened by an extra set of goal posts forward of the adolescent ones, but still, it was the Front Turf, and there in full sight of St Kilda Road, I won a glorious victory under the eyes of all the Prep watching the match.

In Middle II, the form below ours, was a big lubberly chap, as big as any in the Prep. He must have been twelve at least, for he drilled with the Junior Cadets on Wednesday afternoons. His father was a book-maker: that might not be thought to be an aristocratic calling, but he was such an extrovert and so rich as to be a national monument.

The son had none of his father's glamour. Of course he was stupid or he would not have been in such a low form. He was in the habit of undoing his fly buttons under the cover of his desk and playing with himself under the shocked gaze of the surrounding eight-year-olds. He was brutal. He was a slow-mover, but he would catch some little chap and slowly twist his arm behind his back and even the old-stagers of Middle I were frightened of him.

I burst with indignation when he twisted the ear of one of his tiny class-mates, and piled into him. He was unbelievably easy, I think he may have been somewhat spastic. Once under his reach it was a painless pleasure. It was over.

The pleasant cold tinges were running down from my head and consciousness returned. There he lay grunting on the ground with blood pouring from his nose and I had triumphed.

Bwuce treated me with a new respect and it was certain he would never put my name forward for ducking. I got to be quite friendly with Brockhoff and went around to his big house after school, but I never thought much of Bwuce, who continued to humiliate the other new boys. He got me in the end.

Bridger, one of the new boys, was to have a party, and this would secure him a position of respect. Most of us new boys did not have imposing enough houses nor wealthy enough parents to provide parties. Bwuce took it on himself to select the guests and we overheard his talks on the matter. Of course the old hands would all be invited and perhaps one or two of the new boys. I got an invitation; I was near to being established.

But I had to buy a birthday present and it must be an imposing one. I could not convince my mother of the importance of it. All I could scrape up was sixpence and that could buy only an unworthy present, but I hoped for the best.

I went down Dandenong Road by tram to Bridger's house at St Kilda, very nervous about my present. It was received in silence and I hoped I had been forgiven, for now I was on the fringe of the aristocracy.

Then at tea-time with the cakes and jellies splendid on the table, Bwuce told me to shut up; I had only been invited because somebody else had not been able to come and my present had been mean. The humiliation was far, far worse than not being invited.

I slipped out of the room, collected my coat, and caught the tram home. I slipped in through the back door, so crushed that I went to bed without telling anybody or having my Saturday-night hot bath.

Neil went down to St Kilda to collect me at nine o'clock and I wasn't there. There was a fuss until Neil telephoned home and I was found asleep in bed. Going to a public school was a very sorry business.

Between the Prep and the Big School was the playing field to the west and the Back Turf to the north. Field? Turf? Not a blade of grass, just bare soil which washed away in channels after heavy rain. But still, we were part of Wesley and Wesley was not the least of the six public schools, and to go to any one of them marked you out as a person of consequence.

What the Six said and did was important. At the end of the year each speech day was sure of two columns in the papers and every sporting contest was fully reported.

All the Six were rabidly patriotic, but Wesley was the most patriotic. They were suburban imitations of English public schools down to inappropriate details, and especially in the big things like sportsmanship and patriotism. The English seventeen- and eighteen-year-olds were automatically going off to France to be killed as soon as they could. In a dangerous situation, 'the voice of a schoolboy rallied the ranks'.

We tried to do as well, if not better. Already Old Boys of the Six had died on Gallipoli, but they had had little chance of rallying the ranks as they had all been killed as privates or corporals; they were too young for commissions in the A.I.F.

The Six set the pattern which was eagerly followed by the inferior suburban grammar schools. Martin Boyd claimed that his little Ivanhoe Grammar had the biggest proportion of casualties of all Australian schools, a claim impossible to assess, but we disputed it. Wesley's casualties were her glory and each new one added to our score.

What the Heads of the Six said was given more weight than the words of the few articulate professors at the University, and our Head's words were the weightiest of all. He was the most prominent educationalist in Australia; when he dropped a big brick in the waters of Victoria, there were ripples in all other State pools.

He voiced our thoughts and believed what we believed and a bit more. He did not like professional football: 'What would a league of patriotic Germans do in Victoria? It would be no good for them to flash motor headlights to guide zeppelins, no good to signal baby-killing cruisers, as was done in Yorkshire, no good writing letters in invisible ink, as three spies in London did. They could pay 3 pounds to 30 shillings per week to pay professional footballers to keep them here'. A very reasonable amount to keep men from enlisting to fight the Germans.

He had a massive gravity and no trace of humour. He was our war-time leader ahead of his troops, and the five hundred of us at Wesley were his Household Brigade following close behind him. I would see out the war behind Dicky Adamson—like seeing Waterloo whilst perched behind Wellington on his horse.

He was as fervently patriotic as Billy Hughes, our new Prime Minister, but was a more dignified figure. I think that, as an individual, he did more to shape pro-war opinion than anyone else in the State.

He hated the Germans, but after the Dublin rising he hated the Irish Catholics even more. This placed him beside the most vociferously patriotic group of Irish Protestants; Dr Leeper of the University Council, Professor Rentoul of the Presbyterian Church and the Hon. O.A.

Snowball of the State legislature who was President of the Loyal Orange Association.

One single man was more than a match for them. Dr Daniel Mannix, Coadjutor Archbishop of Melbourne was an unusual bishop, for most in Ireland and here supported the war for they were primarily concerned with their church and held that it would gain by alliance with Britain; Mannix, as an Irishman, put Ireland before church policy. He was the greatest anti-war personality in Australia.

Mannix had opposed the war from its start. He fought in the front rank with the rapier of his wit; his opponents fought with the bludgeons of platitudes. They often found that Mannix had reached over their shoulders and punctured their bottoms whilst they had been swinging at him with their bludgeons. We preferred bludgeon fighting; it was something that we could understand. We detested Mannix. To us he was Milton's Satan, handsome, vivid and intelligent, but a force of evil; our Adamson of Wesley was a force for good.

Adamson seemed to have everything and to know all the important people. He was English, and that in itself was good; he had been to an English public school – Rugby – and we were trying to imitate such schools. He was an M.A. of Oxford, and we had a deep reverence for the two old English universities. We did not appreciate that their entrance requirements were such that even a member of the crew with enough money could get similar qualification if he did nothing outstandingly immoral or stupid for three years.

Adamson was a real English gentleman with a substantial income of his own, and Methodist Wesley was lucky to get such an outstanding Church of England man.

We never quite knew why he left England, nor why he did not continue in the law, but became resident master, and finally, Head, in 1902, the beginning of his immense power.

He consolidated the six most prominent boys' schools in Victoria into an exclusive group which provided the equivalent of the Eton and Harrow match and the Oxford and Cambridge boat race.

He organized the training of teachers and used Wesley to do it; he built up the prestige of teachers, although repressing those directly under him.

He promoted amateur sport and amateur football until it became almost as popular as the mildly professional League.

He was early to try new things. He had a great motor-car when no other Head had one, and more, he had his own driver.

He tried to encourage flying by importing an aeroplane but the Customs Department wanted to charge an immense duty so he had the

L. A. Adamson, from a painting by W. B. McInnes

plane dumped at sea. All that remained of it was its propeller on the
wall of the Common Room—a room which he had initiated. That is
the story which we were told at school. Another is that the plane was
landed but did not get off the ground and finally smashed itself at Diggers' Rest.

Adamson was given sole credit for the revival of Wesley after decades of failure and financial loss, but, in fact, he absorbed the reputation of his predecessor and built on it.

Before him, Palmer had held the post for four years and in that time he more than trebled the number of students; he had gathered a staff of very good teachers and established a high academic reputation for the school; he broke the humiliating run of losses at sport; and in 1901, his last year, Wesley won the athletics and the first of the eight-oar boat races. This was the result of the appointment of Charlie Donald as school sergeant; Charlie was a rough old bloke, but an excellent oarsman and coach. The other schools said that this was bringing professionalism into school sport.

But Palmer got into trouble. He was paid a very low salary and received half the net profits, but he took more, £1000 it was said. If he was able to milk that amount from a shaky Methodist school, he must have been a man of some ingenuity. He disappeared quietly in 1901.

Adamson made the school his interest and career and poured his own private funds into it. He initiated a building programme which, between 1902 and the outbreak of war in 1914, provided many useful things: an assembly hall with changing rooms under, a gymnasium, a common room, laboratories and about half-a-dozen new classrooms. A good half of the funds came from his own pocket.

We boys all were in awe of him and respected him as a great man; the only contrary opinion I ever heard, and it was very different, was that of an Old Boy who had begun his schooling under Palmer.

We thought it admirable that our Head should select the English public school as his model for Wesley, a suburban Methodist school, but he had the sense to develop science and mathematics in a very un-English manner, and where the English schools persisted in teaching classics to dull students, Adamson provided book-keeping for them.

On the English pattern he diverted our ambition from learning to sport, but still, the school maintained its high academic reputation – that is why our family went there. We learned that it was discreditable to be a 'swot', but splendid to get into a school team; he wrote the song 'Tommy' as the idol for us to worship. In it, Tommy came up from the Prep and worked hard at games to crown his career by gaining 'triple colours' – respectable places in three teams of the four inter-school sports. Not many got triple colours, even in Vd, the form of dull students but sporting specialists. Tommy's brilliance made him important and popular. Tommy was

> Not too smart at books, yet couldn't call him slow:
> Honest little gentleman and feared no foe.

The Head developed the corporate feeling of the school; in fact, he
formed it into a pack with himself as sole leader. The masters had authority only in the classrooms, and even there, not final authority. No
master was permitted to beat a boy; if a boy deserved to be beaten,
he was sent to the Head, who had the monopoly of corporal punishment
for five hundred boys.

We were flattered that our Head, that great leader of the community,
should give the least of us his personal attention when it came to a
thrashing. And he did it in a masculine Spartan manner, just like the
English public schools. Other schools might cane on the hands or on
the trousers; we got it on the bare buttocks. We called it 'bumming-up'.

Some passed their years at school without this mark of the Head's
devotion, but most got it a couple of times a year. I guess that there
would have been between twenty and thirty beatings each week.

I was luckier than the average and was punished only twice in eight
years; both times I was so ashamed that I kept it secret from the family.
The first time was towards the end of the war when I was twelve and
had tried to be funny in my examination answers; it was a brutal twelve
on my bare bottom with the heavy strap, and I had a suspicion that
the Head enjoyed it.

I escaped the next time I was sent to him. 'Prepare yourself', he
said, and I was unbuttoning my pants when I saw a new picture on
the wall above the sofa. 'That's a new picture, sir.' It was a night scene
of fireworks over the Yarra at Henley.

The Head's pictures were far better than his artistic odds and ends
in Adamson Hall and he appreciated my interest—or sense of self-
preservation. He stopped, told me about it, showed me others in his
rooms and took me across to the Hall and explained the statuary. As
I went I buttoned up my pants and when the bell for change of lessons
rang, he sent me back to class unscathed. No one else had ever done
so well before.

The second beating was after the war, and it was surprisingly gentle
for what I thought was a very serious offence—blasphemy against the
religion of the school.

Our master, Mr Stevens, was dictating a poem of admirable sentiment,
which we would have to learn by heart.

> He wins the prize of prizes,
> Although no prize he gains
> Who through the college rises
> With honour free from stain,
> Who all things base despises
> With silent deep disdain . . .

'Lewis, you said something, off you go to the Head at once.'

And there was no escape, no loitering in the lavatories until the change of lessons, for the Head's door was in clear sight across the quad from our classroom. But it was not nearly as bad as the first time, only a paltry four with the paper-knife; it was almost a pleasant surprise.

The grossest sins were those related to our new puberty, but punishment was secret so that no unhealthy interest would be roused. The type of punishment was unknown to us and we could think of none appropriate; as it was unknown, it was the more frightening.

Stealing commonly meant expulsion; a public beating was the next most severe punishment. I can remember only three in my eight years, but there may have been more. Two were on members of my form and I was friendly with both and knew one of them well.

He was a new boy that year and lived near us in Wattletree Road in quite a humble house near the three isolated shops, a house so humble that it was surprising that it should send a boy to a public school. We often travelled on the tram together, but he really was not public-school material, a skimpy chap who would never make the crew or the football team.

Look, there he is now, standing by the platform at the end of assembly, an under-grown eleven-year-old, always colourless, now ashen and trembling; he sees nothing, but stares ahead, his jaw hangs loose.

The Head is up on his platform alone, for the chaplain has left. Perhaps he does not fancy this sort of thing. The five hundred of us are tense, we feel waves of excitement and we are ashamed that it is a pleasant excitement, rather like those new feelings of sex that the Head had warned us to suppress.

The boy comes up the steps. His crime is announced. A pause, he kneels and bends over the chaplain's chair and the Head slams into him. More impressive than a ducking and quite as exciting.

He spoils it for us by sobbing loudly; he should have taken it in silence, like a man; after all, it was over his apple-catchers and not on the bare.

He had lost status and we avoided him. I was embarrassed if he came on the tram with me. He left at the end of term and I don't think he joined the Old Wesley Collegians' Association.

The other chap I knew was tougher and his family was well-off. He stayed on to be caught stealing again and he was expelled and eventually it made him into a hero. Fifty years later some Old Boys told me about him. Yes, he had been expelled; he had been expelled for fiddling with one of the housemaids of the boarding section. The fable made him into the Don Juan of Wesley.

The athletic successes of 1901 were the start of a remarkable run under Adamson, particularly in rowing under the coaching of Charlie Donald. He was more than a coach; he was a detached pair of eyes and ears for the Head. Outside the classrooms you were safe from the masters, but not from Charlie. 'I seen yer, it's no use arguin', you take a walk to the 'Ead.'

The Head built on the early successes and organized moral support for the teams, and he did it through the boys. It was not possible for him to make attendance at inter-school contests an enforceable part of the curriculum, but the boys could do it. If someone did not voluntarily attend he was ducked and the whole school enjoyed the occasion. No master could interfere for the yelling pack was under the Head's protection and it was a very good way of encouraging everybody to yell at football matches.

Yelling was organized into 'war-cries', very un-English and like American college yells, and the Head approved. Five hundred of us behind our goal at a football match and off we would go:

> Razzle dazzle hobble gobble,
> Zip bomb bar,
> Wesley, Wesley,
> Yah, Yah, Yah.

Each syllable was brought out hard and clear and ending high on the last 'yah'.

Scotch was the only other of the Six to make such use of war cries and Wesley and Scotch yelled at each other and scuffled if there was any opportunity. The two schools made nuisances of themselves and brought the Six into disrepute.

The six Heads, at one of their regular meetings, ruled that war-cries and scuffles were damaging to prestige and war-cries were to be abolished. The Head had encouraged them and now he was forced to disown them. We were not to use our war-cry because of its ending. The Head explained that 'Yah, yah, yah' was German.

He was more lastingly successful in another of his efforts to develop corporate sentiment in the school. He introduced morning assemblies with every boy in attendance.

Other schools might have chapel for different batches on various days of the week but we had our daily assembly with a bit of religion as an *hors d'oeuvre*. When the chaplain had finished his little bit, the Jews came in and joined their forms and we were all at the Head's disposal. Assembly required a special big building. The Head got the scheme

Adamson Hall

moving and gave more than half the money for it and it was rightly
called Adamson Hall. It was a great barn of a place.

Then he set about beautifying it. Most of us had seen some of his
picture collection when we went to be bummed up. He moved the
bulkier things to Adamson Hall.

Central against the wall behind the dais was a 'magnificent sixteenth-
century Flemish sideboard'. My memory is that it owed much to
nineteenth-century England. On the dais too, were his statues and we
were very impressed by all this art; today they would look more like
the unsaleable pieces in the back room of an auctioneer. They were scaled-
down models of famous works, the Hermes of Praxiteles, Michelangelo's
David, a bronze head of the Blind Homer, and the Winged Victory
of Samothrace. She was the only female in the collection and she was
more than adequately dressed.

Not on the dais, but at floor level centre front was a modern marble
head of Adamson himself, and it gave me a very bad couple of weeks
in my first term at Wesley.

I suppose that unconsciously I resented the rigidity of the school.
Still, it was good to arrive very early before the system closed its jaws.

This Monday I was exceptionally early, for Phyllis had a nine o'clock lecture at the University and my lunch was ready to take as soon as breakfast was over.

There was not a soul about the Prep when I got there, and on the ground was a dirty cloth cap which had been tossed over the fence from Punt Road. I went across to Adamson Hall; nobody was about. I put the cap on the marble likeness of the Head and a bit of cloth around the neck and a cigarette butt in the mouth, and got back to the Prep unseen.

At the Armadale State School I could safely have told anyone in the Fourth Grade what I had done and he would have enjoyed it as much as I did and he would never have betrayed me, but who could you trust at Wesley amongst all those hidden enemies? Of course there were close friends, McCallum and Mickey Cohen, but they were as weak as I was and might accidentally have let the secret out; what I had done might be thought of as letting down the school. I told nobody.

It was always noisy in assembly before the Head appeared, but this day it was rowdy and remained restless even after the Head had taken his place on the dais. His table prevented him seeing what was immediately in front of him. I was almost wetting myself with the enormity of what I had done and could not undo.

The trouble came at the next day's assembly. The Head knew which boy had done it but would give him a chance to own up. I didn't believe him, not quite, but I was uneasy, very uneasy, and anyway, I would have been too terrified to go to him. It was weeks before I could feel reasonably safe.

Adamson Hall had art added by the Head's bounty; now the war was giving it a soul. It was being made into a shrine for the Old Boys who had been killed. Perhaps it could never be a really beautiful shrine, that red-brick building with its galvanized roof peeping over the parapet and the locker rooms dingy underneath it, but it could gather spiritual significance.

The brick wall behind the dais was masked by blackwood panels with the names of all the boys who had enlisted lettered in gold and a red star added for those killed – just like the new board at church. The original design became inadequate as the war went on and new panels were jammed on until the brick was covered. But it was not only a red star that the fallen got, they got their names cut in clumsy lettering on white marble on the Memorial Stairway.

That stair came in 1916. It had been rough brick waiting to be rendered in stucco when funds allowed. Now it was smooth and grey with the marble panels and the names, but what made it a grand memorial were the four marble lions, not quite the lions of the school badge, but more like the Venetian lions on St Mark. They had been cut in Venice and shipped across, four of them, two with their left paws on a cricket ball, the other pair with their right paws. They mated suitably at the bottom of the double stair.

Out in front of the stair and central with it was a marble well-head, 'the gift of the Headmaster', dedicated to the 'Old Boys who served in the Great War, 1914-15'. The year '16' was added in my first year at Wesley and '17' and '18' took their places at the proper times. We did not appreciate that well-head; it was Byzantine, a copy of one in Venice and perhaps ordered from the same catalogue as the lions. The stylized birds looked clumsy to us; art, for us, began in early Victorian times and this was earlier still. Water was to be expected in well-heads and this one had water; inside it was a complication of pipes and when you pressed a knob there was a spout of hygienic water; with a bit of luck you could press the knob before the other bloke was ready.

As the war went on other things were added to Adamson Hall until it had by far the best collection of memorials of any school. The old wooden stair on the north was replaced by a rendered brick one as a memorial to the Old Prep Boys who had enlisted. There were eighteen of them and we in the Prep had decided that it should be built, but I can't remember anyone asking my views. This stair included another little addition to the art collection – an early Italian Renaissance-type shield with the school coat of arms outlined in black on the marble.

Then the tongue-and-groove hardwood doors were replaced, one by one, with blackwood doors as memorials to individuals; they were in the Adam style, but I doubt if the Adam family, father or sons, would have admitted paternity.

The Head got a new blackwood table and the chaplain a new black-wood lectern, memorials to important Old Boys who had been in the crew or football team. A stained-glass window was placed in the front of the hall, copied from one at Eton, showing Sir Galahad; it soon got a matching one on the other side.

Many Old Boys were not distinguished enough to merit an appeal nor were their families wealthy enough for a really big memorial. They could get a memorial chair at the back of the hall with a little brass plate with the name on it for only £5. Chairs did not merit a special dedication service.

We had to wait until 1918 for the biggest personal memorial – the double stair on the south side. The Head must have given personal advice and help, for who else could have produced two miniature bronze statues of a pygmy Octavius and a dwarf Julius Caesar in kilts? Those

Morning Assembly in Adamson Hall

two-footers perched on the top of two fat piers look as comical today as they did in 1918.

The war brought European art to Wesley, even if it was out of scale.

The team spirit of Wesley was produced by the daily assembly and assembly focused on the Head. From his central place on the dais he dominated all those hundreds of dots of faces which filled his hall—Adamson Hall.

From our second day at the Prep it was routine. After roll-call in the classroom we surged out of Middle I, out of the door under the little veranda, along the fence of the Prep ground beside the Back Turf, and past the physics lab. There were the wooden stairs up to the hall; into the hall we went, to the central rows of seats at the very front. Here sat the Prep under the eyes of the Head.

The hall filled, the boys like starlings returning to their roost, bickering and screeching until some group organized a war-cry for their form and other forms followed with theirs. It was noisy, but the sound gradually lessened until it got near to ten past nine. Sudden quiet fell as the Head walked through the door by the dais, the same one that we of the Prep used. He was on the dais, a short stocky man with a big jowled face, looking like a mastiff, but rather a bad-tempered one; his bright little eyes showed that he might bite. Yes, he did look like a dog with his short quick steps across the dais like a dog heading for a lamp-post.

Diffidently behind him walked Mr Nye, the chaplain, a humane and popular man who taught scripture and also Greek to the few wanting to study it. He had no trouble in keeping order by using reason. Both wore black academic gowns, the only time they were used in the school.

They sat down for a moment and then Mr Nye stood at the lectern and led off with the usual prayer, one of the best in the Anglican collection: 'Almighty and Everlasting God, who hast safely brought us to the beginning of this day; Defend us in the same with thy mighty power'. It passed over our heads as part of the daily routine, but perhaps some were unconsciously appreciative of the words. This had been the usual end of the chaplain's public religious duties for the day, but the war had added something else:

> More especially we pray for our own Australian brothers who are now facing their country's foes. In swift or lingering death be near them; if it be thy will, touch their wounds and make them whole again, and be to each and all their inspiration in the day of strife, teaching them patience in adversity, gentleness in the hour of victory and compassion for the fallen foe.

I don't know who composed that prayer—it could have been the Head, he was capable of writing lucidly and well, but if he had written it, it masked his real sentiments. The 'foe' to him were those born in Germany who now lived here. They were down, and the Head was the first to kick them. He had gone to some trouble to get himself elected to the University Council where he was one of the pack that yelped for the dismissal of all German-born members of staff; yet right through the war he stood by his old fellow-teacher, Otto Krome, and no one could have been more German than he. Germans to the Head were more obnoxious than masturbation or 'gels'.

From the end of April in 1916 the chaplain occasionally had another addition: 'On this day, so and so, an old boy of this college, died for the cause of freedom and righteousness in the world's war. May the memory of his sacrifice help each of us to make our lesser sacrifices for the good of others'. This really moved us; sometimes some boy snivelled at the name of his elder brother and sometimes the older boys remembered him at school.

Then it was the Head's turn. He read notices about lost things and made announcements; then he made a précis of the day's news or read something appropriate from the English periodicals which he got, and he gave his views on the Germans; later in the year he included the

Irish and Archbishop Mannix. It was the Easter Day Rising in Dublin
which set him off. Some days he would read a letter from an Old Boy
away at the war, and of course, he would particularly mention any recently
wounded or killed.

We got our opinions on the war from daily assembly, but we got
our sentiments from Friday's assembly; it took up the whole of the
first teaching period and we had singing, a loosely used term, for there
was no instruction in music and we shouted purely by the light of nature.

We had a school songbook, which we had to bring with us on Friday;
it was a prescribed textbook. The Head could write and compose, and
most of the more popular songs were his; they were simple and forceful.
We sang a couple of the popular songs first. The favourite was the
Head's 'Football Song', where we could shout as loud as we liked. In
the third verse we sang a parody of 'Scotch may come against us with
their championships elate' rendered as 'They are bolting shut the gate',
and the Head beamed. He was probably the only one to remember some
incident of long ago.

The popular songs had got us into a mood for singing and now
we could take on the war songs. A pamphlet had been printed for insertion in our songbooks and there was another later insertion, and all
the new songs were about the war. The Head had gathered them from
London *Punch*, the *Graphic*, the *Cornhill Magazine* and *Country Life*;
he had composed the tunes for them and for a couple of even better
war songs of local origin. The common theme was the poignant beauty
of young men dying for their country. The titles show what we sang
about: 'To the Living', 'To the School at War', 'Sleep on Beloved',
'Our Undying Dead', 'Hail and Farewell', 'God Speed', and 'To the
Fallen'. Just writing those titles brings back that Friday feeling of fore-
boding misery. Four brothers were on the way to the war.

Some of the songs were very rude about the Germans—one said that
they used 'Every mean device of treacherous hate'—and the accompaniment for them all was played by Nichterlein, a boy in form Va.

The most moving and miserable was not sung by us: it was a solo
by de Lacey. De Lacey was a good tenor and sang with more than pathos,
he used tremolo and dropped his voice right down at the very sad bits.

> Somewhere in France there is a gra-a-ave
> Where wild flowers bloom and gra-ar-ar-arses wave,
> And at the head a woo-oo-oo-den cross
> To mark our own and England's loss.
> No more his arm shall wield the lance,
> Dear God, Dear God, Somewhere in France.

This, I think, was a real treat for the Head. He deeply felt the loss of the boys he admired, those athletes of the crew and fooball team of a few years earlier. He enjoyed an ecstasy of sorrow.

The deep feelings of the war produced much verse and most of it now seems trite and shallow, or even silly. Some would now be regarded as blasphemous: for instance, 'Our Boys–Christs All'.

> Ye are all Christs in this your self-surrender,
> True sons of God in seeking not your own.
> Yours now the hardships, yours shall be the splendour
> Of the Great Triumph and THE KING's 'Well done!'

This was written in England where conscription was coming in and it would be a rare young fellow who would not be made a compulsory Christ. In Australia too he would be a shirker one day and a Christ the next, and then, like a Crusader, he would have a very good chance of ending up in heaven, and no questions asked.

Some of the songs have lasted and will last. We had Binyon's

> They shall not grow old, as we that are left grow old:
> Age shall not weary them, nor the years condemn.
> At the going down of the sun and in the morning
> We will remember them.

The last three verses are just as good, but they were hard to sing and were only used as a solo. The words, so suitable for the loss of a generation, were written in September 1914 when the losses had been about the same as in a sizeable train collision.

I think one song in our songbook was the best patriotic verse of the war, more moving than anything by Rupert Brooke. It was 'For England', written by an old Scotch College boy, Corporal Burns. The first stanza began, 'The bugles of England were blowing o'er the sea'. The last verse:

> Oh England, I heard the cry of those that died for thee,
> Sounding like an organ-voice across the winter sea;
> They lived and died for England, and gladly went their way–
> England, O England–how could *I* stay?

This was what we felt. It was an honour and a duty to go to fight for England; not for Britain; not for the Empire nor for Australia, but for England, and we were proud to be able to help.

By the time we sang it, they had gone their way. Burns had been killed on Gallipoli and Rupert Brooke had died on his way there. There was no more verse of elated patriotism; patriotism was now patient suffering and there was a different sort of writing.

I wonder what happened to that war-time songbook? It had been

the litany of the school for four years and then the years discarded it.
It certainly lingered for a while and the sad songs were sung on Anzac
and Armistice Days. It was still current at the end of 1921, for I got
a leather-bound copy as the scripture prize for the fourth forms. It was
the only real prize I got at Wesley. But even then it may have been
because the chaplain liked the coloured maps at the back of my scripture
note-book and the drawing of the Israelites crossing the Red Sea clustered
behind a Cohen's furniture van.

The Head was proud of the school assembly which he had instituted
in his own Adamson Hall, and on Fridays he was very proud indeed
to hear five hundred boys singing the songs which he had written, as
well as the new pathetic war songs from English magazines. He invited
guests to Friday assembly, often quite important people. Uniformed
guests were particularly welcome; brigadier-general was the lowest rank
unless the visitor had been to Gallipoli and then it dropped as low as
captain. The most important guest of 1916 was no soldier—it was Dame
Nellie Melba. The Head knew her well enough to ask her along to
hear our singing. Singing? We shouted the Head's songs with zest. 'Magnificent in rhyme, rhythm and attack', said Nellie Melba, but nothing
about other qualities.

The name, Preparatory School, might sound as if it were a different
place from Wesley, but it wasn't; it was a sort of colony and what we
did and thought was settled by the Big School. We did have our own
set of teachers, but one man served both sections—Mr Frank.

The Head had a gymnasium built and gym was a regular twice-weekly
class for all up to the Intermediate level. Mr Frank ran all the classes
right up from the tiniest in the Prep. I think he was Norwegian, but
we liked him so much that we never said that he was a German spy.
We liked his direct dealings.

Of course we acted the fool when we came into the free air of the
gym, but if we were very silly, we were not sent off to the Head: we
got a rubber shoe thrown at us very hard from the other end of the
gym and we stopped being silly.

The Prep had a headmaster, Mr Kennedy—'Bill', we called him behind
his back—but he was not really a Head and was not allowed to beat
our bare bottoms like the real Head. We liked him; he was human
but not super-human. I can't remember him ever sending one of us
off to the Head.

He coached us at football after school and bowled at us at cricket
practice. He had charge of Upper I, the top form. If you were in academic
trouble, he would move the other chap out of the paired desk and sit
very close and sometimes rub his bristly face against yours.

We were sorry for Bill Kennedy. His brother was away with the
A.I.F. but Bill had been rejected at his medical exam. He had had some
sort of operation, but was still rejected. Jerry Hattam was the only other
regular male Prep teacher and he was obviously medically unfit. We
liked them both and they were quite as patriotic as anybody.

Bill Kennedy was really Head of the Prep at the last period on Friday
afternoons. He took the whole hundred or so of us for a special lesson
on the war.

We felt good with the week behind us and we fooled about as we
went across to our usual front seats in Adamson Hall. The hall was
all ours: the Big School benches were empty behind us. Bill stood in
front of the platform at our level with a board on an easel and pictures
on the board. He showed us pictures from papers like the *Illustrated
London News*, and when those on the ends squeezed up we could see
them all quite well, and he told us about them.

Our ages ranged from eight to thirteen with a very few odds and
ends beyond those extremities. We had all seen dead dogs and cats;
now we saw pictures of dead men. There seemed to be an awful lot
of them, but they were only Germans.

Then at 3.30 the week was over and there were two clear days before
the Wesley war started again at Monday morning's assembly.

Every boy at Wesley was medically inspected each year. Middle I
set out for Adamson Hall and as we straggled along we met the tiny
little fellows of Lower I straggling back. We did not go up the stairs
to the hall, but in through the doors to the locker-rooms at the lower
level. Middle II was dressing itself; we took their places and undressed
and put our clothes on the seats in front of the lockers and went into
the next room. There was the school visiting doctor; this year it was
not Dr Fetherston; he was away on a special trip to the war as a medical
officer, and it was a stand-in. There beside him was the massive and
dreadful figure of the Head, but today he was not dreadful, he seemed
jolly and even joked with us. Naked as fish, we took our turn against
the pole to get our height measured, and then on to the scales. Then
a tape was placed around our chests, 'Keep it there, now a very deep
breath', and there was competition to see who had expanded his chest
most. It was all written down on a special card with our name and
the form on it; each year another set of entries would be made on it.

All day it went on; from the chubby little pink chaps of Lower II
going up with ages until the classes got to form Vd. This was the climax;
after them the Sixths and Honour Six were anti-climax.

Vd was the prime font of the crew and football team. Vd was the
dam caused by the Intermediate exam: a pass at Intermediate was needed

before going on to the Sixths and the matriculation examination for
the University. There in Vd they stayed until they were eighteen and
too old for school teams; then they went back to the farm or into the
family business, except for a very occasional and wealthy one who went
on to Cambridge, a university rather more tolerant than Melbourne.

All through the day it continued, five hundred naked boys of all
sorts, shapes and sizes, and the Head waited for them all. But it was
Vd that was most important: those broad hairy athletes, who in as short
a time as twelve months might be killed at the front and mourned by
the Head.

15
More of the War

Ireland: we did not know what to think of the place. Some of our Irish said that they were very loyal and others kept doing disloyal things. We had heard about Sir Roger Casement who had been in Germany trying to recruit Irish prisoners of war there for some sort of force; we were not sure if that force was to fight for Irish Home Rule or for Germany, and we had thought that Home Rule had come anyway.

On 20 April: TRAITOR – SIR ROGER CASEMENT. GUN RUNNING PLOT FOILED. IRISH COAST INCIDENT. Casement had come from Germany in a submarine accompanied by a steamer carrying arms. The steamer had been captured but Casement had come ashore in a collapsible boat; once he had landed he made a mess of things and had been picked up. It sounded like ridiculous melodrama.

A week later it was real drama. It had happened on Good Friday, and we thought the Irish were a fervently Catholic people who would not do this sort of thing on a particularly Holy Day. It must be the Sinn Fein; we had them here and they were a wild lot and against the war, but now it seemed that they were actually fighting on Germany's side and killing our British troops and we had thought that everybody in Ireland was happy now that Home Rule was certain.

We got a rather muddled picture; it sounded rather bigger than we had been told. The rebels had seized five different localities in Dublin, including the post office, and there they had cut the telephone and telegraph lines, and the Four Courts – the law courts – had gone up in flames, but the troops from the Curragh had reasserted control.

Our papers never told us how many had been killed in the fighting but there must have been quite a lot. One item was that 200 rebels had been buried and one mourner allowed for each, and 2000 had been deported.

Martial law was proclaimed and the rebels were captured or chased

REBELS IN DUBLIN

PORTIONS OF CITY SEIZED

MOB AND TROOPS EXCHANGE SHOTS

TWELVE SOLDIERS KILLED

"Situation Well in Hand"

away and three of the leaders were shot. This we felt, was quite reasonable, for it was a rough game and police and soldiers had been killed. One of them was Pearse, a silly sort of show-off who had got himself a green uniform and had been very dramatic about it all, and it served him right.

But the troops kept on shooting people in batches. FIVE MORE EXECUTED. That seemed a bit much. TRAITOR'S MARRIAGE. ON THE EVE OF EXECUTION. BEAUTIFUL WOMAN AS BRIDE. A WIDOW AT DAYBREAK.

There was pathos in this and the new widow had a sister already made a widow in the shooting of the first batch. And the poor chap who was so badly wounded that he could not stand up to be shot so they gave him a chair. We did not like the sound of it at all and felt that the troops would be better in France shooting Germans.

But that was not the only shooting; they shot Skeffington and he was a Pacifist and not a Sinn Feiner. His widow said that he was 'unarmed, non-combatant, an earnest and well-known pacifist', and had been putting up posters when he was caught. They had shot two journalists and all this before martial law had been proclaimed.

We thought it shameful that there should be a rebellion when we were so busy fighting the Germans, but we were shocked at the violence of the military. They sounded trigger-happy, like our own sentries at the beginning of the war when they shot at anybody they did not like the look of.

The commander of the British troops had been on Gallipoli and we had not thought much of his troops there, but this lot in Ireland seemed as brutal as they were incompetent; if the Germans had blundered in shooting Nurse Cavell, the British blundered in Dublin.

Mob hysteria. In the Commons a member asked the Prime Minister, 'whether the traitor Casement should be shot forthwith?' But he had his trial, was found guilty and condemned to death. The *Argus* did not think he would be executed, as that would give him a martyr's crown—but he was. First they removed his knighthood and other honours and it seemed petty to make such a fuss of an eccentric and helpless man. His legal adviser, George Gavan Duffy, said it was a monstrous act of indecency to refuse to give his body to his relatives, and we were interested in that for the Gavan Duffys had always been prominent in Victoria and at least one of them was serving with the A.I.F.

Then we got the whispers—not that we youngsters heard them—he might have been spared if he had not been homosexual. This put him beyond pity, but nobody had worried about the whispers concerning Kitchener. Casement gave one last kick to the Establishment before he went: he was admitted into the Catholic Church.

Mr Redmond, the Nationalist leader, said that the rising was a criminal German plot. 'My first feeling on hearing of the Sinn Fein revolt was one of horror, discouragement and despair', and he said that the Nationalist Volunteers were ready to assist the military in restoring order, but the crude brutality of the soldiers swung the Irish from the Nationalists towards the Sinn Fein in Ireland and in Australia.

Our Archbishop Mannix blamed the 'Carsonites', those in the north who had armed themselves to resist the decision of their government. Carson was not put in prison for inciting rebellion, but before the year was out, he was given a place in Cabinet. It was an affront to the moderates of Ireland and Australia.

We had been shocked by the way the army had behaved in Ireland but we were appalled by the rebellion. At the beginning of the war we had called every northern European a 'Hun'; now we called all Irish 'Sinn Fein', and that was worse than being called a Hun.

On 5 June we read: GREAT NAVAL ACTION. SERIOUS BRITISH LOSSES. Of course ships would be sunk in a sea battle but the Germans must have suffered as much or more. On 6 June: ENEMY LOSSES THE HEAVIER.

On 9 June: THE NORTH SEA BATTLE. 'A REAL BRITISH VICTORY'. It was the Battle of Jutland.

So they had done it at last. We had waited two years but now the German navy was wiped out. We could picture it all; great dreadnoughts moving on implacably and little destroyers dashing around them, all trailing great banners of black smoke under a lowering sky, and bright flashes from the guns, great and small, and the thunder of war. As the days of June went on, the victory seemed to shrink. We had lost a lot of ships. There were hints that we might have lost more than the Germans, but still it was a victory and we had many more ships to lose.

The battle had started with the dashing Admiral Beatty leading his cruisers against the German cruisers. We were not told that he had not informed his commanding admiral, Jellicoe, that he had contacted the Germans; it seems he was thinking of other things. Admittedly he had lost three of his cruisers, perhaps recklessly, but he had attacked in the old and glorious tradition. He was a real naval leader, perhaps the one we had been waiting for. We put up pictures of him all over the place: a gallant figure with a square jaw, both hands in the side pockets of his jacket with just the thumbs sticking out, his jacket with an extra pair of shiny brass buttons; his cap jaunty on one side of his head, not square on his head like other officers, or like Admiral Jellicoe, who had disappointed us up till now. Beatty looked dashing and fearless, and his unusual dress, which would not be permitted in a lesser man, made him a public idol, safe from any intrigue, an example followed by Montgomery in the next war. He moved with the best people and had his country estate and plenty of money from his wife, a divorcee – and we forgave both of them for that.

When it was all washed up, the British lost more ships than the Germans and 6274 men against their 2545. We were not ever told the details and we had nagging suspicions, but that did not stop us remembering the great victory of Jutland.

Then a crashing disaster. Lord Kitchener.

Lord Kitchener was the great solid rock of our war. The waves beat against him and he was unmoved. We had read how Lord Northcliffe had personally written a savage attack on him in his *Daily Mail* but it had been just another wave and the rock had not toppled. We knew Kitchener. His stern face with its bulging eyes and handle-bar moustaches still told all young men that their country needed them. He was part of us. We trusted Lord Kitchener as we trusted God; between them, they would win our war.

Then in June we read:

LORD KITCHENER

Tragic Death at Sea

WARSHIP DISASTER

All on Board Perish

World-Wide Sorrow

He had been on his way to Russia where he was trusted as much as he was here. He was going to revive the Russian war effort, and he might well have done some good, but his ship hit a mine in foul weather off the Orkneys, quite close to shore.

Perhaps some had survived; perhaps Kitchener had got ashore in some remote place and would be found in a day or two. We waited for news and it did not come. Perhaps he had been pulled out of the sea by a U-boat and was now a prisoner in Germany – at least this would be better.

We kept hoping although we knew that our hope was ridiculous. We still hoped through the bloody shambles of the Somme and our own thousands killed at Pozières. We never quite gave up hope.

Over a year later, on 28 July 1917, the *Argus* published a statement by his sister, Mrs Frances Parker: 'It is my firm belief that my brother is still alive and will return'. And letters from prisoners of war in Germany told of a very distinguished fellow-prisoner whose name could not be mentioned as the censor would delete it.

In the House of Commons an attack on Kitchener a month earlier had been led by the Australian, Colonel Lynch, who blamed all our muddles and reverses on Kitchener. Now there was to be a week of mourning and a great service in London's St Paul's. I wonder if Lynch and Northcliffe occupied their reserved places? Here we had a service in the Exhibition Building; 1500 got inside and another 5000 could only wait outside.

The Russians were really doing something. In April we had read that they had entered France at last: a 'strong force landed' – we never were told how many – and Russia had sent 'some of her bravest soldiers' as a pledge of her devotion. For nearly two years they had won victory after victory but our maps showed no great gains. Now in June there was another Russian victory, just like the earlier ones, but this time it seemed to last – yes, it kept on going and this had not happened before.

Brusiloff had moved against the Austrians without any great preparations and their front had collapsed. He took 40 000 prisoners on the first day; we had heard that sort of thing before, but they really kept on going and in two weeks it was 200 000 prisoners. The prostrate giant had given a last convulsive kick and the Austrians were on the run. It might be the final Allied victory.

Romania thought so and came in on our side, just as Italy had joined in when she thought Gallipoli was ending the war; like Italy, she did little good for herself. Down came the Germans in a couple of weeks and Romania was hopelessly beaten before we had had time to learn to recognize her national anthem.

The Australians were now in France, 90 000 of them; a similar number were in England ready to join them. Now our papers showed pictures of the wrecked French countryside. This was what our men were facing, like the others. And like all the others they now had steel helmets like pudding basins and they carried gas-masks, and aeroplanes were overhead all the time. They were now in a big amorphous sort of war, not their own Anzac.

Haig did not think much of the Australians and soon they did not think much of Haig. 'They were not nearly so efficient as the Canadians, . . . they put revolutionary ideas into the heads of our men'. They had an abnormally high proportion of military prisons 'because Australia refused to allow capital punishment'. 'They look on themselves not as part of the English army but as allies beside us.'

That fondness for capital punishment of the British army irked us. We remembered Dublin; we had read how the British wanted to shoot conscientious objectors who had been forced to go to a war they hated and were unwilling to obey orders to shoot other men. And the occasional poor chap who broke down under the strain; he was shot after a court-martial before officers in neat dress who had never had any strain. Officers were not shot, that was part of their privilege; but how much more logical to shoot some of those whose happy complacency had killed hundreds.

The attack was coming, the great attack; it was not for any clear objective, but it was the great attack. It looked promising, for Haig had under his hand seven times as many men as the German defence. On 1 July he wrote to his wife, 'I feel that every step in my plan has been taken with divine help. The wire has never been so well cut, nor the artillery preparation so thorough'.

A million and a half shells were fired from 1537 guns in one week but, divine help or not, the wire was still there and the shells had made the ground into a German defence obstacle.

Successive lines of men, shoulder to shoulder, each carrying 66 pounds of equipment, scrambled through the churned mud to the un-cut wire. At 7.30 in the morning they started as the artillery changed targets. At 7.31 the Germans carried up their machine-guns from deep shelters and mowed them down.

It was the worst day of the war. Of 100 000 men who moved forward, 60 000 were shot down; 29 000 bodies lay between the lines, and, I suppose, Haig went down to breakfast.

The Battle of the Somme went on month after month, with 7000 casualties each day. When it was over we could see the gains on the map in the breakfast room, nearly six miles in one place, but the main German defences were still intact.

Late in July our 5th Division made a feint attack at Fromelles and lost 5533, but it was only the start. Haig then set them 'an easy task', the capture of Pozières, and they did it. There were 5000 casualties in four days and another division was thrown in. In less than seven weeks the A.I.F. lost 6842 dead and 17 513 wounded. This was worse than all the eight months on Gallipoli.

The news of the attack on Pozières reached Melbourne one evening and the State Governor, Sir Arthur Stanley, said, 'It was a Happy Night for Australia'.

Our church caught it. Mr MacRoberts, the man who did not want to kill another man, was killed. The story is that he was in some rear unit, like the Army Service Corps, well behind the front, which was very quiet then, just an occasional rifle shot. His job took him forward; his curiosity took him further, right to the trenches. He wanted to see what no-man's-land looked like. He looked over the parapet and was struck at once.

He was important enough to get the only personal memorial on the church wall, and so he should, old enough to be old for the army but young enough to be remarkable as our Senior Elder. His brass plate is beside the first honour board on the right-hand side of the pulpit.

Poor Mrs MacRoberts. Her face showed resignation and sad beauty. There she sat in the choir each Sunday where we could all see her, still young, gentle, with pure white hair.

Then Innes Gun went in the main attack. Poor blind Innes with his thick glasses and in the infantry; he was a stretcher-bearer, and that was an unhealthy job. In the mist behind his glasses he would not have seen what got him.

We had not expected either to enlist. Seldom could there have been two more unlikely soldiers, but they thought it seemly to go to the war and the war took them.

And still the Battle of the Somme went on. Of course, it was successful; there had not yet been a battle or an attack which was not. The first day: EARLY SUCCESS ACHIEVED; the second day: ALLIES GAIN GROUND; the third day: ALLIES ADVANCING. Every day we were doing well as we had always done; it was a pity that our maps did not show it.

Then came something new: an invention, the last of the war. BRITAIN'S MOTOR FORTS. NEW WAR ENGINE IN ACTION. BRILLIANT SUCCESS. We would call the things 'tanks' later, and in fact, the name had already been used to mask their real purpose. A 'brilliant success', the headlines said. There were 150 tanks in France but the crews had only had weeks to get used to the first clumsy machines. It seems that Haig thought he might get into trouble if he did not produce some results from the months-long slaughter, and the new tanks might be enough to break the German lines. He gave the order for their use despite strong protests at the gross mishandling of the new weapon.

There were 49 tanks but only 32 reached the starting point. Of these

9 went with the infantry, another 9 eventually helped in the clearing-up, 9 broke down and 5 were ditched.

The Germans had released gas before they were ready to exploit it. We did the same with tanks, but luckily for us, the Germans were very slow in finding a counter.

Philip Gibbs, the correspondent of the *Daily Chronicle*, the man whose jolly schoolboy journalism was to win him a knighthood wrote about the new machine and the *Argus* quoted him: 'The British went over the parapets excited by a smell of victory, and also in the greatest good humour, laughing as they ran, because the new toy inflamed their fancy'. So the men, carrying 66 pounds, ran; so the men expecting to have their guts blown out by high explosive or to be cut in half by machine-gun bullets, laughed. Philip Gibbs must have seen and heard them from miles away in safety at Haig's headquarters.

The tanks 'are proof against bullets, bombs and shell splinters and take ditches like kangaroos' and yet only one-fifth of them were able to go into action with the infantry. 'The actual sight of them is monstrously comical. They are like enormous toads. The only effect on our inquisitive troops when they appeared was to create shouts of laughter, but they did good work, and scared the Germans dreadfully'. The few that got through did good work, but how much more good work would have been done if they had been used in full numbers by fully trained crews on solid ground, and not churned-up mud?

The War Office decided that they were a failure and ordered that the contract for a thousand new ones should be cancelled. But Major Stern persisted and they were built. Stern was excluded from conferences and sacked from the Ministry of Munitions and his place was taken by an admiral, who had never seen a tank.

The fighting on the Somme continued. On 1 October: THE ALLIED PLAN. DESTRUCTION OF MAN-POWER. RESULT OF THE SOMME BATTLES. FIGURES THAT TELL. So we were not fighting to push the Germans back; we were fighting to kill enough so that there would be too few left to fight. I suppose Haig and his staff knew that it cost thousands of pounds in ammunition and almost two British lives to kill each German.

On 18 October: THE SOMME, AFTER THREE MONTHS. FIRST GOAL REACHED. DISASTER AHEAD FOR THE ENEMY. But it was a long way ahead and the rains of November drowned the Battle of the Somme. Our battle of Pozières was one of the few things to stand above the mud.

We did not think logically about it then, for our thinking was controlled by the massive propaganda machine, a grossly clumsy machine, wheezing on blindly and throwing us false statements, which we were only just beginning to question.

What had the Somme meant? It had meant the most gigantic defeat that Britain had ever sustained; those hundreds of thousands of uncomplaining dead had achieved nothing, absolutely nothing. Those who had sent them to their deaths were still smugly in power ready to plan further defeats.

The casualty lists in the papers made it all clear to us. Every day we saw men and women wearing bits of black, and we knew of others wearing no sign at all. The pattern of the war was set.

It had been horrible on Gallipoli, foul with flies and stench of unburied bodies, but it had been romantic. It was an ancient storybook land and we had been fighting a fairy-tale sort of people. It evoked the *Arabian Nights* and that sort of thing, and with just one bit of luck there would have been a startling victory. It had been human; the enemy could be seen occasionally and it was rather a personal matter between him and you. Now there was no hope of quick victory; the nearest enemy was a distant machine-gun and death crashed at random from the skies. It had been unburied bodies on Gallipoli, now it was ragged fragments of bodies scattered in the mud.

On Gallipoli we had had chirpy Birdwood as a leader and he could be seen every day. Now Birdwood was remote and now his popularity dropped – he was thought to be too subservient to the British staff which ordered his men to useless death and Birdwood did not protect them. He had become part of the clumsy machine which swallowed men and tossed out dead and wounded – the machine which did not move forward but only made pieces of meat out of the happy friend of yesterday.

What had seemed to be strange incompetence at Gallipoli now seemed to be normal British army procedure. The letters from France told that 'men had been murdered through incompetence, callousness and personal vanity of those high in authority'. Haig in his polished riding boots became as unpopular in Australia as he was in the A.I.F.

At school the Head still announced that some Old Boy had died gallantly for his country, but gallantry was now a word which meant nothing: we were beginning to think that he had gone uselessly and inevitably to slaughter.

At home, there was no rush for the paper before breakfast to read of the new victory; there were victories in the paper but we did not believe in them any longer. There might be some new place-name, but it soon fell back amongst the other place-names as somewhere where thousands had been killed. On and on the war was going; it would go on and on and no end was in sight.

We had started and would have to see it through, and if our luck was good, there would not be any close friends in the casualty lists. Now it looked as if the Allies would never set foot on German soil.

The losses at Pozières showed that if there were more such battles the normal flow of reinforcements would be insufficient to keep our divisions up to fighting strength.

Billy Hughes was in England. He was a curiosity there; he showed no sign of subservience to the English but he got on very well with the gentry, and this may have had an effect on him. He, the man who had said that he was firm against conscription, told 3000 Australian troops at Weymouth camp that 'he stood, more than any other man for compulsory military service because there was no other way whereby a free people could strike a blow for liberty'. Like Lloyd George, he was more fluent than logical, in suggesting that compulsion was necessary for freedom.

The army authorities gave him an inflated figure of the number of men who would be required and he had an inflated idea of the number of fit single men still in Australia. His figure was 150 000, but opponents of conscription made it 50 000.

He was a Labor Prime Minister but the Labor Party had been consistently against conscription and 'No Conscription' banners had been carried through Melbourne in the last Eight Hours Day procession. It turned out that only about a quarter of the Labor politicians were for conscription. One of them was Senator Pearce, the Minister for Defence. The War Precautions Act had superseded democratic procedures and free speech, and he used the Act to authorize a raid on the Melbourne Trades Hall to seize anti-conscription posters.

To introduce conscription a Bill would have to be passed by both Houses. The Lower House was in favour, but the Labor majority in the Upper House would be certain to reject it. The only way round would be to hold a referendum. There would be a referendum on 28 October and voting was to be compulsory.

The Irish in Australia were strong in the Labor Party and their distrust of England and dislike of her war had increased after the brutalities of the military in Dublin, only six months earlier. The Roman Catholic Church was becoming identified with the Irish feelings. Old Archbishop Carr, an Irishman, had originally stressed the justice of Britain's cause and he remained neutral on the conscription issue: 'The Church neither advocates or opposes it. She leaves it to her members to freely decide how they should vote'; and 'Conscription is purely a State matter'. Archbishop Kelly of Sydney, who had previously appeared on the platform at recruiting meetings, now appeared at the fund-raising meetings 'to relieve Irish distress and to assist Ireland to become a self-governing part of the Empire'. Carr's coadjutor, Mannix, spoke often and fluently against the war and against conscription. In March a deputation of leading Catholics protested that Mannix's statements were 'disloyal and inimical to the interests of the Church'. Carr took no action.

The Premier of New South Wales expressed the hope, through his Agent-General in London, that Britain would make a statement that martial law in Ireland would cease and that Home Rule was still the firm policy. The only satisfaction he got was the assurance that shooting of civilians had now stopped. This was not good enough. The Catholic Church split on conscription, as had the Labor Party, and in both cases the majority was anti-conscription.

The Protestant churches were 'pro', and the Church of England was very 'pro'. Dr Leeper moved at the Anglican synod in Melbourne:

> That this synod is so convinced that the forces of the Allies are being used of God to vindicate the rights of the weak and to maintain the moral order of the world, that it gives its strong support to the principle of universal service, or the conscription of men and income, that the enforcement of such universal obligation is the only equitable way of employing our national resources of manhood and wealth.

The motion was carried with cheers and two verses of the national anthem were sung.

The Presbyterians were less enthusiastic. At the General Assembly a vague motion was passed–'the words should not be considered as condoning or condemning conscription'. The Rev. Burgess said he would vote 'No' because of the moral issue–and he had given five sons to the war. This was five more than Dr Leeper had given.

Anticipating that the referendum would establish conscription, the Commonwealth government issued a proclamation at the end of September, 'calling upon all men who on the second day of October, 1916, are of the age of twenty-one years and upwards and under thirty-five years, who are unmarried or widowers without children, to enlist and serve as required'.

Magistrates could grant exemption. Archdeacon Hindley, acting on behalf of the Council of Melbourne Grammar, applied for the exemption of the headmaster, R. P. Franklin, on the grounds that his services were essential. Franklin was thirty-two, three years too young to escape the terms of the proclamation, but public opinion was that once a man was thirty he should not be driven into the army by shame, but could go of free choice. Plenty of older men enlisted, but plenty of younger ones stayed without feeling too bad about it. In Franklin's case exemption was refused. Lieutenant Vines, representing the Defence Department, said that Franklin 'sought to despise the honour of the women of France and Belgium' and that it was 'demoralising to the boys he looked after'. The decision was reversed on appeal to the Supreme Court, but we were shocked that a headmaster of a public school was not setting an example of loyalty. Franklin enlisted in the next year.

It was a bitter conscription campaign. In the old days feeling had been high over free-trade and protection, but now there was vicious hatred and violence.

We told each other that I.W.W. stood for 'I Won't Work', for it fomented the strikes which hindered our war effort. Officially it was the Independent Workers of the World; it was based on the Anarchist and Syndicalist movements of Europe and was not anti-war so much as anti-capitalism. It had originated on the west coast of America, and oddly enough, was strong in patriotic New Zealand. It advocated, and used, arson and sabotage; four members were jailed for treason on 3 October and another dozen on 12 October. We lumped the I.W.W. in with the Sinn Fein.

The referendum produced violence and both sides condoned it. Conscription meetings were patriotic but too rough for the Boy Scouts: guards of honour of men in military uniform took their place. Any uniform was good, but returned soldiers' uniforms were very good; best of all was that of a maimed returned soldier. No magistrate would show any pity for anybody who assaulted one.

Meetings were held to preach to the converted and could be held only where one party predominated. The Yarra Bank was traditionally reserved for the left-wing, and anti-conscription meetings were held there. In the industrial suburbs no pro-conscription meeting was possible; it was almost as dangerous to have an anti-conscription meeting in a middle-class suburb. On the opposite side of Kooyong Road from us there were many small houses and sometimes a risky meeting was held on the Church of England corner; quite big ones were held near the Malvern town hall.

We knew it was our duty to break up meetings and we did our best. Neil, usually rather careful of himself, was quite successful. He would put iron filings in a cool-drink bottle with sulphuric acid and screw down the stopper. At a meeting he would unscrew the stopper and the chemical action would begin and out would come sulphurated hydrogen. The rotten-egg stink was strong enough to clear a big space around the bottle—it was the same process that had been successful in Sunday school.

For political purposes rotten eggs were more valuable than good ones;

they provided a valuable counter-argument at any meeting and a well-aimed egg could silence the most eloquent speaker.

The conscriptionists, the 'Yes' party, included the solid establishment and a majority of the church people, like ourselves, a majority of women and of men above military age. We were a very dignified lot but we accepted that the rantings of Billy Hughes expressed our views.

The 'No' party had the rantings of the Labor politicians; it also had the logic of Archbishop Mannix, but feelings were so deep that logic was unimportant. Because of Mannix, the Catholic Church in Victoria was identified with the 'No' party. In the other States the division was more on the old political grouping.

Of course those of enemy alien origin, whether naturalized or not, were not allowed to vote in the referendum. Instructions were given that any man who appeared to be eligible for the call-up was to have his voting paper distinctively marked.

Of course 'Yes' would win. But it didn't; it lost by 1 087 557 to 1 160 033. Conscription gained a majority only in Victoria and the two small states of Western Australia and Tasmania. Worse still, was that when the overseas A.I.F. votes were disclosed, the 'Yes' had only a small majority.

In a year of disappointment, this result was one of the biggest. Australia had shown that it was not the most loyal bit of the Empire; it had decided that it was to be the only large bit which would not have conscription. The government's premature action had left a mess to be cleaned up: all the men called up under the proclamation had to be released and all convictions quashed.

The year 1916 was going out dismally. The only victory of the year had been Brusiloff's defeat of the Austrians and he was very pleased with it. 'War Won Today' he said, and 'Russia had not yet reached the zenith of her power' but it was not very convincing for we had heard nothing from Russia in the past months.

'Our New Ally' of August, Romania, was finally extinguished by the capture of its capital, Bucharest, on 7 December. Four other capitals had fallen to the Germans so far – Warsaw of Poland, Belgrade of Serbia, Brussels of Belgium and Cettione of Montenegro. That last might be only a little unimportant place, but it was bigger than anything we had captured.

It had been a disappointing year and something should be done about it. The Northcliffe press thought that Britain should get a new Prime Minister and that Lloyd George was the man; so did he. He resigned from the Cabinet, complaining of indecision in the conduct of the war; two days later the Prime Minister, Asquith, was deposed from the War

Cabinet and Lloyd George was put in his place. No Prime Minister could be expected to accept such humiliation and Asquith resigned. After a bit of shuffling about, Lloyd George was made Prime Minister.

Asquith had seemed a decent and reasonable sort of man to us and had the respect which we always gave to British Prime Ministers, but he had little glamour and was a sad man after the death of his son., Raymond, on active service.

Lloyd George's son had had a very comfortable war and the papers said that he was going to be made the second-youngest lieutenant-colonel in the army after only eighteen months' service. This was a bit too much and a fuss was made in the Commons; it did not come off and he was to end the war as a major. The rank was, of course, temporary, and would cease on demobilization, but he kept it throughout his political career; in some ways he was like his father.

In Australia Lloyd George was never outstandingly popular, probably never as popular as Asquith had been. In England an attempt was made to build him up as a figure to replace Kitchener, but a large minority always detested him.

He was a fluent and emotional speaker, like our Billy Hughes, and a quick and shallow thinker. As Chancellor of the Exchequer he had brought in radical budgets which hit the privileged classes, and we approved of that, but in 1914 he had cut the naval vote on the grounds that 'the international sky had never been more perfectly blue'. On 23 July 1914, the very day of the Austrian ultimatum to Serbia, he had told the Commons that our relations with Germany were better than they had been for years and that war in Europe was unlikely.

He had lived down the Marconi scandal of 1912, when he, the Chancellor, with the Solicitor-General, had bought Marconi shares below the market price just before the company was awarded the huge government contract for installing wireless throughout the Empire.

He was a Prohibitionist and we thought he was a wowser, with his own peculiar moral standards. He could not be accused of being a drunkard, but then, wenching was much cheaper than drinking in North Wales.

He might well have been blamed for ammunition deficiencies, both as Chancellor and as Kitchener's successor as Minister of War, when that Ministry included the Office of Munitions. What he said he had done in five months after the Office had been promoted to a Ministry under him, gained him immense credit.

Churchill was usually an ally of Lloyd George. He wrote, 'Lloyd George in the War Office is fatal. He destroyed the Treasury and the Munitions Office is in chaos. The ideal is that he should have some job like the Duchy of Lancaster and be on the War Committee, where he would be of value because his brain is fertile.'

We knew that the Germans were unscrupulous and we thought that it might be a good thing to have an unscrupulous leader against them, but in Australia Lloyd George never replaced Kitchener in our minds.

But was he really our leader? Northcliffe supported him on his appointment in a statement to the United Press Association of America: 'Mr Lloyd George has given a knock-out blow to the gang of aged and inept mediocrities who have prevented the British Empire from exerting its full force in the war. Whatever happens, those malevolents can never get together again'.

Northcliffe told him that he was to do as he was told. 'It would be impossible to continue [my] support for the government if they continued to scatter their forces in the Balkans when all sound military opinion urged a concentration on the Western Front'. The 'sound opinion' was that of Haig who had become Commander-in-Chief just a year before with some help from Northcliffe. Both of Northcliffe's creatures would see out the war mutually detesting each other but unable to do much about it because of their common dependence on him.

Northcliffe threatened to force Lloyd George to resign if he did not keep on the right lines, and this he might have been able to do; but he said he would do more. He intended to overthrow the French government if M. Briand, the Premier, did not mend his ways.

So Northcliffe thought that he was the leader and Lloyd George was his puppet. Our papers did not give us any hint of the position and we accepted Lloyd George as the leader, even if we thought he was a very grubby substitute for Kitchener. We preferred our Billy Hughes to him, and this was the first time that we had placed our own Prime Minister above Britain's.

There was no substitute for Kitchener. Haig could not fill his shoes, a remote and shallow man. The best that his supporters could say in his favour was that all other generals were worse. He was 'every inch a soldier to the top of his polished riding boots', Lloyd George said of him.

Things had changed since the Boer War when every general had been a hero until he was sacked. In those days we bought postcards with portraits of the British generals and posted them to each other; the postcards had been designed in England and printed in Bavaria, but they showed our heroes.

One of the portraits was of Major-General French, our first Commander-in-Chief. Now major-generals were pretty thick on the ground and we even had some of our own. We knew that real heroes got the Victoria Cross and we also knew that no general could get near enough to danger to be given one with decency. We looked elsewhere for our heroes.

We got our first Australian hero when Corporal Jacka won our first V.C. on Gallipoli; he seemed to be entirely genuine. The English had already had a generous issue of Gallipoli V.C.s but Jacka's showed that the A.I.F. was recognized and eligible for decoration.

We heard about another hero who was killed before he got any recognition; Simpson and his donkey. Simpson was a recent English migrant who had knocked about in Australia before joining the A.I.F. On Anzac he had commandeered a donkey and, without instructions or authority, used it for carrying wounded men to the beach through the mist of rifle fire. He did it once too often. Whatever we had been taught to think about English troops, the most colourful Australian hero was English.

In December 1916 we read:

KAISER AND PEACE

Preposterous Offer

British Feeling Scornful

"A COLOSSAL BLUFF"

The following is a copy of a message sent by the Kaiser to all his Generals in the field: 'Soldiers,–In agreement with the Sovereigns of my Allies, and with the consciousness of victory, I have made an offer of peace to the enemy. Whether or not it will be accepted is still uncertain. Until that moment arrives we will fight on'.

There had been talk of peace from Germany in April and the Chancellor had asked for terms from the Allies. Apparently all the Germans had considered vital was safety from another two-front war. That would mean that Poland and the Baltic states would be established as a buffer between Germany and Russia; Belgium would not remain in the French-British group but would be neutral. There was even a hint that a plebiscite would be held in Alsace-Lorraine.

Every now and then throughout the year there had been paragraphs saying that both Turkey and Austria were on the brink of collapse and wanting peace. This time the offer of peace had come from the Kaiser himself and this was the Kaiser's war.

If we had had just one great victory to our credit we might have been ready to bargain, but now it would look as if the Germans had won the war. We hoped that time would give us the victory which we had not won by fighting. Perhaps the real reason we refused the peace offer was that we would not accept Germany as the dominant nation in Europe.

Whatever the peoples of the countries whose men were being killed thought about it, they could not express their opinion: it was a matter for the politicians.

The British government did not like the idea. One theory, possibly an unjust one, was that Lloyd George, as the new Prime Minister, did not want peace until he could get the credit for it.

Right from the beginning there had been a small but quite respectable minority in England wanting peace. Ramsay MacDonald with his little International Labour Party had done his best and tried to meet leaders of similar views in the European countries. Lord Landsdowne had spoken in favour of it in the House of Lords, and he seemed to be a very reasonable man. If Britain decided on peace negotiations, France would have to concur and Russia was not in a position to express an opinion. It was possible that a press campaign could have moved the people to demand peace from the new government.

Northcliffe was against it. 'The German peace move is due to shortage of food in Germany, Austria and Turkey. There is also the fact that Germany knows that in 1917 Great Britain will have three times as many shells and guns as she will possess. The proposals have been received in England with contempt'.

We had seemed to have had plenty of shells and guns on the Somme but they did not seem to have done us much good, but Northcliffe spoke for England; 1917 would be the year of victory. We could not see that the French army would mutiny, the Italians would run and the Russians would collapse.

It was odd that the Germans who had planned and started the war should now want peace after all their victories which had knocked out the teeth of France and Russia. It was strange that they were now willing to grant all that we said we were fighting for.

The Allies were unwilling to put on the brakes and it would be two years before the war-machine stopped. Two years of dull war, the same new things no longer new—aeroplanes, tanks, submarines, gas and flame-throwers; the same muddy uniforms and the same terror; no new atrocities, nothing to match Nurse Cavell and the *Lusitania*. The same shortage of food in England, but not nearly as short as in Germany. At school more new deaths to be announced at morning assembly, but they would be just routine additions to the school's score. Adamson Hall was already well stocked with memorials.

16
If Peace had Come

From this distance in time it is possible for us to form an idea on what would have happened if peace had come with 1917.

The dominance of Germany would not have been replaced by that of the United States; the Reichsmark and pound would have competed with the dollar and Wall Street could have crashed without ruining the world's economy. European peoples would not have become so impoverished; their standards of living would have risen and that of the United States would not have increased so quickly. They would have had better home markets and could have competed in such things as car manufacture and film production.

Millions more soldiers would have lived and there would not have been the conditions conducive to the rise of Spanish influenza, which killed so many millions more. Those two extra years of fighting heaped further indignities on millions of men; without them we would have remembered more of their sacrifice and less of their hopeless suffering.

The map of Europe would have been more logical, for the new states would not have been formed for the punishment of the defeated enemy. The chain of buffer states between Russia and Europe would have been larger and stronger with the addition of the Ukraine: no bad thing for Europe and the Ukrainians. Vienna would have remained as a great city and the Emperor of Austria-Hungary would have been the focal point for a federation of national states with national languages. There would have been no artificial barriers to block the trade of the Danube basin. The easy tolerance of the old Empire would not have been replaced by the bitter animosities amongst the minorities of the new synthetic nations.

Germany would have kept her Kaiser, for the success of German arms would have strengthened the military party against the democrats and it would have been a long time before the Kaiser became a constitutional monarch.

Russia might have kept her Tsar for some time longer, and he just might have become a constitutional monarch. If the revolution had come, it would not have been so violent and would not have set a pattern for the communist revolts of Germany, Austria and Hungary.

It is just possible that Turkey could have survived as a Moslem power in Asia incorporating the Arab states, but they would have been German-dominated and not divided between the influence of France and Britain. A revived Turkish empire would have controlled the Arab oil resources.

There would have been a lot more kings in Europe. The new states of Poland and Lithuania already had kings and other new states would have followed them. It had been the established practice for every new state to be issued with a king, not only Greece and the Balkan nations, but Norway as well.

An imposing figure was 'regal', 'kingly', or 'queenly', never 'Presidential'. Wilson, the American President, did not look imposing or kingly: he looked like an albino prune stuffed with teeth. Even in America God was 'the Almighty King', and the Virgin Mary, 'the Queen of Heaven'. They were never addressed as 'Mr and Mrs President'. Presidents were regarded as shoddy things. In Europe there were only three—in the notoriously politically unstable countries of France and Portugal, whilst Switzerland had some sort of anonymous one.

We thought the American president was inevitable in his country, but unsuitable for international conditions. The long months that elapsed between an old president and the new meant that the world could only guess what American policy would be. He had more power than most kings but was not trained to use it. His main concern was with his support in internal matters, rather than with his nation's place in international affairs. The intrigue and exhibitionism essential for his election did not necessarily produce a statesman.

If a president got into trouble it meant trouble for his political party. He was part of politics and not above them; as one of the most powerful men in the world, he would shelve his international responsibilities to intervene for his party in an election. Few presidents would have made good kings, but a lot of kings would have made good heads of the American state.

If a king gave trouble he could be sent home and another one got from one of the dynastic stud-farms of Europe. Kings were not such silly things. Practically all of them knew something of the history of Europe; they could speak French and other languages and could talk with their relations across the national boundaries. The Kaiser had done his best with his cousin, the Tsar, when war had seemed likely.

If peace had come, what would have happened to Britain? She would certainly have lost her trade supremacy to Germany, and not, as eventually, to the United States. She still would have been very important in trans-ocean trade and the Empire would have remained as a strong base.

Here in Australia, Germany, not America, would have been our most important influence after Britain.

When the American fleet had visited Australia in 1908 we had made a tremendous fuss of it, but our fear of Japan might have had a lot to do with that. We feared Germany almost as much, but we did not fear the United States. We regarded the Germans as being more sophisticated and more solid than the Americans, who, in many ways, appeared as huge versions of ourselves.

The German navy would have persisted after a peace in 1917 and our fears of it would have preserved our reliance on the Royal Navy. There would have been some hope of an Empire federation, which had been vaguely talked about. Already the war had prompted Britain to make formal consultations with dominion representatives in London, and the dominions were the larger and more independent of the colonies.

The colonies of non-British stock would have moved slowly towards greater self-government. The most important was India, which was still a colony, no matter what it was called. It would have set the pattern for the others. There was already a halting policy of granting more self-government, but the Indians selected to do the governing were those most similar to the English ruling class. India would have become a nation of princely states, but there would have been a longer continuation of impartial central power which might have prevented the break-up of the country and the religious slaughter. The glamour of the princes would have been no more wasteful of manpower than the present civil service and would have looked far more attractive.

How would Australia have done? We certainly would have claimed our conquest of the German Pacific colonies, but our voice would have been weak. Our only hope would have been that Germany could have been bought off somewhere, perhaps east of the Ukraine. But that would depend on how the peace conference treated Russia.

Internally we would not have reached the later extremes of sectarian bitterness, which related so much to what happened in Ireland. There would have been no excuse for the British coalition government to refuse the promised Home Rule to Ireland, and any settlement could not have been worse than the later one.

As for us, our real war was over at the end of the Gallipoli campaign. Anzac had been our very own, and after Anzac the war had become impersonal and out-of-scale.

I pray that soon from Anzac Cove
His ship may cross the foam,
And may I, too, go down to see
Young Galahad come home.

Already Pozières had stopped a lot of young Galahads from Anzac ever coming home and the extra two years of war would mean that very few ever would. But France had already added something to our military education. On Anzac men had died for their country; in France they had learned to fight for it, and if they fought intelligently, they might not die.

By the end of 1916 it was no longer glorious to sacrifice yourself for the Empire and it was better not to die uselessly. No more close-packed lines of men being herded into attacks, but teams of men using initiative to get forward with minimum loss. Already it was accepted that Australian attacks succeeded with fewer casualties than those of the more conservative armies.

The tremendous Australian successes in France in 1918 added little, or nothing, to what we felt about our men of Anzac. They might have increased our military standing abroad, but it was already established at home.

In 1917 the bridging bond of the returned soldiers over the splits of the community would have been stronger than it was at the end of the war. If our troops had returned then there would have been a greater proportion of inspired volunteers and fewer of the poor fellows edged into the army by social pressure to fill the dismal gaps of 1917 and 1918. The war would have been remembered more for knight-errantry and less for despondency. Our war memorials would have been just as imposing. We had already paid a sufficient price to make reunions of returned soldiers more than meetings of privileged men who had enjoyed overseas travel and carefree adventure during the happiest years of their lives. Already by 1917 they were men who had shared danger and were happy to be still living; men who had learned to know and trust each other more in a matter of weeks than they would in years of civilian life; men whose forced companionship would last the years; men whose leaders had emerged through competence and not intrigue; men who had denied themselves for the group good. They were already a new force in the community.

We were already as proud of the A.I.F. as ever we would be; it was a new sort of army and it was our own pattern of what an army should be. We had already lost our old reverence for the Brahmins of the English army caste system.

Our men were already known as 'diggers' by the British; the word had nothing to do with 'de guerre' or digging trenches, it was a long-established word of amiable address to a stranger, just as 'Blue' was used for anyone with red hair, or 'Titch' for anyone below average size, or 'Cocky' for any farmer, irrespective of how big his farm was. 'Digger' had survived from the gold rush; the pub and village outside Melbourne on the way to the gold fields was on the maps as Diggers' Rest. The diggers were people of dignity, the first artisans to be given full democratic voting rights, and they all felt independent and proud. Their success depended only on luck and application and any digger was as good as any other. Every man in the A.I.F. was proud to be a digger and no better than any other digger.

The Australian state educational systems had made the A.I.F. the best-educated army of any in the war. We did not think that parental money spent on sending a boy to an expensive school for a couple of years' extra schooling necessarily made him a good leader of men in danger, but rather that a man who had survived danger might be able to help others to survive.

A good potential leader might be a simple sort of fellow and unable to cope with the paperwork. That sort was sent off to be educated sufficiently to become officers, and of all places, they were sent to Oxford and Cambridge.

All English officers were expected to speak in a way similar to that of all other officers, and it was often very different from the speech of the men. In the A.I.F. there was no distinctive officer tongue. Some used a strong nasal accent, a 'Sydney accent', we said in Melbourne, but it was no handicap to an officer, nor was an approximation to standard English any advantage.

There was no great cultural difference between officers and men: they came from similar backgrounds. The financial disturbances of the 1890s had dispersed old wealth, and little hereditary privilege survived.

Mother's brother, Uncle Sam, was rich, stinkingly rich, and had married more money. He had been in the Upper House in Western Australia and still liked to be called 'The Honourable'—mother did not quite agree with the adjective. In 1918 his only son, Bert, was old enough to enlist if he got his father's consent, but he did not go.

Mother's younger sister, Ethel, had married a consumptive carpenter who took a long time to die and did not earn much while he did it. Her son, of about Bert's age, became Private Henderson.

It was hard to sort out the rich from the poor because they did the same sort of things. One of the Coles, one who was killed later on Gallipoli, was on his horse and tossed sixpence to an old swaggie who had opened a gate for him. That swaggie was the immensely rich 'Hungry'

Tyson, who often inspected his properties by rolling a swag and setting out on his two feet.

Respectable people did the same thing on holiday. They rolled a swag and worked for a while and then moved on. Fruit picking was static and could be done from a fixed camp, but harvesting required mobility. We and our friends often used bicycles, but we met the pedestrians.

We met them in the usual camping places where news of possible work was exchanged. One was under a bridge about a mile out of Sale and there we got to know a huge and amiable Maori, and a pair that always went about together–a little chap in his thirties who mothered an old chap in his seventies.

When we first met them they were very pleased with themselves after a comfortable couple of days in a returned soldiers' hostel in Bairnsdale. It was in 1920 and returned soldiers were still getting consideration as they settled back into civilian life. The little chap really was a returned soldier but the hostel had doubts about the old bloke. 'Dad, you look pretty old to be a returned soldier, what war were you in?' 'The German war' he replied, and was allowed in. He had been in the German war; he had fought for the Germans against the French in 1870.

Rich and poor had gone camping in the bush, cooked their own meals and improvised their living conditions. War required improvisation, and the better it was managed, the more chance of survival. Every single Australian, city or country, had used an axe and a spade. In 1940 a lot of the British troops arriving in the Middle East had never dug a hole in the ground and, like those in the earlier war, it took time for them to adjust themselves.

The few English who had used fire-arms had used shot-guns in the caste-ritual of slaughtering semi-domesticated poultry; most Australians had used light rifles to shoot rabbits for the pot or for profit and heavier rifles for killing vermin, such as foxes and kangaroos.

By the end of 1916 most junior officers in the A.I.F. had served as N.C.O.s, and when a good N.C.O. was promoted to lieutenant there was a good private to take his place. Reinforcements arrived as privates and served in action before being promoted to N.C.O.; once promoted, they served a further term in competition with others before gaining a commission.

The pictures of 1916 show that officers in the line carried rifles and wore the same issue uniform as their men, with only their little black shoulder pips to show their rank. There was no barrier and it was unthinkable that a junior officer would not eat with his men and share their conditions. The tradition established by 1916 lasted throughout the next war.

In 1914 we knew that real soldiers—British soldiers—wore gaudy ceremonial and walking-out uniforms. Our local imitations were drab in comparison. By the end of 1916 we knew that real soldiers—Australian soldiers—wore only utilitarian dress and yet were quite as martial as those in fancy dress. After the war some British ceremonial dress survived and when the Duke of Gloucester was Governor-General it added nothing to his popularity that one of his staff went about in absurd cerise stove-pipe trousers. To us he looked like a fop and not a soldier.

Every man in the A.I.F., from generals down to privates, carried his paybook, which recorded his current entitlement of the rank he held and his accumulated credit—and all pay was drawn against the credit.

It was reckoned no disgrace that the pay-corporal should see that an officer had once been a private on five shillings a day. His paybook contained his full military history and would have been of interest to German intelligence, so he was not allowed to keep it on his person on going into action. Then all he had was the common meat-ticket with his name, military number and religion, but not rank. It was enough to bury him and his next-of-kin would get the balance in his paybook back at base.

The British pay system was cumbersome and elaborate, with allowances for all sorts of things. The British officer was regarded as a gentleman, even if temporary, and was thought to be above money. He had a sort of bank account somewhere but he did not know what it was, and as many youngsters had never had a bank account before, they got into trouble. It was complicated for them as there were all sorts of extras to which they might be entitled. Some of those who got to Archangel in 1918 found that there was a very high summer temperature which entitled them to the Tropic Allowance whilst the simple ones only drew the Arctic Allowance.

In the A.I.F. a colonel commanding a battalion was not ashamed to have a brother who was a private. If Keith or Owen went out with Ralph, they lent him their greatcoat with the pips on the shoulder. The British system did not approve of fraternizing; a new lance-corporal was broken and a private punished for addressing him by his Christian name.

It might have been expected that even an officer would adjust himself to primitive conditions, but as late as 1918 Monash had complaints from the British that Australian officers in France were not wearing gloves nor carrying canes. No British officer was permitted to ride on a bus in London or to carry a parcel, but seventy miles away he was expected to live in a muddy hole.

There were quite a lot of English in the A.I.F. and some Australians in the British army and the hereditary background of both armies was similar, but it was the immediate social background which produced two very different types of fighting men.

The war which had produced a new sort of army by 1917 had already stimulated or produced social changes at home.

By 1917 the temperance movement had got as far as it ever would go and it was general for pubs to be shut on Sundays and only open from 9 a.m. until 6 p.m. on weekdays. Outside those hours it was necessary to be a traveller and the locals would flood into railway refreshment rooms when a train stopped for a meal break. Of course a lot of back doors were open, but they had to rely on the attitude of the police to stay open.

The attitude of women and the attitude to women changed during the war. Odd ones, like Vida Goldstein, had done quite well when they stood for parliament, but they were not taken very seriously. Our women had had the vote ever since federation but had not been very concerned about it—free-trade or protection made little appeal to them.

In England they did not have the vote and the suffragettes had done startling things until the war prompted them to keep quiet during national hostilities, but they were edging into positions which had previously been entirely male. We followed haltingly.

Three women were made magistrates in Adelaide and when two took their places on the bench, counsel asked, 'Who are these women sitting in judgement of men?'

British women were encouraged to do war work, but ours had little they were allowed to do. The cab drivers of Bendigo protested that Mrs Jackson was driving a cab; Mr Jackson had a licence but he and his son were in the army. Mrs Jackson was allowed to continue.

Our women could knit socks or make pyjamas, but it seemed unlikely that either would turn the tide of history. There was one thing they could do which might, just possibly, be useful. They could learn first-aid.

There were classes in every suburb. There was a class on Wednesday evenings in our Sunday-school and it was just the thing for Mother.

She had lived in the bush for years far from any doctor, given first-aid to hundreds and helped a lot of babies into the world, but now she really learnt first-aid. She had a little black St John's Ambulance book with pictures of men with drooping moustaches having water squeezed out of them or having broken legs and arms put into splints. As well as the little book, she had a square of calico, or some such material, with pictures on it showing how it should be folded and tied into a sling or used with two flat pieces of wood for splints.

The war was serious and mother was conscientious and took a lot
of our time when she practised tying us up. She passed the course and
got some sort of certificate. She added the little black book and the
odds and ends to the medicine cabinet on her bedroom mantelpiece – the
one made by the mine carpenter at Derby from a piece of fiddle-back
blackwood.

The war hurried on the rebellion of women against the smothering
of their bodies in excessive clothes. It was all very well for the girls
in convent schools to have to wear shifts in the bath in case their patron
saint was embarrassed by nudity – you would have thought he would
have got used to it by now – but it did seem ridiculous for a woman
to take off her underwear only after putting on her nightdress in case
the father of her children should see something of her body.

Once it had been daring to show anything above the ankle, but now
women went swimming, even if in places reserved for their sole use.
In the big cupboard in the dormitory at home was a communal heap
of bathing suits. The ones that mother and Phyllis took exposed their
legs right up to the knees, and their arms right up to the elbow; above
those extremities heavy cloth and frills masked all else. Women were
in rebellion and were willing to hint at their underlying nudity.

In 1915 *The Sentimental Bloke* was published; the hero, a Melbourne
tough, and his Doreen were drawn as plump naked cherubs, giving
some hint that nudity was not to be entirely confined to high art.

Infant male nudity had been a feature of religious art for hundreds
of years; now infant female nudity was to be displayed to the laity.

'Kewpies' – Cupid dolls – had been contrived in America well before
the war and the conditions of the times made them popular everywhere.
They were little nude figures of Cupid, but incomplete. Nudity might
be all very well in churches but it would offend lay morality, so the
poor little chaps had been castrated, and not only castrated, but completely emasculated. Kewpies ended up as plump little girls, hands shamelessly at their sides and looking up through the tops of their eyes, coyly
inviting attention.

Female nudity had been commercialized and kewpies were everywhere. They were given as dolls to children, and unmarried females
decorated their dressing tables with them and wore tiny celluloid ones
on their dresses. Girls wore them to the school boat-races with ribbons
of colours wound around the kewpie's waist and trailing below, but
leaving the plump belly bare and all essentials exposed. Even at League
football matches kewpies attended on miniature walking-sticks with
the colours of Carlton and Collingwood.

Kewpies lasted out the war and into the years of peace as part of our mating ritual. Their population far outnumbered that of females in Australia.

Women's dress became simpler during the war.

I can remember being called to the front gate in 1914 to see a lady in a hobble skirt going down Kooyong Road. She bulged in the proper places but the bottom of her skirt was so narrow that she could walk only with little mincing steps. It was a recent European fashion but the rationalization brought by the war prevented it being widely followed here.

The first pictures of an Australian General Hospital arriving in Malta showed a straggling procession of nurses in voluminous skirts, wide hats and veils enclosing their faces. The huge skirts went with the war and the big hats and veils were only used by women riding in the dusty and windy motor-cars. Starching went from women's underwear; there were no starched frills and elastic was used instead of linen tapes.

By 1917 the shape of women was being flattened; the bulges of 1914 had already disappeared. The great burst of hair was the first to go; we followed England where long hair was dangerous in the machinery of the war factories and hair was cut to almost the shortness of men's. The bulge of the breasts—the bust—was flattened so that our pattern of female attractiveness became that of an adolescent boy.

The most distressing thing we heard from England was that women were smoking: bright young things were parading in public shamelessly smoking cigarettes. Smoking had been a purely male vice and we were shocked; at least in Australia, women did not smoke in public. The first time I saw one doing it was early in 1919; I was appalled to see a young woman puffing a cigarette in the seclusion of Cataract Gorge in Launceston, but all else about her looked perfectly respectable.

Almost as distressing as women smoking, we learned that some women in England were enjoying sex. Previously, we had regarded sex as an unfortunate male weakness forced on ladies as the humiliating price of marriage. Now we learned that young women in England had learned to enjoy it and were sharing their pleasure with young men they would have married in happier times. They were talking of birth-control. Here a discussion on birth-control was only permissible in private between consenting adults of the same sex. In England it was being discussed by quite young girls. There was already the arid clinical work by Havelock Ellis, which was on some of our bookshelves, but always masked by a brown-paper cover. A more entertaining work was produced in 1918 by Dr Marie Stopes, a mature virgin, but she was already being talked about. Marie Stopes was merely a squalid name to us.

War work in England was making women independent of men and

they were leading independent lives. In October 1916 Lloyd George announced that those working in munitions would get the same pay as men for similar work and already many were doing men's work on farms, on trains, trams and buses. Quite young girls could afford to live away from the supervision of their parents. Girls who could not have spoken to a man unless in the presence of a chaperone were now free to be kind to men who might be killed in a day or two; the fears and excitement of the time had produced a new moral code.

Middle-class women had been set on a pedestal and had been schooled to disdain the urgings of sex with marble disdain, like a statue ignoring a dog pissing on its base. Now the statues had stepped down and become warm and human to those who might have only a few more days to live. Nice young ladies were giving birth to children whose fathers had been killed in France. Here, if any girl anticipated the marriage ceremony, the long sea voyage allowed time for a proxy wedding.

English women were offering themselves to men. Here, the *Age* of 24 August carried a startling headline: LADY OFFERS HERSELF AND HER MOTOR CYCLE. The lady lived in the north of Victoria at a place called Watchem, yes, that really was the name of the place.

Male dress was changing too. Once father had worn a frock-coat and top-hat to church, as some men still did in the richer congregations. A few very dignified professional men still wore them into the city. Then frock-coats deserted the churches and were worn only by undertakers and politicans, although not all of them: only some Liberals and the members of the Labor federal Cabinet.

Bowler hats became restricted to publicans and foremen; by 1917 city men wore black felt hats with a bound brim and all others wore grey with a black band. Those grey hats had displaced the cheaper and more convenient cloth caps, which were now only worn by the really lower-class. Straw hats had gone out by the end of 1916 and university students wore the common grey felt hat; schoolboys wore their little coloured caps.

Men's shirts began the war with starched cuffs and collars. The collars and cuffs were detachable and went to the wash each evening; a shirt would last a week and even the starched pieces might make a couple of appearances. Starching was a tedious and skilled craft beyond the capacity of many housewives. Chinese hand-laundries dotted the suburban shopping streets and did a most proficient job, but as starching declined during the war, those shops became rare, and rarer still when soft collars came in for very informal occasions.

Boys' school shirts began the war with soft cuffs but detachable starched collars. Then celluloid collars came in; they could be cleaned with a rubber, but eventually became brown at the edges. They were flammable and dangerous. Once mother lighted an old one to show the danger and it gave a bright burst of flame.

Then soft collars became general. A shirt was bought with two collars and those two could see out the week of a shirt, if care was taken.

Little boys wore stockings and shorts, showing their bare knees. At the beginning of the war, boys who had turned thirteen covered their knees with long black stockings and these saw them out until they put on long pants at the age of seventeen. There is a photograph of the Honours Sixth at Wesley, all in long pants, except Owen, who still wore the juvenile long stockings.

The war brought the fashion of 'apple-catchers' to cover the knees; loose pantaloons fixed with buttons which the stockings hid. This fashion had come from America; it died soon after the end of the war and boys went straight from bare knees to long pants.

Even death was losing its glamour by 1917. There were too many deaths overseas to make those at home seem important.

Before the war the one certain great occasion in a man's life was when he was no longer living. No matter how unsuccessful and ineffectual a man had been, he had his last great public celebration.

He was put into a shiny coffin and flowers were piled on top. We could see it through the side windows of the hearse, expensive plate-glass windows with pretty decorations etched around the edges.

Already in 1914 there had been motor-hearses but they were regarded as interfering with natural function, just like birth-control.

The proper hearse was a shiny four-wheeler drawn by two black stallions as shiny as the hearse. That last turn-out was magnificent in its ominous way; through the streets it went with at least two black carriages, for they were a mark of respect and needed to make up a procession. There would be more carriages if it was someone important. Behind them came a string of polished motor cars followed by horse-drawn vehicles, other carriages, four-wheelers and jinkers, but all these were private and not paid for out of the deceased estate.

A really important funeral was half a mile long and went at walking pace. Carts and cars pulled to the side of the road and the drivers cursed. The boys of the Armadale State School stood motionless on the kerb with their caps off.

But now random death was obliterating the most virile and they would never have a grand funeral. We lost interest in other people's funerals and they would never be the same again; they were expensive, anyway.

Those young men who were killed in the war might not even have a grave. The bodies of some of them had been dispersed just as effectively as a heretic's scattered ashes, and yet we expected them to be resurrected. Apart from its initial expense, cremation did not seem so silly to those who were not worried about the theory of rising at Judgement Day.

It had once seemed reasonable to make a family burial group with a family monument, and that monument was as much a status-symbol as a family piano. Temporary immortality could be secured by a monument of everlasting granite; marble looked nicer if it was cleaned up on Sunday visits and there could be a marble statue: an angel pointing upwards in admonition or leaning on the anchor of hope. A child might get a personal monument in the corner of a family plot; it would be a cherub, suitable for any child under the age of puberty.

It was all right if someone was drowned, for his name would be cut on the family monument. There was a recognized procedure for getting him to Judgement, even if he did not go in the family party.

The names of those killed on Gallipoli or in France were not cut on the family monument. It was thought right that the government should look after them and that they would be resurrected in military formation. We could do nothing about their graves.

Interest in graves waned and fewer people went along with flowers on Sunday to tidy them up. The number of monumental masons clustered around the cemeteries dropped almost as much as the Chinese hand-laundries.

The war by 1917 even affected God. We knew that he was above, unseen by us, but seeing us. He was up there in the sky, but no matter how high He was, how could He see our relations in France and us at the same time? And how far up was He? Balloons and early aeroplanes had caused concern, but now there were a lot of planes flying very high indeed and getting in His way. He was getting very remote and we lost some of our respect. He should have stopped the war by now.

Taken all round, the two extra years of fighting did little good. They gave only the neutral countries anything on the credit side of their ledgers.

America was slightly involved but her great profits were from her earlier nominal neutrality. She became the great world power, not by national effort, but by the suicide and murder of other world powers. As the only affluent nation in a bankrupt world she was able to dominate the peace settlement which produced a map of Europe carrying the inevitability of war, as had the map of 1914. It is probable that the map made in 1917 would have been better. America was applauded for it as a rich man is applauded by beggars hoping to flatter him into giving a handout.

Of the European neutrals, only Sweden did very well for herself, but her wisdom in avoiding the folly of war may have been at some cost to her self-respect. She certainly felt morally inferior after her second successful neutrality in the next war, and was despised by her Scandinavian neighbours. Her material gains were at a moral cost.

The first years of war had made Russia unstable; the last two years made all mainland Europe belligerents unstable and the world became a mess.

We had made gains in the first years of the war but we had paid a high price. We paid a comparable price for the final two years and they yielded us nothing, absolutely nothing.

1917

—

17
Brothers at War

School was much better this year. Our Middle I moved up to become Upper II–but not all of us. Those old lags who had given us a bad time were all pushed into the 'Shell', a form for those who could not keep up with their age group and needed special treatment to be admitted to the Big School at a reasonable age. They would do easy subjects, not French and Latin, like us, and they would never matriculate. They would end up in Vd; but even then, none would get into any of the school teams and they already had a smell of failure about them. It might be undesirable to do too well at lessons but you should be adequate.

We now felt superior to them, especially on Wednesday afternoons, for they had reached the age of military duties and were in the Junior Cadets and they drilled. That was one good thing about leaving the State School, for now we were regarded as being too young to be of use to our country.

We watched them at it, straggling in lines across the Back Turf and upsetting Willie Watson's pony. He was the only boy still to ride a horse to school. He was also the only boy to have a first name, but it really was not his, he had to put up with it because of the federal politician known as Willie Watt.

That barrel in which the boys were ducked was for the use of the single pony and he really owned the Back Turf. He shared it with us at lunch-time when footballs were kicked about, but he was undisturbed in his corner. But on Wednesday afternoons those Junior Cadets made every corner unsafe and the pony trotted bewildered ahead of the ranks and broke into a gallop when he thought they had him cornered.

That year in Upper II was the best of my eight years at Wesley, for we were now a solid group and the new boys who joined us were just like us; none came from disgustingly rich families and none of us felt badly about our poverty. But it was an indirect result of the war which made it so good.

Before the war it had been essential for the teacher of Upper II to be a man who had recently left school and had played in the football team. Sometimes he was not quite bright enough to face the University, or he would be doing his course part-time and earning his way through, but whichever sort he was, he had been invariably a good teacher and a happy link between school and maturity. All of that sort were now in the army.

Last year, from the time we had pushed through the creaky wooden gate until it clanged behind us in the afternoon, we had been in a part-time monastery. Our Miss Connor of Middle I would have given no worry to any monastery and she was the only female about the place—except for the Head's bull-terrier bitch, Nancy, who had morals which, if she had been human, would have justified the Head's opinion of 'gels'.

Our new teacher was not only a woman, she was a Mrs, and there had never been a Mrs in the school before. She was very feminine, young, under thirty, fresh complexioned with fluffy curly hair. She shamelessly let us know of her home-life; for us home-life was a shaming secret not mentioned at school. The really odd thing about her was that her husband taught at Scotch; only the war could have made a family bridge between the antagonistic schools.

Mrs Tomlinson was a heretic. She did not seem to care if Wesley won the boat race or the football. Last year we had been infantile adolescents; now she treated us as her own thirty little boys. She talked about her home to us, and we met her children. She invited the class to a Saturday afternoon party in the Botanical Gardens with her small son and his sister, a pretty little thing with colouring like her mother. In later years we were to meet kindly masters, but none was to be as intimate with us as was Mrs Tomlinson—I don't think the Head would have liked a master to establish a close bond with his class. That year, Upper II was a cosy harbour safe from the reefs or shoals of school life.

Not only did we get Mrs Tomlinson, but now, or possibly the next year, we got Miss Eastaugh, and the Head had appointed both. It was more dramatic than if the Pope had suddenly ruled that women could celebrate the mass.

Miss Eastaugh not only taught in the Prep; she taught in the lower forms of the Big School. She taught French in a funny sort of way, using a French accent, which was a completely novel thing in a boys' school. She taught for decades and eventually taught the highest French class.

There was another new teacher, Mr Crooks. He was well over military age but we had our suspicions of him. He had been in Europe and knew the world, so we thought he must be a German spy. We called him 'Herr von Crooks' and gave him as bad a time as we could. He was very decent about it and did not send us off to the Head for a bumming-up as often as we deserved, but he was fair game.

Once when the class was playing up, he told me to come to the front and stand facing the blackboard, but it did not settle me. Some people have the power of moving their ears; I was exceptionally gifted and could move each ear independently. Standing in front I was applauded when I waggled each ear in turn; Herr von Crooks had no hope of finding out why the class was still giving trouble.

We of the Six had been embarrassed for Melbourne Grammar with a headmaster of military age who had not enlisted. In February he put things right: MR R. P. FRANKLIN ANSWERS CALL. He got quite a big article in the *Argus*. From the beginning he had been anxious to enlist but his friends and advisers at Grammar had insisted that he would be of more use as a headmaster than as a soldier. Now that conscription had been rejected, there was no compulsion for him to go, but off he went, and the public schools felt better about things. Before the end of the war he rose to the rank of lieutenant.

At church the first Sunday of 1917 was not much different from that of the previous two years. The three Jones brothers stamped in as they had before but now we resented their uniforms. Only one other man of full military age was left in the congregation and he seemed ashamed to be there. Those under twenty-one were getting their parents' consent and joining up.

Young Eddy Shemilt enlisted and that was hard to understand. We thought he was barely sixteen, but he had given his age as twenty-one and his mother was upset. She had only two sons: Jack was not very bright, but Eddy was dashing. She tried to get him out of the army and went to see an officer. He told her that Eddy was so keen that he would run away and enlist somewhere else, so she let him go. I suppose he had had a very bad time with people saying that Shemilt was a German name. In fact, they had come from South Wales and Mrs Shemilt was descended from Captain Hardy, in whose arms Lord Nelson had died at Trafalgar.

Alan Gibbs' brother, Maurice, was eighteen, perhaps rather a harum-scarum sort of chap, but he got his consent, and in he went.

These two were the youngsters, but older men felt the same pressure—men I later knew as solid architects.

Alec Egglestone was thirty-three, married, with three children and a new and thriving practice. He was a particularly religious man whose office had prayers on Fridays. He thought it wrong to kill people, but more wrong to prosper whilst his rivals were doing what they thought was their duty. His partner agreed to keep the practice going and to look after his widowed mother, and he volunteered for the Medical Corps. He was rejected as physically unfit, but this did not stop him. He joined the Y.M.C.A. to serve the troops, but this, of course, did not put his name on any honour board nor earn him any deferred pay. In the next war, his son, married with two children, enlisted at the same age.

John Gawler had returned from America in 1912 with an American wife who was lonely in her new country and when the war started she was pregnant. John Gawler had been one of the party pressing for compulsory military training for everybody else, and now he was at home with his wife. His first daughter was born and his wife thought he should go but she did not like the idea of being left a widow with a child in a strange country. He waited. When his second child was born it was time to go, so off he went into the army. He got five shillings a day, plus the allowance for his wife and two children, but it was a financial sacrifice. He rose to be a sergeant in the Engineers and on his return he organized and administered the new Faculty of Architecture at the University as a part-time lecturer. He was paid £250 a year whilst a professor was paid £1000 for similar duties, and Gawler gave the five or six lectures a week expected of a professor.

Only one Melbourne architect I knew had deliberately avoided service and got a practice going whilst the others were away. No one was very sorry when his practice did not flourish.

The local Royal Victorian Institute of Architects supported its members overseas by sending parcels and recognized their service by putting their names on an honour board in the Council Room and providing memorial chairs and a table. It helped its members on their return, but a lot of the brighter ones did not return.

Harold Griggs of Adelaide, now a very respectable architect, falsified his age and was accepted, but was found out and not allowed to go overseas. He was sent as a guard to a military prison. The prison was inspected by a headquarters major, or someone of that sort. The further from the war, the more martial the appearance; this one was glorious with red tabs and polished riding boots. He came on Griggsy, who, with loaded rifle and fixed bayonet, should have been guarding a prisoner breaking up stones. The bayonet was sticking into the gate, the prisoner was holding the rifle, and they were both sitting on the pile of stones and smoking.

The only way to punish Griggsy was to send him to France – and this was just what he wanted. His transport crossed the Pacific and entered the new Panama Canal. Griggsy knew that his transport would pass a hospital ship with his brother on board – and there it was, tied up at the side to let the transport pass. How would his brother see him among all the hundreds of khaki figures?

The foredeck was out of bounds and empty; his brother would see him there. He would see him better if he stood on something. Giggsy stood on a piece of machinery, and there was a tremendous din and a cloud of rust: Griggsy had anchored his transport in the middle of the canal. He did not see daylight until his ship got to Liverpool.

At home things were easier now that mother was getting the boys' allotment pay regularly and the household numbers were so small, but we were sailing close to the wind and it was worth while picking up odds and ends. Phyllis and Ronnie made quite a bit of money by coaching students for the exams, and even Neil coached boys older than himself; five shillings an hour they got for it.

There was something left to sell. Father had no use for his assaying equipment now that he had no assaying to do, and his platinum beaker would fetch a lot. He took it along to Selby's, the scientific equipment shop, and got £15 after negotiations.

In 1914 Selby's had been Silberberg's. No firm could be expected to prosper with such an obviously German name and it was a mouthful over the telephone. But Silberberg, like a lot of German names, was not German. The Jews of Poland had been required to assume surnames by government order and German-speaking officials had registered them. Sometimes the name was crudely insulting, but usually they were new fabricated names: 'gold', 'silver', 'rose' or some other flower or fruit, with 'garden', 'castle' or 'field' added. Occasionally a slip was made and an existing German name was used. Rosenberg, non-Jewish, was a particularly nasty Jew-baiter in Hitler's time.

The Polish Silberbergs had lived in Victoria since the early days of the gold rush, but in Sydney was a German Silberberg who made the name infamous by flying the German flag at the beginning of the war. He made things awkward for the Sydney branch of the Polish Silberbergs and the name was changed.

The Selbys might have got a more convenient name, but right through the war most of those odd-sounding, German sort of names persisted. The Irish had provided us with leaders in quantity disproportionate to their numbers in our early days; now a similarly disproportionate number was being supplied by the children of European gold-rush migrants, particularly of the Polish Jews. They were prominent in commerce, law and medicine, and in the A.I.F. Monash and his friend, General Rosenthal, were by no means lonely. The list of Wesley's war dead is sprinkled with those names. We regarded them as almost as good as ourselves and better than a lot of other groups.

As well as selling things, we economized on household expenses. We saved on fires. Coal had been the usual fuel for the single fire in the study, but it was getting rare and expensive; we tried a new thing. We sifted the ashes, washed them, drained off the water and after a difficult start, they gave a splendid glowing fire which lasted the whole evening.

Pretty little Sylvia had been a paying guest (not a boarder of course), and the money had been a bit of a help. Someone at the church put mother in touch with the parents of Gordon, a seventeen-year-old from Gippsland; they would like him to live in a good Presbyterian family whilst he did his pre-university year at Wesley. It was hard on Neil. He had the dignity of being in the Honours Sixth, the top form of the school; his cap had a special badge, a tiny lion with a sort of belt all around. Neil, with his dignity, had an older boy in a junior form, going to the same school by the same tram and nothing could hide that he was a 'paying guest'.

Neither of us liked Gordon and I doubt if we would have in any circumstances. I suppose that he was shy, but he was certainly reticent and solitary. Although we all travelled to school on the same tram, we never went with Gordon. We had our regular duties about the house, and Gordon did nothing, not even make his own bed. He was getting his money's-worth out of us.

When we came into the breakfast room at night to do our homework after doing the drying-up, Gordon was already there with a little bag of lollies under his left hand. He sucked them noisily through the evening and never offered us one. If any of us had a bag of lollies it was passed around the family in turn until it was empty. We never offered him anything of ours. It was much happier when he went home for the school holidays.

In March 1917 began the happiest weekly occasion of the war. Friday's tea was over, father had read the chapter of the Bible, and we had all knelt for the Lord's Prayer, the clearaway and drying-up was done and then Neil and I joined the others in the study. Gordon was left sucking his lollies in the cold breakfast room and we were sitting by the warm fire.

The boys all wrote a weekly letter and the overseas mail seemed regular and unfailing. The letters had been delivered in the morning but kept unopened until now. We settled comfortably by the fire.

Ralph Lewis

First came Keith's letter, written in a running hand, breezy and cheerful and very human with no hint of any unpleasantness. Father read
it to us, and put it down and took up Athol's.

Athol had lost his sergeant's stripes and reverted to the rank of gunner,
but he seemed to find life fun. He was in demand as Prisoner's Friend
at court-martials and enjoyed it. Anyone with a reasonably quick mind
and a rudimentary knowledge of the law could change the solemnity
into a farce, and Athol was very successful. He was the one least suited
to army life but seemed to enjoy it most.

Owen Lewis in 1917

Ralph's letters were in a small neat hand; of the four he suffered most from the inhumanity of bulk organization, but was happy with new friends and with the interest of seeing new places.

Owen's writing was very clear, a sort of copperplate. He had left as a lance-corporal and then transferred to the Engineers—the 10th Field Company—and had become a corporal. It was good to be a corporal in the Engineers, for corporals ate in the sergeant's mess, when there was one, and ranked as infantry sergeants. The only difference was a bit less pay and greater vulnerability to the military police—they usually let sergeants alone—but this would not be a great matter to Owen.

That year he had met Keith in France and talked about trying to get into the Flying Corps; Keith thought it a reasonable idea, for it would carry a commission; it was more dangerous, but if your number was coming up it would come up anyway.

Owen was accepted for the Flying Corps and had a spell of training in an Oxford college and was able to get about the country more than the others. He met father's relatives of Bute, on the Clyde, and mother's in Derbyshire, and made friends all over the place.

Sixty years and more afterwards we are still friendly with a Presbyterian family he met in Southampton. His camp had been on Salisbury Plain, at Lark Hill, I think, and he had borrowed a bicycle and ridden a good forty miles into Southampton. Going to church must have been only part of his plan, but he was keen on church and Presbyterian churches were rare in south England. After forty miles in the rain he was soaked. He dried out by sitting on a radiator during the service and this interested the Huttons and he often visited them later. We saw them a lot when they moved to Melbourne after the war.

Those letters which father read to us on Friday were carefully preserved. He got four box-files and pasted 'Keith', 'Athol', 'Ralph' and 'Owen' on the fronts and every week the latest letter was put on top of the others in the file. Each letter was a journal of the week's happenings, and we had them all, from the day when they went into camp until the day they returned. Four personal accounts of the war, all written in a different style and all written vividly. The four files had a fixed place on the top of mother's desk right through the war and after it. There they were, even after the family moved to the new house, right up to mother's death in 1947. Then by accident or intent, someone threw them out without asking the three surviving brothers if they wanted their records of the war. Only a few scraps remain in the pieces copied out for the aunts, and Athol's diary and letters to Elsie.

All four brothers were in danger and we all prayed for them. I certainly did, and in my bed on the balcony I listed to God all the contingencies I asked Him to preserve them from. Mother had her regular daily session in the morning, and probably at other times.

One afternoon she got a shock. She happened to look out of the window; Mr Millar had clanged the front gate and was walking up the curving path to the front door. It must mean tragedy. On their enlistment forms all of them had listed Mr Millar, the parish minister, as the man to break the news in the event of their death. In his short black coat he looked like a raven coming from the field of battle and the piled bodies of the slain. He rang the bell and was shown into the drawing room and mother tried to compose herself before entering.

But Mr Millar was bland and amiable; mother waited for him to get over the preliminaries and get on with it, but he continued bland and amiable. Mother was tense; she suggested a cup of tea, this would hurry him up; he accepted, drank his tea and rose to go. He went. No bad news after all, not this time, just a normal parish visit. He had no idea of the anxiety he had caused. Mother asked that he be good enough to telephone before his next visit.

We, in Australia, felt very deeply about the war but our interpretation of the newspapers gave us different views from those in Britain on the Irish question. We read the paragraphs taken from the London papers and they did not convince us. We thought Ireland should have Home Rule at once and should have had it years ago. More: we thought it should be Home Rule for all Ireland and not just the Catholic south; we knew that the Catholic minority here was in about the same proportion as the Protestant minority in Ireland and it had got on quite well with us until the Irish troubles of last year. We thought that the Ulstermen with their assumption of being ultra-patriotic were, in fact, mere troublesome dissidents, and very nearly rebels, and were doing a lot of harm to the war effort. It hurt us that the wildest group was called Presbyterian and they were primitive and savage, not bland and broad-minded like us; we were embarrassed by them. Give Home Rule to Ireland without any strings and let us get on with our war against the Germans, and not the Irish.

Last year's conscription referendum would have been won if it had had substantial Irish support; the silly military shootings in Dublin had alienated Irish opinion there – and ours as well.

On 4 January we read that Sir Edward Carson had been made First Lord of the Admiralty. It seemed odd to us but shocking to the Irish Nationalists. Admittedly he was a very capable man, but he was the leader of the group proposing resistance, if not rebellion, against the British government, and now he had been made a member of that government. It looked as if the policy was no longer Home Rule for all Ireland.

Then in February we read that Sir Roger Casement – we still thought of him as 'Sir' – had left his entire estate to his sister and it amounted to £135. It had seemed unnecessary to hang such an unpractical romanticist, but he had been hanged. His small estate hinted that he had been rather a pathetic little man and no figure of terror: his name was now added to the list of martyrs shot by the military in Dublin in 1916.

On 10 March: HOME RULE CRISIS. SENSATION IN COMMONS. NATIONALISTS WALK OUT. EFFECT OF LLOYD GEORGE'S SPEECH. Lloyd George had been a member of the Liberal Cabinet which had promoted and passed the Home Rule Bill and now, as Prime Minister of the coalition government, he was withholding it.

In the debate Australia was quite important. Mr Devlin asked whether the Australian Senate had passed a resolution in favour of Home Rule for Ireland by 28 votes to 2–and if so, would the ministry give due weight to this expression of Australian opinion? Mr Lloyd George replied that no official information had reached the government.

Mr O'Connor moved, 'That, for the purpose of strengthening the hand of the Allies in achieving recognition of the equal rights of small nations against the German principle of military domination, and of government without the consent of the governed, it is essential to confer Home Rule on Ireland without delay'. We thought that Mr O'Connor had something there.

On 10 May: IRISH PROBLEM. CHURCH OPPOSES PARTITIONING. The Catholic Church in Ireland had been a moderate supporter of Home Rule. Now three archbishops and fifteen bishops, together with three Protestant bishops, were asking for Home Rule for a united Ireland–and from a British point of view, they had more sense than the Ulstermen.

The Irish Protestants had an empire outlook and were even something like an English garrison. Although there were not many of them in the south and west, they were some balance against the Sinn Fein, and behind them was the powerful support of the Protestants in the north. If Ireland was divided, they would become weak and isolated, just as would the Catholics in the north, and the extremists would become more unrestrained in both the north and the south.

The war was not going too well and it was getting very dull. Then came the last new atrocity of the Germans–admittedly they were carrying on with their old atrocities, but this was to be the last new one. GERMANS AND THEIR DEAD. PRUSSIAN CORPSE FACTORY.

> No horror in the war excited such universal indignation as the announcement that factories had been established in Germany for extracting oils, fats and pig food from the bodies of German soldiers killed on the battlefield. When the statement was first made most people refused to believe it. We had long known that the Germans stripped their dead behind the firing line, fastened them into bundles of three or four bodies with iron wire, and then dispatched the grisly bundles to the rear for extraction at Seraing, near Liège–and everything else was ground down in the bone mills into a powder which was used for mixing with pigs' food and manure. The Germans made no secret about it and published an article on the factory in a Berlin paper.

Of course the Germans denied it. They said the article had described a mill where the bodies of mules were transformed into oil and that 'the anti-German propaganda is the acme of stupidity'.

But some still believed it in 1918. In the Australian advance a dug-out by the entrance to the St Quentin Canal tunnel was found to have a domestic copper with bits of Germans in it, all ready for boiling up. This domestic copper was a corpse factory.

Keith saw it and wrote home; he said that a shell had caught the dug-out and in tidying up afterwards, fragments of bodies had been put in the copper and it was not even a small-scale factory. Father sent a copy of the letter to the *Argus* and it was published, but we still believed in corpse-factories.

The war produced a new sort of story which all enjoyed and shared. Every one of us enjoyed the war stories and we ten- and eleven-year-olds were told them by the grown ups.

An American was sitting in a train in England, reading in the paper about some tremendous battle in France. He was excited; he tapped the knee of the Englishman opposite; 'Some fight', he said. The Englishman looked up, and replied, 'Some don't.' We thought that the Americans should be in our war.

In 1914 our overwhelming strength had made us think it would be an easy and quick war; now our victory seemed remote. Our allies had been knocked right out, or broken, and the Russian steamroller seemed to have run out of fuel. America was our last hope and she should join us in destroying the evil of Germany. The U.S.A. owed us a lot. Our war was making America prosperous and she should do something to help. Our war was to destroy Germany's supremacy in commerce and we were deliberately transferring our claims to America. Those shipments of gold – forty tons in one go – were sapping the foundations of sterling as the world's standard currency and building up the dollar in its place.

America was for the Allies. Nearly all her war news came from London, for the British controlled the Atlantic cables. Her European trade was controlled by the British, and English was the language of the country.

But it was not as easy as all that. The Germans in America were the biggest minority group; they were very respectable and also politically powerful, especially in the Middle West and around the Great Lakes where Milwaukee was a German city.

The Allies' blockade was giving slight offence to America compared to the German counter-blockade. Those Americans drowned in the *Lusitania* were still remembered, and the submarines were still sinking American ships. The Germans were in an awkward position; submarines were the most fragile of ships and it was dangerous for them to surface to ask questions. We knew of one which had been sunk by an armed British ship flying the Stars and Stripes, but we had not heard of any protest by America about the misuse of her flag.

Then the British did something refreshingly effective. They intercepted and decoded a message to Mexico from von Zimmerman, the German Foreign Minister. On 2 March: GERMAN PLOT AIMED AT AMERICA. OFFER TO MEXICO AND JAPAN. SENSATION AT WASHINGTON. Mexico was to come in with Germany if America came in with the Allies, and was to use her influence to get Japan in as well.

Japan had collected her payment for joining in: she already held the German bases in China and the northern Pacific Islands. Now Germany might be able to give her more.

Mexico was promised Texas, New Mexico and Arizona. All three were now States of the Union, even if the last two had only got in in 1911 and 1912; they were the first-fruits of America's wars of expansion.

The first war of expansion, aimed at the annexation of Canada, had been a disgraceful failure, especially because, at the time, Britain had been fully stretched as the only nation standing against Napoleon. But Mexico had been weakened by attempts at internal reform and had no overseas country to help her. In 1848 the U.S.A. won the war and extended her frontiers down to the Rio Grande. Apart from winning the war, she had paid fifteen million dollars for this great slice of the continent.

The American public was incensed at the thought that the three States might again become part of Mexico. In Texas it would mean that local Mexican police would be allowed to arrest whites, as well as Mexicans and Negroes. In a nation based on the theory that all men were born equal, this was worse than imagining that the President could be a Jew or a Catholic.

This Mexico was the nation which the United States had blockaded in 1914; she had made a needlessly brutal naval attack on her main port of Santa Cruz and occupied it for six months, in order to bring down a government of which she did not approve. The President of the time, Wilson, was the very same man who would insist on the sovereign rights of the newly erected nations of Europe.

The Zimmerman message gave President Wilson and the pro-Allied party what it needed. On 8 April: AMERICA AT WAR. CONGRESS DECIDES. SWEEPING MAJORITIES. INTERNED SHIPS SEIZED. The President signed the joint resolution and orders went out for mobilization.

It was just as well, for now America replaced Russia in our hopes. No encouraging news had come from that country lately, and what there was was sparse and confused; our hope was that she was using the winter lull to build up her strength.

On 12 March: RASPUTIN MURDERED. We had heard nothing of him since just before the war; then he got a lot of space in our papers when a woman had tried to stab him to death. It was explained that he was a 'Miracle Working Monk' at the Russian court where he had the support of the Tsarina. There was no scandal there: she trusted him to help her son, who was a very sick boy, a 'bleeder'; the safety of Russia depended on his being fit enough to inherit the throne.

Rasputin was a hefty man of forty with a big black beard and the most unclerical appetites and morals. He was important politically. The Russians had no House of Lords for redundant politicians and were obliged to assassinate them, but Rasputin proved difficult to dispose of. He had drunk enough poison to kill an elephant and it had not worried him. This time, although unarmed, he had put up a tremendous struggle before the gang of aristocratic assassins had been able to finish him off.

The Tsarina had been a German princess and she and Rasputin were supposed to head the pro-German party which was held to be responsible for the lack of Russian success. We felt that it was a good thing that Rasputin had been murdered.

On 16 March:

REVOLT IN RUSSIA

THE CZAR ABDICATES

Pro-Germans Overthrown

War Fervour Unaffected

ENCOURAGING OUTLOOK

This was a bit sudden. We had learned that the Tsar was a good chap, perhaps a bit simple, but doing his best; Russia might still do something really big in the war, like she did last year. The Tsar's brother was to be Regent and the Tsarina would not be able to hinder things. Bonar Law, not a very grand figure, but the leader of the British Conservatives in Lloyd George's coalition government, said, 'the discontent in Russia is not due to any desire for peace but because the people are not satisfied that the war is being conducted with sufficient energy'. And after all, the British Prime Minister had got the sack some months before for not being energetic enough. Now in Russia the pro-Allied leader had been made head of a provisional government.

Somehow it was not convincing. It was comforting to think that the Russians were still keen on fighting the Germans—even though they were not doing too well and having a lot of men killed—but it seemed drastic to make such a violent change in the middle of the war.

The news was confusing. In the political upset 'there had been no serious loss of life'; then a bit later: 'There were many civilian casualties'. M. Sturmer, who had been Prime Minister some months ago, had been murdered; the headquarters of the Secret Police had been burnt down and police stations had been looted.

But 'Washington officials' said 'it was the greatest democratic victory of the century, ensuring, as it will, closer political sympathy with the democratic ideals of the Allies and a more tenacious prosecution of the war to liberate Europe'.

Yes, it was all right. Next day it was RUSSIA. SPEEDY VICTORY AIMED AT and on 23 March BRUSILOFF APPEALS TO TROOPS. Brusiloff was the only successful Russian general that we knew about, and the army would certainly support him.

In April we read: RUSSIAN PEOPLE WANT A REPUBLIC. Natural enough, but it would make for confusion, and what about the Regent of Russia? In May: RUSSIA'S DUTY. 'WAR TO VICTORY'. NO ALLIANCE WITH GERMANY. On 28 May: GLOOMY OUTLOOK. ARMY RETREATING IN ARMENIA. KERENSKY THE ONLY HOPE. Who was Kerensky, anyway?

But two days later: WILL ARMY FIGHT? PROSPECTS IMPROVING. On 2 June: HOPEFUL SIGNS. SOLDIERS RETURNING TO FRONT. 'We are going to fight, not fraternise'. We had heard nothing about any fraternization; it may be that some of the Russians were getting friendly with the Germans. On 6 June: KRONSTADT. REVOLT AT NAVAL BASE. That did not sound very good, but GOOD NEWS OF THE ARMY. MORE THAN EVER IRRESISTIBLE. On 15 June: RUSSIA NO SEPARATE PEACE. DEFEAT OF EXTREMISTS. So the Russians had mastered that group who wanted peace.

We need not have worried. On 5 July: RUSSIAN BLOW. AUSTRIAN ARMY REELS and it was BRUSILOFF AGAIN, just like a year ago. 'The Austrian line has been definitely broken and our advance continues. General Brusiloff has ordered the entire Russian army to prepare'.

The Russian provisional government suggested that the Allies should reconsider their conditions for peace. That seemed very reasonable, now that Russia was so shaky, and the British government said it would communicate with other Allies. Its representative in Petrograd said that Russia was not yet ready for socialism and should 'cooperate with the bourgeoisie in order to secure freedom's triumph'.

By the end of July Petrograd was quieter, the Cossacks had fought the mob. Against that was to be set the fact that the rebel sailors from Kronstadt had entered the fortress of St Peter and St Paul.

Next day, the 24th, there was mutiny in the army and Kerensky went to the front. After their advance against Austria, the army was retreating and Kerensky had been wounded; it was RUSSIA'S HOUR OF TRIAL. They were still fighting the Germans; there was a women's battalion and it had captured a hundred prisoners. The Russian workmen and soldiers' delegates issued a manifesto, saying that 'there was a serious defect in the army and general panic, preparing the poisonous seeds of counter-revolution, and the terrible break in the front had been caused by open treachery and mutiny'. So the Russian revolutionaries were still going to fight the Germans.

But things got no better. By the middle of August it was WHY RUSSIA COLLAPSED. ARMY DISCIPLINE ABOLISHED. THE COMEDY OF MILITARY FREEDOM. The Russians abandoned Riga and the new Commander-in-Chief, Korniloff, resigned. Then, chaos: RUSSIAN CRISIS. A GRAVE SITUATION. Russia was on the verge of civil war and Korniloff made himself dictator.

Then things looked up. UNEXPECTED GOOD NEWS. Russia had made an advance on the Riga front and there was not going to be a separate peace with Germany. But there was still a muddle. Alexieff resigned before we knew who he was or what he had resigned from. By the beginning of October it was TURMOIL. FIGHT WITH EXTREMISTS. KERENSKY'S SUPREME HOUR. On 8 October: THREAT OF CIVIL WAR. But M. Trodzky, a Maximalist, said that although civil war was unavoidable, his party would not forcibly seize power. The Russians, occupied with the internal struggle of the October Revolution, could no longer take an effecive part in the war.

A lot of people with German names had tried to hide their shame by changing them to high-sounding English ones; it saved them from casual public insult but their old acquaintances remembered. I fancy more changed their names in England than here, but that is only an impression. All our old German friends kept theirs; at church Mr Schneider and Mr Himmer persisted, and so did Mr Hartung, the music teacher in Malvern. Aunty Dora, now a widow, was still Mrs Kussmaul.

At Wesley, Fokken had enlisted under his own name in 1914, but he evidently found it to be a nuisance in the army and changed it to Falkiner when he transferred to the Flying Corps. Amongst the names of the fallen cut in the marble slabs at the entrance to the assembly hall, Fokken appears – that was the name he was known by at school – and there are quite a lot of German names as well as his.

By the middle of 1917 it was difficult to get into the army with a German name, despite the urgent call for men. A Ballarat man who had enlisted was discharged because of his name; when he was said to be a spy he brought a libel action and won, and the Minister for the Defence said that he could enlist all over again.

Place-names were another matter. When the war began the capital of Russia was St Petersburg, in the German form. Now it was Petrograd, the Russian form; finally it would be Leningrad. In Australia in 1914 some enthusiasts wanted to change the name of the suburb of Heidelberg, but the move was derided in the papers and the name has persisted.

A few place-names were changed in Victoria, but South Australia did a thorough job. The Nomenclature Act of 1917 changed forty-two of them. Blumberg became Birdwood; Germantown, Vimy Ridge; Hamburg, Haig; Kritchauff, Beatty. The Chief Secretary suggested that Kaiserstuhl Hill should become Mount Lord Kitchener, rather a mouthful, but the wines from there still carry the old name: no one has yet drunk a Mount Lord Kitchener claret or hock. Two little creeks, the North and South Rhine, became the Marne and the Somme; if the blood which had flowed beside those rivers could have flowed down the creeks, it would have made the biggest flood in their histories. It might not have been entirely necessary to change the name of Bergen, for after all, it was Norwegian, but it had a German sound about it.

At the end of July our King set an example. He summoned a special meeting of the Privy Council and signed a proclamation relinquishing all his German titles, and those of his relations in England, and changing his family name to Windsor. One of those attending was Mr Schreiner, the South African High Commissioner. We had never thought of our king needing a surname like us ordinary people, but it seemed that it had been Wettin, a branch of the house of Saxe-Coburg-Gotha.

A sense of humour was not something which we attributed to the Kaiser, but he rose to the occasion, or so it was said. It seems that the

Germans were still broad-minded enough to stage English classical drama. The Kaiser ordered the production at the State Theatre of Shakespeare's *Merry Wives of Saxe-Coburg-Gotha.*

Those Protestant Irish patriots were as embarrassing as the other sort of Irish.

Dr Leeper had used his position on the University Council to try to purge the University of all German contamination, to rid it of German textbooks and staff of German origin; now he wanted all students of military age out of the University and into the army.

The war was very serious in 1917. Leeper wanted to know why all German schools had not been closed – this meant Lutheran schools; he wanted to know the number of undergraduates who had enlisted, and who hadn't. He ordered a census of those who had entered the University that year.

There were thirty-three below the age of twenty-one, who needed parental consent before enlisting; there were thirty-three over the age of twenty-one, and this figure included medical rejects and returned soldiers. In all, it did not seem to be enough to make a fuss about, but he got Council to put up notices in all departments 'Urging upon men students the duty of rendering to the Empire all personal service of which they are capable'.

We did not want our Ronnie to go off to the war – not yet anyhow, not until we knew more about the other four brothers. Yet Ronnie at the University was getting Leeper's full blast.

Leeper had two sons of military age who did not require parental consent: Alexander, aged thirty, and Reginald, twenty-nine. The nearest they got to France was the Office of Information in London, where they were of much more use than if they had been in the trenches. Perhaps some in the University were better where they were.

18
Famous Friends

We were a middling sort of family but we seemed to know a lot of prominent people.

In father's time at the University the students had been a smug group. It was quite sure of its importance and so exclusive as to have its own songs, which others were not allowed to sing. 'There is a Tavern in the Town' was bohemian, and better suited to the old universities of Europe than to our puritanical colonial one; 'Riding Down to Bangor' was an American student song and rather daring; there were also some jolly ones of local origin. These songs were still University property fifty years later.

The group was so small that all knew each other personally and father was still friendly with handfuls of men in other professions and, of course, there were his particular friends, Arthur Lynch and John Monash.

Arthur Lynch was now being rivalled as the most prominent Australian in London by Oscar Asche, the Shakespearian actor, whose Othello had been reckoned as the greatest of the time. He was not German, as his name might suggest, but Norwegian, and as a young man had gone to study drama in Oslo, then called Christiania.

Father had once known him and we knew his family. I think his brother was a Presbyterian medical missionary; a niece was a friend of Phyllis at the University and her family lived near us on the Toorak side. Father had known Oscar when they were boys of about twelve and both boarding at some little school in South Melbourne; his diary described him as being a fat and greedy boy.

Asche had turned actor-manager and had staged the two most successful spectacular shows of the time: *Chu Chin Chow* and *Kismet*, both typical of Edwardian opulence. *Chu Chin Chow* had been revived after its first run to become a real part of the war. The Tommies would go to music-halls on their leave; officers on their last night would dine expensively and then go to *Chu Chin Chow* and lose themselves in its romantic glitter. The next night they would be shivering in the trenches, only seventy miles away. The Edwardian age was sinking in the mud of Flanders.

I saw Oscar Asche when he staged *Chu Chin Chow* in Melbourne a couple of years after the war, a man with a presence but bald, and so fat that the only Shakespearian part which would accommodate him was Falstaff.

Mother had met and known the greatest Australian of all. She had been a boarder at Miss Wigmore's superior school for young ladies until she had to leave in a hurry when her father over-spent. She had been friends there with the Mitchell girls. She visited their home where they all resented being told to keep quiet whilst Nellie sang. Nellie was now our Dame Nellie Melba.

Then there was Harry Power, the bushranger, who had been the handyman about the place when father's family lived on the mine at Whroo. He worked well except for occasional absences on his real job of horse-stealing. He was a very gentle sort of bushranger and a lot of people were sorry when he was taken off to gaol. Some said that his pupil, Ned Kelly, had betrayed him to the police, but this was probably wrong.

Father's people knew the Kelly family, although they were not on visiting terms. Aunt Katie, who had met Ned when she was out riding, spoke highly of his good manners.

One Sunday afternoon a group of friends visited grandfather and tethered their horses to the fence; someone noticed them and assumed that the Kelly gang was holding up the house and organized a group to capture the gang.

Another family story is that there was a tip-off that the Kellys were going to hold up the wagon with the month's gold aboard. As it came down the hill, the driver whipped the horses to rush the slope on the other side—and a wheel came off. Fortunately there were no bushrangers about.

We got to know a man who was to become great and already showed signs of it. Phyllis became engaged to Bob Menzies. How could it have happened? Phyllis herself seemed surprised and her friends were astonished. Few people could have less in common, for Phyllis was flippant and impertinent and Bob was massive and dignified.

He had been at Wesley for a couple of years at the same time as my elder brothers, but had not been a great figure there. He was there to learn and to do well at his exams—and he did. He did not waste his time in playing games in the manner prescribed by the headmaster.

At the University he was a big fish in a pool depleted of males by the war; most of the males who were there were waiting to enlist at the end of the year. He was president of most things at the University, including the Students' Christian Union.

He was leading the union in prayer at a lunch-hour meeting and Phyllis and Norah Crawford went up to the gallery and squirted him with water-pistols borrowed from Neil and me. The angry Christians swarmed out of their meeting and up the stairs, but Phyllis and Norah had got clear, leaving a cup of water and a pistol behind a nice lame girl who was sitting on the stairs by herself in quiet study. Bob would not think this sort of thing funny.

Bob was efficient in everything he did—coldly efficient. He could shape a poem and handle metre better than most, but poetry was beyond him; he was unable to strip off his defensive armour and expose his innermost thoughts.

He was a keen amateur soldier and was a corporal in the University Rifles and in September 1914 he published a sonnet in the *Magazine* on the departure of the first troops overseas:

> 'Farewell, brave hearts'. The simple words proclaim
> The passage of swift years, and the swift leap
> Of worlds to arms . . .

Admittedly it was rigid and used the clichés of academic verse of the time, a type of verse which would become out-moded in the later horror of the war, but it demonstrated his exuberant loyalty.

This was what was puzzling. He displayed a pre-Boer War loyalty to England and to the Crown, then, as throughout his career, but he showed no signs of wanting to enlist.

It is impossible to recapture the feeling of the time. Today it would seem very reasonable that a family with two sons in danger should feel that it had given enough, but the public then had no such feeling.

In the next war there would have been no fuss about a man in Bob's position not enlisting, and anyone with his capacity could be sure of walking into a respectable 'reserved occupation' where he would be of more value to the community than in the army.

Bob continued in the University Rifles where most of the others were doing preliminary training before they entered the army. He became a lieutenant, which was creditable, and finally became a captain, which was very rare for a student, but he did not enlist.

He entered the Students' Union in his grand new uniform and what somebody said is still remembered after all those years. 'C'est magnifique, mais ce n'est pas la guerre'. He is credited with saying that his brains were too good for cannon fodder, but I have not come across anyone who personally heard this.

Bob Menzies remains a puzzle; there were few better natural soldiers. One story is that a family meeting decided that his two elder brothers should go provided Bob stayed at home with his parents. But one Friday, Athol's letter from France said that he had met one of the Menzies boys who asked him to write to Bob suggesting that he should enlist; Athol did not because he would not meddle with the affairs of another family. That letter has been destroyed but my memory is clear and has family support.

I believe that Bob had a deep reason for not going but could not reveal it without hurting others. I believe that he deliberately damaged his career knowing that he was making a sacrifice in so doing.

It told against him from the outset of his political career and it brought him down when he was Prime Minister for the first time at the outbreak of World War II. He had returned soldiers of capacity in his Cabinet, and as returned soldiers, they rebelled.

Mother and father were puzzled by him. He seemed to have all that a future son-in-law should have; he came of a respectable Presbyterian family and was clearly going to be a success. They approved of Phyllis's engagement but felt constraint.

The brothers in France all knew Bob to some degree, and my memory is that they approved without any great enthusiasm. Athol, however, always liked him.

Neil and I liked Bob a lot. He showed no stiff dignity with us and was easy and natural; he did not condescend but dealt with us in an adult sort of way, and was good fun. Neil remarked that the bell of the Church of England opposite could not be secured from the local boys and challenged Bob. Bob rang it, an action quite out of character with his reserve towards adults.

Ronnie gave some trouble over the engagement, perhaps because he was suffering from pressure to enlist and resented Bob's apparent complacency. One Sunday night after tea Ronnie suggested music, and music meant singing. Phyllis unwillingly played the accompaniment; Bob's robust baritone in the drawing room was really something, and as we were all tone-deaf, we enjoyed it immensely.

Bob did his best, but never fitted easily into the family. That August, broke as we were, we took a small house at Mornington for 7s 6d a week. We lived carefully and often caught fish for our main meal. It was winter and boats could be hired for 2s for two hours. There we were, mother, Phyllis, Ronnie, Neil and me, all pulling in flatheads in dozens in sight of the Mornington pier, when we saw Bob waiting on the pier. We pulled up the lines and rowed back to the pier to load on Bob, city clothes and all. We went back to our fishing, but it was choppy and Bob felt sick, so we had to pull up the lines again and row back to the pier. We lost a good half-hour and a lot of fish. We were embarrassed because Bob was embarrassed. He seemed ashamed that his seemingly formidable figure had been brought down by a petty physical weakness which lesser people did not have.

We accepted that Bob and Phyllis were engaged but it did not seem quite real; there was no obvious affection between them and none seemed to develop. Both were prominent at the University and there was the air of an arranged dynastic marriage; time seemed to draw them further apart but neither took action to end it.

It happened suddenly. On the first Friday of July Ralph's letter sounded very good. He had got a safe job at the headquarters of his Tunnelling Company. On Monday came the notification that he had been severely wounded. It was six weeks before Keith's letter gave details. He wrote that Ralph had a lot of wounds and the worst was in the leg, but that the leg was likely to be saved.

It would be Ralph who caught it badly; he had no luck. Like Athol he had no wish to go into the army, but whilst Athol seemed to enjoy it all, particularly getting out of trouble with silly people, Ralph just suffered them.

His luck was really bad. He had passed his officers' training course before going overseas as a corporal, but had reverted to sapper on joining his unit. Owen had been promoted in France but there was no vacancy for Ralph, despite his holding acting rank in the absence of some N.C.O., so he was wounded as a sapper.

But his luck had not been all bad. He was always diffident and, when his party ran for shelter in a cellar in a heavy bombardment, he had hung back. A shell got the cellar and he was the only wounded survivor.

His luck still held after he was wounded. He was taken to a Belgian hospital, for his company was in the Belgian sector of the extreme left of the line, and there he was a curiosity as the only Australian. The French and Belgians competed to be in the next beds and there was a solitary Australian sister who looked after him. Keith visited him and took the sister back to unit headquarters for tea.

Then after two weeks his bad luck returned and he was fit to be moved to the big British hospital at St Omer. There he was just one more to be moved out as quickly as possible, alive or dead.

He developed a temperature of 105° and syphilis was diagnosed, and it really would have been something if Ralph had collected it. He was isolated by himself in a tent in the cold with very occasional visits from an orderly, but eventually, a medical officer did turn up.

Of course it was not syphilis, it was trench fever. He was moved back to a ward, and that was almost as bad. He had his high temperature for days and the only thing given him to eat was bread and mutton dripping, and all the time, all day and every day, a gramophone played the same single record of Harry Lauder.

But at last he was moved from St Omer, rather worse than when he had entered that hospital, and sent to Harefield, outside London, which was much better. He could not get out of bed but his neighbour, who could walk, borrowed his Australian uniform as it made him more successful with the girls about the place.

Then Owen was wounded. He had been wounded once before, but this time it was more serious.

He was in France with the Australian Flying Corps—but it may have been included in the British Corps, for his name did not appear in our published Australian casualty lists. Athol's letter gave us the first details and then Owen's gave more.

He was flying as an observer and his pilot had taken off on a misty morning and climbed up into the clear sunlight leaving the smokey lines of trenches hidden below.

'God's in his heaven, all's right with the world'—Owen normally did not quote poetry. There came a sudden burst of machine-gun fire and things were not right.

Thirty German planes hunting in a pack had dived on to his slower plane; the pilot got it back, shot full of holes. There were twenty-six holes in Owen and he had lost a couple of toes.

Owen, as an officer, did rather better in hospital than Ralph had. He had quite an interesting time. The man in the next bed had lived in India and believed in reincarnation—that after a man died his soul would move into another body. In his letters, Owen showed that he was impressed. I heard mother and father discussing it. If Owen, the most formally religious one of the family, thought there was something in it, it should not be condemned. It was against church doctrine; but was it?

After Christ had been transfigured on the mountain, He asked His disciples who they thought He was. They replied, 'John the Baptist, Elias, Jeremiah, or one of the prophets.' So the disciples thought that Christ might be a reincarnation of an earlier leader. Apparently Christ had not thought their theory odd, and could almost be said to have given it tacit approval.

But the Church had not built on those words and reincarnation had not become one of our doctrines, although we had others with less foundation. Reincarnation might be quite reasonable, but we would do nothing about it and we hoped that Owen would get it out of his system.

Then Athol was in hospital for a couple of weeks, but not because of anything the Germans had done. It was thought he had appendicitis, but he did not have even that.

There was no hiding that things were not going well in Russia, and things in France were little better. Joffre had kept our approval for the first years of the war and had seen our General French get kicked out. Joffre was a rough peasant sort of man, unshaken in adversity and promising victory; a jovial chap, elderly and plump with a great fat white moustache. His promised victories had not come; perhaps he was not going to provide them after all.

A new hope: Joffre was replaced by Nivelle, a much younger and brisker man who had done very well at Verdun. We liked the look of him. Best of all, he was a Protestant, a sort of outlandish Presbyterian; nothing but good could come out of his appointment.

Nivelle let us know that he had the key to winning the war; we heard about it, even in Australia. He made no secret of it; he would do it with the French, without British aid, and all the glory would go to France. He was going to make an irresistible attack. The Germans were as interested as we were.

The long-advertised attack was made but the Germans had quietly fallen back to strong defence positions and there was a deadly muddle. We were dispirited and so were the French but we did not know then how dispirited they were; we knew nothing of the widespread mutinies which wrecked the French armies.

Perhaps the despair was the reason for the Third Battle of Ypres, just something to keep the Germans occupied – for if Haig was choosing a place for a battle he could not have picked one where conditions were worse for attack and gains from a victory would be so slight.

Ypres was the place where things were tried out for the first time. At first Ypres in 1914, trench fighting started; at second Ypres in 1915 the Germans used gas for the first time.

Third Ypres, 1917, really started very well. The Messines Ridge dominated the area and we captured it; it was a success, a preliminary to the victory we expected later, and it was the nearest thing to a big victory up to that date.

On 7 June, after seven days of intense barrages and no worry about any surprise, we blew up nineteen great mines and wrecked large sections of the German lines.

We had been tunnelling under the ridge for two years. Keith, Ralph, and the 2nd Tunnelling Company had worked there.

Tunnelling was not as secret as all that, for signs were hard to hide above ground. If a tunnel was started by one side, the other would counter-tunnel to intercept it and blow it up before it could do any damage. Both sides had listeners to catch the noise of tunnelling, and all the time men with microphones in quiet places listened for any enemy noise. If they heard something, a drive would be made towards it. The 2nd Tunnellers got right on to a German sap and could look into it, and this was very interesting; the second-in-command was called down to see the curiosity, whereupon he panicked and fired his revolver into the German sap and gave the game away. He was the brother-in-law of the commanding officer and got a medal.

Ralph said that the German tunnels were really rough affairs, with uneven levels, untidy and crude, not at all typical of the notoriously tidy Germans.

Sometimes a raid was made above ground to capture the head of a tunnel and our cousin Archie sent a copy of an English paper describing 'The Most Successful Raid of the War'. It was by the London Scottish and Keith accompanied them. When the tunnel-head was captured Keith went down and set charges to destroy the tunnel. All the London Scottish officers got decorations, but Keith missed out.

At Messines every German must have known that he was sitting on top of a lot of mines which would go up when we pressed the plunger, and it cannot have been a nice feeling.

Up went the mines and the noise was heard in England. The infantry advanced and overran the whole wrecked front defences and kept going in the face of stiffening resistance. The ridge was captured and the New Zealanders cleaned up the whole intricate fortification system. The Australians were there too, and so was an Irish division fighting alongside one from Ulster.

It was a short battle. By 4 o'clock it was over with all objectives gained and 7000 prisoners, and of course, a lot of other German casualties. There were only feeble counter-attacks, and when a big one came next day, it failed. The Messines Ridge was in our hands and we were in a fine position for the real start of the Third Battle Ypres.

Lloyd George, like many in England, was appalled by the losses which had brought so little gain, but he was a civilian and the military were fighting the war and Haig was the leader. Haig promised victory and agreed that he would only attack in partnership with the French and stop if there was a severe check. He knew of the mutinies in the French armies and the government did not. The French were in no position to do anything much and gave notice that they could not join in. Haig kept that to himself.

The objective was supposed to be the German submarine bases thirty-five miles away on the Belgian coast. The biggest previous advance had been about six miles when the Germans were falling back to strongly prepared positions.

There were two months of preparation for an obvious attack; it was almost as well advertised as that on the Dardanelles. There was shelling by day and night, 4½ tons of shells for every yard of the German line. Off went the infantry on 31 July and an advance was made. The Germans were not greatly worried about their front trenches, for behind them was a novel defence system in depth composed of concrete machine-gun posts and safe shelters.

On 1 August: NEW OFFENSIVE IN WEST FLANDERS. ALLIES BEGIN WELL. But the days passed and we were told of no new gains. They kept plugging away until each attack dissolved in slaughter. Fresh attacks were made where there had been failure. Fresh troops came up through the mud and attacked through the wire with the dead of earlier attacks still hanging on it.

Here we were told nothing of it, but in England there must have been a fair idea with the great casualty lists and the flow of wounded to hospitals; but a lot of wounded never got to hospitals, they just died in no-man's-land. The British army was bleeding itself to death. After the war we read survivors' accounts of the utter hopelessness and misery of men being sent to their deaths. Haig's dispatches told of happy victories.

On 1 September: NEW BRITISH ATTACK. VALUABLE POSITIONS TAKEN. But we could not see them on our maps. On 21 September: HAIG'S NEW ATTACK A 'GREAT SUCCESS'. VALUABLE POSITIONS TAKEN. We still could not find them. On 6 October: HAIG HITS. A TERRIFIC BLOW. VICTORY EVERYWHERE. FIGHT FOR THE LAST RIDGE. The casualty lists in Britain and Australia showed the price which had been paid.

On 13 October: HAIG'S LATEST ATTACK. CHECKED BY HEAVY RAIN. It was not checked for long; they moved again on 26 October with the mud jamming the rifles and Lewis guns, but, at least, muffling the shell bursts. The Canadians reached the site of Passchendaele and it was the end. Passchendaele, once the name of a harmless village; now a word for futile slaughter.

The submarine bases were still thirty miles away; the gain of five miles had cost 244 897 casualties and 75 000 dead. The Tyne Cot cemetery at Passchendaele has 11 512 graves with names and 8366 of unrecognized bodies; there was not enough left of about 34 500 to merit even an unknown grave. Liddell-Hart says that 'in the swamps of Passchendaele was squandered the faith which founded an empire'.

Haig had blamed his previous lack of success on his shortage of artillery; at Third Ypres he could not advance because he had too much of it: men and tanks could not get over the shell-tortured mud. It was unsuitable for men and impossible for tanks, and both men and tanks were being knocked about.

Four days after the opening of the battle, on 3 August, Colonel Fuller at Tank Headquarters wrote, 'From a tank point of view the Third Ypres is dead, present conditions will not only lead to good machines and better personnel being thrown away, but also to a loss of morale by infantry and tank crews through constant failure'. Fuller then proposed a different use for tanks, a revival of the old cavalry raid, for tanks were a new sort of cavalry immune from rifle and machine-gun fire. The raid he proposed was 'to destroy enemy personnel and guns, to demoralise and disorganise and not capture ground'. It would last only eight to ten hours, to allow no time for the organization of counter-attacks. It was to be a real tank raid with only one division of infantry to tidy up, and some extra artillery.

What Fuller proposed was not tried, but the Germans used the scheme in 1940 and disorganized and demoralized the British and French armies, and all other armies they came across.

It might have worked in 1917, for Byng, the Army Commander, approved of it. He went along to Haig, and he approved the plan; then they changed it, the professional experts took it over. Instead of a raid it was turned into a frontal attack and ground was to be captured. Cambrai was to be taken by six infantry divisions supported by 381 tanks.

Off went the attack over land suitable for tanks. It was a surprise and a success, but the tanks were not used as Fuller had proposed. Instead of concentrating on selected important points, they were spread out along the line of infantry. But the attack worked; the tanks flattened the barbed-wire and silenced the machine-guns. The main defences were overrun and the line moved forward, but not as far as planned. Cambrai and the Hindenburg Line were still ahead, for the men who should have exploited the success had all been killed on the way to Passchendaele. Yet it was a victory, the first great British victory in France, and the bells of the London churches pealed out in glad thanksgiving.

Within a week the Germans counter-attacked and the troops were driven back, back beyond their original starting point. Only a stand by the Guards saved the defeat from becoming a disaster. The line settled into a different shape and that was the only result from all the new graves.

And this was not our only victory which had turned out to be a defeat. Italy was in a bad way after earlier splendid news.

In May the Italians had attacked and advanced on the plateau north
of Gorizia and captured a lot of Austrians. On 1 September: ITALY'S
VICTORY. 'TURNING POINT OF WAR', but the war did not turn.

On 28 October: BLOW AT ITALY. HUGE TEUTON ARMY. ENEMY'S
EARLY SUCCESS. 60,000 ITALIANS CAPTURED. There was no huge army,
just a few German troops; the Italians had a massive superiority in numbers. Ludendorff had thought it necessary to support Austria in case
she collapsed, but he was short of troops, for Russia had not yet capitulated and the British were still attacking in France. All he could scrape
up were six depleted divisions which had been fighting for months on
the northern Russian front.

The six German and nine Austrian divisions prepared secretly, and
suddenly attacked through the mountains on 24 October. Four days
later they were at Udine, clear of the mountains. The Italians scuttled
back behind the Tagliamente River, then rushed behind the Piave only
just in time to save their flanks from being cut off. There were 200 000
Italians captured, and twice that number of other casualties. The Italians,
like the French, had been demoralized by their huge payment in deaths
for petty gains of ground. Luckily the Germans just did not have enough
men to finish off Italy.

A British and French Army Corps was rushed to Italy. There was
talk of the Australians going, and some must have gone, for there is
a single reference to them fighting in Italy. By December the new arrivals
had gone forward and taken over particularly vulnerable points. The
snows of the 19th stopped the campaign.

Haig and Northcliffe must have had second thoughts about their
1915 policy of concentrating all forces on the Western Front. British
troops were now in Italy; British troops were in Ireland shooting the
Irish to encourage them to fight the Germans; another lot was sitting
in Salonika, waiting for something to turn up; some were already marked
for Russia; a force was pushing up the Euphrates, although what it
did there could have no effect on the war; another lot was pushing
across Sinai and this really did something.

There was a flash of light in the dark days at the end of 1917. We
did win a real victory; we captured Jerusalem.

Allenby had done better than most British generals in France. He
was moved to Palestine and took over command in July. He was one
of the few generals respected by the Australians, but he did not approve
of their lack of formal discipline. The campaign was a cavalry affair,
horses and camels, and the Australian Light Horse and New Zealand
Mounted were his most effective troops, very different from the British
Yeomanry.

It was a successful campaign after a bad start. In April 1915, before Allenby's time, the Turks had again driven towards the Suez Canal, but this time our defences were on the eastern side. The Yeomanry held the Qatiya oasis and the Turks overran the advance post in a way not at all creditable to the defence. Miles back the main camp panicked and ran, leaving the oasis to the Turks.

Next day the Australian Light Horse went off to regain the oasis, but the Turks had left. The main camp was just as it had been the day before: the officers' tents had carpets, chairs and wardrobes, even chamber pots; the champagne was still in the coolers. They had been having a comfortable war.

We said that the cavalry relied on their horses for intelligence and the Yeomanry were imitation cavalry – social holiday-soldiers drawn from the fox-hunters. The Australians were able to send back the bulky luggage of five lords. Not all the Yeomanry were quite gentlemen; the only one that I knew personally was a substantial corn-chandler who sold horse-fodder to his betters but was allowed to go hunting with them – he tried to appear more of a gentleman than they were.

The Australians did not think much of the cavalry or Yeomanry in that war or the next. In 1941 one lot of Yeomanry turned up in the Western Desert, but they had tanks, not horses. Their mess-dress included spurs, but they were not really much good for hurrying up tanks. That lot took mess-dress, mess silver, everything for a dignified mess dinner. Other officers ate rough and wore only trousers, shirts and jerseys.

When Gallipoli began to look discouraging in 1915, it was decided to keep the Turks busy in Palestine. More divisions were sent out and a railway and pipe-line built to support an advance. When these got near Gaza, two muddled and unsuccessful attacks were made on the town.

At that stage Allenby took over; he planned to roll up the Turkish line by a mounted attack on the right of his line in the wilderness near Beersheba. It was essential to win because the only local water was in the wells of the town. Late in the afternoon the Light Horse charged and overran the Turks. The line was outflanked and untenable; the Turks were too slow in starting their retreat and got into bad trouble.

It was, probably, the most significant cavalry charge of the war, remarkable in that the Light Horse were mounted infantry rather than real cavalry. I suppose it was the turning point of the Palestine campaign.

The Turks were pinned down on the coast by renewed infantry attacks on Gaza whilst a mounted column swung around through the wilderness and cut them off. They tumbled back in a hurry, but not fast enough to organize a stand on the hill passes, and Jerusalem fell on 9 December.

The capture of Jerusalem was a substantial victory, but moral rather than strategic. Constantinople and the Turkish Mediterranean ports were still under no threat, but the Turks had got into the habit of accepting defeat.

It all had the air of fiction about it, an adventure story of an old small-scale war rather like that with the Boers; no poison gas, no great number of planes nor weight of artillery; a war of movement.

We church-goers were pleased. Our men were fighting in the Holy Land where once the Israelites had fought, and we now shared their battle-names. Our advance was taking us out of Old Testament places into New Testament towns, and our Light Horse was putting us in the mainstream of world history.

Turkey was dented but not broken. There may have been the thought that a similar effort with troops of similar quality and experience might have smashed the Turks on Gallipoli in 1915 and saved Russia.

At home there was to be another referendum on conscription.

A year ago it had been rejected by a substantial 70 000 and we had been told that the issue was dead and buried. In October there was talk of a new Bill, and it would easily have passed both Houses, for there had been a Nationalist, or pro-war, landslide at the elections in the previous March.

But one of the election pledges of Billy Hughes had been that if he got a majority, he would not use it to bring in conscription. He may have thought that his immense majority in the election indicated a changed attitude to the war and to conscription.

On 7 November Hughes announced that there would be a second referendum and the voting would be five days before Christmas; he staked his political future on the result. In the event he avoided paying the stake.

There was no obvious indication that there had been any great swing of opinion.

The Labor Party, which had been divided on the question last time, were now solidly against conscription. This was perhaps not quite logical for the party which supported compulsory unionism; but then, it was far more dangerous to a man to be forced into the army than into a union.

Some might have been exasperated by the frequent strikes, said to be engineered by the I.W.W. and Sinn Fein, and might vote patriotically against them. The electorate would be slightly different, for the short notice meant that itinerant workers would not get on the rolls in time, and they were reckoned to be against conscription. A sizeable number of Irish Catholics were expected to vote 'No' but there seemed to be

no way of stopping them. It was expected, rightly or wrongly, that
the German-Australian vote would be 'No' and naturalized Australians
of German origin were barred. Naturalization did not provide them
with full citizenship. More remarkable, their Australian-born sons were
also barred. If General Monash had been in Australia he would not
have been allowed to vote, but he got his vote as a member of the
A.I.F. overseas—and there were plenty like him. Anyone with a foreign
name was likely to be in trouble. A man of Dutch origin was very offen-
ded when he was turned away from the polling-booth.

Casualties in France were high, but not worse that those of the previous
year; the war news was grave, but not much graver than last year.

New Zealand had brought in conscription in the meantime, and Canada was on the verge of doing the same. We thought we were the most
patriotic of the lot and perhaps some might be shamed into voting
for it.

The sectarian savagery of Ireland was stronger and the Sinn Fein was
more hated by us than a year earlier. Once the Irish Catholics had ranked
about equal with the Jews on our social scale; now they had dropped
well below, but that would not make more of them vote 'Yes'.

The most powerful 'No' voice was again that of Archbishop Mannix,
but at this second referendum he spoke from a stronger position. Old
Archbishop Carr had died in May and Mannix was now sole archbishop.
It did not seem funny at the time, but it produced the greatest comedy
of our war. He was made Chaplain-General in the place of Carr.

Australia had no official religion, but Christianity was thought to
be a very good thing and all sorts had to be accommodated, so in 1914,
four Chaplains-General were appointed: Church of England, Roman
Catholic, Presbyterian and Methodist. As it happened, three of them
were located in Melbourne, convenient to the federal government and
the headquarters of the Defence Department. But religion was not confined to Melbourne and the Church of England Bishop of Adelaide
was one of the four.

The Catholic Church must have made the choice of Mannix as
Chaplain-General, for Mannix was the last man in Australia that the
government would have chosen. The only thing in his favour was that
he had succeeded Carr in the diocese of Melbourne. Kelly of Sydney
was much more senior; he was a bit pompous and had an almost medieval
opinion of the importance of his position, but his views on the war
were in conformity with those of most Australian bishops. He had come
from a very distinguished career in Rome, whereas Mannix had an entirely
Irish background. Kelly would seem to have been an obvious choice.

The nomination was probably made by the Apostolic Delegate,

Bonaventure Ceretti, who was nobody's fool. His appointment as the first Apostolic Delegate to Australia was only one of the very responsible jobs he held in his lifetime. He was centred on Sydney and must have been familiar with Kelly and would have known all about Mannix.

It may have been that Mannix's views on conscription coincided with those of the Pope. Benedict XV was a firm opponent of conscription and held that the huge conscript armies of Europe had a lot to do with the outbreak of war. During the war he consistently worked for peace, and although he may have been right, his views got him a bad press in the Allied countries.

So Mannix was to be Chaplain-General; he was to be a commissioned officer, but the Governor-General refused to sign the commission. Mannix would be required to swear the oath of allegiance to the King, and that might have been difficult. It would be interesting to know how they got around the problems, but he was appointed and took his duties very seriously. He was still Chaplain-General until his death forty-six years later and on the day of his funeral he was given an official gun-salute fired from the Domain. His military cap is still preserved, perhaps as a curiosity, in Mannix College at Monash University in Melbourne.

The bad feeling of the first referendum became bitter hatred with the second. It was not impossible that the violence might have developed into local civil war.

Probably because of Mannix, Victoria was the most bitter of the States and the bitterness was very marked near Sale, in eastern Victoria, where Irish numbers approximated the others. The business arrangements of generations were scrapped. No Protestant would trade at a Catholic store and vice versa, and neither party would meet the other socially. Groups met at farms in the evenings ready for some little thing to spark off a fight. They were still meeting three years later in 1920 and I attended one such meeting on a farm where my Irish Christian name had got me a job harvesting at almost an adult wage.

Mannix, for good or bad, was isolating the Irish. At a meeting on 20 December he said that 'it would be a surrender of freedom by accepting conscription'. This was a quite reasonable statement, but 'at the close of his great speech, the audience rose and sang 'God save Ireland'.'

Not all Catholics supported him and our solidly 'Yes' press made the most of it. PRIEST'S STIRRING APPEAL. SPEECH BY FATHER O'DONNELL. 'We must all stand together—he knew that a high dignitary of the Church in Melbourne had had a great deal to say on the question of military service—he had always stated that he did not speak as a Catholic priest or bishop, but as a citizen. (voice—"Cheers for Dr Mannix").'

Chief-Justice Sir John Madden, a good Catholic, born in Cork and educated at St Patrick's, Melbourne, said that 'The Government should be petitioned to deport Mannix—he was loyal only to Sinn Fein and some of its adherents in Ireland had been deservedly shot'.

We all felt very strongly about the referendum, and that included us eleven-year-olds at school. What we said was solidly 'Yes', for all our families said it. From my balcony bed at night I called the common catch-phrases to those passing in Kooyong Road, but the only reaction I can remember is that a couple of people laughed.

Those small houses on the other side of the road might have hidden Labor supporters, they might harbour 'No' voters. Our side of the road was solidly 'Yes'.

Bob Menzies was at tea with us and a sudden and sordid 'No' meeting was improvised on the corner by the Church of England. It was foolhardy to have a 'No' meeting in Kooyong Road.

The view from the balcony at 'Remo', looking towards the Malvern Town Hall—drawn some time late in the war by the author whose father had written on the back: 'B.B.L. about 1916 or 17'.

Bob, Neil and I went across and Bob countered the arguments with brilliance. We were in a majority and would settle the intruders. Somebody threw a rotten egg at the speaker; but if his politics were right his aim was bad and Bob stopped it. He came home with us and we sponged him down, yet we felt it odd that Bob should be concerned with sending unwilling men to the war.

But the 'Nos' won, and actually increased their vote. It did not hurt as much as last time – perhaps it was not so unexpected, even if feelings were more bitter. Billy Hughes did not step down as he had promised, he merely side-stepped. The Governor-General went through the motions of calling other people to form a government, but he gave it to Hughes again.

It was lucky for us and our views that we were defeated. The war was not going to last long enough for the unwilling conscripts to have had any effect. If they had been sent they would have smeared our image of our fighting men's self-sacrifice. Our Armistice and Anzac Days would not have been so moving.

The A.I.F. was as bitterly divided as we were. It voted 10–9 in favour of conscription, but Billy Hughes, 'The Diggers' Friend', was as unpopular with some as Mannix was with us.

The only time I heard John Gawler, the architect, use doubtful language was when he said that in France he 'did not want one of those buggers beside him'. His Engineer Company made an effigy of Billy Hughes, hanged it on a tree and then burnt it.

I think that few of the troops wanted conscription. Those who voted for it wanted the men at home tipped out of the jobs which their safe security was building up for them. Public opinion was behind this attitude and after the war returned soldiers were given preference, both officially and unofficially. Of those who stayed, some of individual brilliance, like Bob Menzies, got a flying start, but it told against them long afterwards.

Even the universities, with their regard for seniority and bits of paper, appointed professors whose seniority had been lost by war service. It was different after World War II.

That referendum gave us a nasty Christmas present. We would not have conscription – and our men in France would not get adequate reinforcements.

A miserable Christmas and a sad end to a very bad year.

Romania had done nothing; she had gone. Italy had been saved by the winter and was propped up by men who were needed in France after the terrible losses of Passchendaele. And Russia was out of it at last.

All through the year we had been told that Russia might revive and again do something useful against the Germans. We had thought it quite a good thing when the Tsar had abdicated; now we hated the Bolsheviki and wanted him back. On 19 November: RUSSIA TURMOIL. BOLSHEVIKI HAVE UPPER HAND. On 24 November: LENIN'S PEACE MOVE. CENTRAL POWERS RESPOND.

But still we hoped. On 1 December: LENIN'S DOWNFALL. REPUDIATED BY CONFERENCE. On 8 December: ELECTIONS FOR AN ASSEMBLY. BOLSHEVIKI MAY BE BEATEN. On 15 December: REPORTED ESCAPE OF EX-CZAR.

But the Tsar had not escaped, the Bolsheviki had not been overthrown and Lenin was still in power.

On 20 December: RUSSIAN ARMISTICE.

All that fighting and all those dead and we had done nothing much in France in 1917. Now the Germans would be able to send troops from Russia and gain superiority in power and numbers for the first time. It seemed as if it would have been better to have made peace at the beginning of the year, for now it looked as if we might have peace forced on us on German terms.

1918

19

The War Goes Sour

1918 and a gloomy New Year. All other New Years of the war had been bright with the expectation of victory within twelve months, but both sides had remained too strong to be strangled by the other. Now the Germans were stronger than ever before and all we hoped was that defeat might be avoided until things got better in 1919 or 1920.

The veil of propaganda had worn thin and could only distort, not hide, what was behind it.

The Kaiser had been pictured as a buffoon or as a fiend; we were beginning to think of him as a man. We had been told that our troops were stainless knights, that they were happy boy scouts holidaying in France, that they were nonchalant clowns tumbling in the mud of no-man's-land; we were beginning to think of them as hopeless men moving to their deaths because they could see no escape. The 'sweet red wine of youth' had become blackened blood. We had been given a picture of the 'fallen' as lying clean and serene before being committed to the gentle earth so that flowers could bloom above them. We were beginning to know that they would be lucky to be pushed into a hole and not remain as rotting hunks in the mud.

We were fighting 'England's war' but we had come to believe that English troops were inferior to the Scottish, our own, the Canadians and the other colonials. We had thought that the French were heroic; now their civilians were leeches and their troops were sheep driven to profitless slaughter. The Belgians were worse; sublime in 1914, now they were despicable; and the Italians were ridiculous.

We still hated the Germans but no longer with any great enthusiasm; we hated them less than some of our Allies. So much propaganda had been shovelled on us that we were trying to crawl from underneath. We hoped for survival, not victory; we could see no good thing coming from the war and we wanted to be out of it.

We, like all the Allies, had been exuberant and hysterical in August 1914, but that was a long time ago and we had quite forgotten.

The war was a new adventure to the Americans and they were more blatant than we had ever been. Their excesses were published in the press of all the suffering nations. Early in 1918 their most popular song was blared from the tiny gramophones: two stanzas and the chorus sung three times:

> Over there, over there,
> Send the word, send the word over there
> That the Yanks are coming,
> The Yanks are coming . . .
>
> We'll be over, we're coming over,
> And we won't come back till it's over,
> Over there.

Those bloody Americans were shouting that they would win the war which we had been fighting for years. All our dead had accomplished was to keep things going until the Americans won the victory.

It gave deep offence at home and at the front. Nothing which the Americans could ever do could remove the resentment.

A minority of us were still fervently enthusiastic, but few of that minority had direct involvement or personal anxiety; the majority of us were pessimistic.

The big headlines and main articles in our papers were the official handouts and we accepted that they had been passed by the official censor and were false in their ridiculous optimism. Our own correspondents were more factual and frank, but they, too, had to get their news past the censor. The letters from France which we passed around had been censored only by officers in the field and they were often very frank indeed – and some had been printed in our papers. There had been official complaints from England about the Australian press.

But even our letters spared us the true picture of the conditions. The only hint the family got from the brothers was in one letter from Athol. His battery had halted for lunch beside a water-filled shell-hole, and on an island a few yards away was the decayed body of a German with a bayonet in the throat. That small item added something to the official picture.

The people of England were quite as divided about the war as we were. We had many who were opposed to it but they had many who were enjoying it. Manufacturing was booming with war contracts, steel and coal were flourishing, farmers were prosperous and the munition workers were having a splendid time on excellent wages. Theirs was one sort of England.

The other sort was that of the families whose man was on a shilling a day in France. Their man who had not killed a mouse in his life was now expected to clumsily kill a man just like himself because he spoke a different language; kindly men who had always lived comfortably who were now forced to endure indignities; men who had expected to quietly do the job they were born to but were now driven to do things they hated.

They returned on leave from France and what they told was very different from the France of the newspapers. There was less reason for them to write letters when they were so near their homes, but a letter by one of them survives. It has nothing to do with Australia but it shouts what we were beginning to whisper. I have been given a handwritten copy of it, undated. I don't know where it came from, but I feel it is genuine. It has not been published, as far as I can ascertain. It should be published. At the beginning of the war it was believed that only officers could read and write adequately, but this letter, written by some insignificant private who died in agony more than sixty years ago, still lives. The rigid insincerities of his Field-Marshal Haig were dead before the ink had dried on his paper.

It was written from Private Simpson to Corporal Wilfred Saint-Mardé, both, probably, of the Somerset Light Infantry.

> When you receive this I shall have gone west, for although they try to keep the truth from me I realise I'm a goner. It is curious that I survived the journey down, for my legs were shattered, and there is a deep body wound that they try to drain with tubes, but it is too deep, and I know from the pain that sepsis is setting in. I hope the end will come quickly for the pain is almost unbearable and I cannot sleep.
>
> We have had some good times together and some bad ones. My wife will be informed in due course that I died like a hero. How absurd it all seems! We lie in holes shooting men in the back if no other part of the body is visible, bombing them when invisible, blowing them up at all times, and poisoning them with gas when the wind is favourable. And of course they do the same to us. It all involves great courage of a kind, but we ought to refrain from boasting about it and thinking about it as a glorious achievement. I doubt if the legend of war's glory will ever die. When this one is over some spasmodic and half-hearted attempts will be made to promote better understanding between the nations of Europe, but gradually the old order will re-establish itself and the terms of peace will inevitably sow the seeds of the next war. I would like the shirts we threw off

in the brewery to be kept and supplied to any youth who may think of it as a glorious lark. If he can stand a thousand lice biting him night and day without losing his enthusiasm, make him lie in a hole in the garden in winter exposed to rain, hail, snow and frost. While he lies there; shoot, bomb and gas him. Then take him to the operating theatre of any large hospital and make him watch the amputating of limbs.

The letters from France which we passed around were not so outspoken nor so hopeless and pathetic, but they carried a hint of what he said.

Private Simpson no longer had any enthusiasm for fighting; neither had we, but we didn't know how to stop. He was disillusioned about the war and its aims; so were we. To him the war was futile and peace would bring no grand solution; things would be much as they were before. We had not thought of what we wanted from peace, all we wanted was for the fighting to stop. He felt that the Germans were fellow-sufferers caught in the same cruel trap. We were beginning to think that we had overdone our hatred of the Germans.

We had no hope of victory. We had counted on Russia for victory, and now the most we could expect of her was that she would keep some Germans from France until her ill-equipped hordes were replaced by hordes of untrained Americans.

We knew that already the Germans had transferred troops from the Russian front to France, but we hoped that the Russians might revive and renew the fight after the present armistice, even if they only made a fighting retreat deep into their country, as they did in Napoleon's time. But now it looked as if the Germans would not chase them but would make peace with the Bolsheviks—we no longer called them 'Bolsheviki'—but there was hope that the Bolsheviks would be over-thrown.

Then in January a separate peace was made between Russian and Bulgaria. Prisoners of war would be returned and the reinforced Bulgarian army would be available on the Italian front. Mr Lenin, the Russian Prime Minister, was negotiating with the Germans at Brest-Litovsk, but yet there was hope. There would be a 'holy war' to repel the German advance and the Russians 'would fight Imperialism'.

But on 15 January Sir George Buchanan, the British ambassador, on his return to Britain from Russia, said that the Bolsheviks had attained such a position that nobody could overthrow them, that the Soviets were the holders of real power, that Mr Trotsky was trying to make a separate peace with Germany and that 'Russia had finished her role as an active power in this war'.

Russia was falling to pieces. The Ukraine broke away as an independent

nation and made peace with Germany. German troops would be withdrawn and Ukrainian wheat would go to hungry Germany. The Finns
were actually fighting the Russians.

By February the Bolsheviks were quarrelling with the Germans over
the future of Poland. WILL FIGHT BE RENEWED? There was no hope
for peace as the German terms were 'Murderous', so the German armies
swept on.

On 26 February: RUSSIA YIELDS. ACCEPTS ENEMY TERMS. So no more
help from Russia. But then came hope; on 9 March: THE CZAR MAY
RETURN. STRONG REACTION IN FAVOUR OF MONARCHY. A year ago
we had been glad to see him go; now he seemed much better than
the Bolsheviks. But even if the Tsar returned, it seemed, there would
be a lot more German troops available for France.

All four brothers sent home postcards of the places they had been. We
took the family cards out of the fattest album and put in the new war
postcards and still more came until there were three albums on the wickerwork fitting in the corner.

There were garish coloured photographs of English towns, smudgy
grey photographs of Belgian and French towns. There were a lot of
copies of some items, the Tower of London, St Paul's Cathedral and
the Cloth Hall at Ypres. There were even more of the cathedral tower
at Albert in Belgium: a ruined town with the tall tower and on the
top a statue of the Virgin knocked sideways so that it looked as if she
were leaning forward to throw her Child down. The story was that
when she fell, the war would end. There were postcards of black and
white drawings with sunsets painted in sentimental colours as a background to the smashed trees and barbed-wire of no-man's-land.

On the mantlepiece among the vases were two miniature shells, only
about an inch in diameter, possibly high-velocity anti-tank ammunition;
they looked very well when they were highly polished. There was also
the rather ugly nose-cap of a much bigger shell with a bit of jagged
metal around it.

Athol sent home a bundle of magazines which never got to the drawing room but were kept under the curtain in the study. They were from
Paris and I think they were sent to tease mother; they were not a bit
like our patriotic magazines and I gathered that I should not look at
them.

A twelve-year-old friend and I were on the balcony with *La Vie Parisi-
enne*, trying to translate it with our school French. We got the meaning
'He who goes hunting loses his place'; it went with a picture of a luscious
young woman starting up from her bed, an officer in only his pants

getting out of the side of the picture and a furious old husband with white moustaches, in hunting clothes and a gun slung over his shoulder, entering the room. We were puzzled about what it meant. Phyllis came out and caught us.

Athol also sent home odds and ends from prisoners – the ribbon of an Iron Cross, a piece of German sandbag made of paper (this showed that the blockade was hurting), and a chocolate wrapper. 'Old Gold' the chocolate was called – funny, because that was the name used by MacRobertson's for a new sort of chocolate. Our Mr Schneider at the church worked for the firm; with his German name it was just possible that he really was a German and had suggested the name for the chocolate.

Ralph was on the way home. All we knew about it was that he would not lose his leg. Now after six months in different hospitals he would be safely home with us. We were told that his hospital ship would arrive in February and the censor even allowed us to know the actual date.

We would meet him; Mrs Shepherd would lend us her car and we would pay the driver, a girl she regularly employed, for neither she nor Mr Shepherd could drive. Mrs Shepherd hired her every Saturday morning to drive her to the Prahran market and mother usually went with her; Mrs Shepherd would save the money by buying things cheaply; she might spend as much as ten shillings and pay the girl a pound for her services.

I was allowed to stay at home from school and go along with mother, father and Phyllis to see the heroes' welcome at Port Melbourne. All returned men got splendid welcomes, even those sent back as undesirables. Ralph again missed out; his homecoming was far from splendid.

The ship pulled in to the grey wharf where a quiet clump of relatives waited in silence. The gangway was put down and men with empty sleeves, men on crutches and men hobbling with sticks came down it; at least their kit-bags were carried down for them. Then down came the stretchers and parents were able to talk for a minute or two before they were put into the ambulances.

Ralph came down, getting along with a stick, and was allowed to travel with us in the car. Off we went in a miserable procession through the unnoticing streets of Melbourne and along to the Victoria Barracks in St Kilda Road where Ralph limped off whilst we waited to take him home to a late lunch.

He had always been quiet. Now in the car he seemed very quiet and a bit shaky; in the next war we would have said that he was 'bomb-happy' but in this war only officers got 'shell-shocked' and it was not creditable, even for them. He looked different. His face had little scars and dents where the shrapnel had got him and in his curly black hair were a couple of pure white streaks which made him look very distinguished.

At home we had done our best for him and he was able to have Keith's old room; he had never had a room of his own before, and each of us had done something towards furnishing it especially for him. He had to put up with a wastepaper-basket which I had made out of a wooden soap box with drawings pasted on the outside, things like the Rising Sun of the A.I.F. and the badge of the Tunnelling Companies, but I had done my best.

As he settled back into the family he spoke of things not mentioned in his letters. The Belgian hospital had been very good, but not the people of the Belgian villages, dirty, money-grubbing people who were not a bit concerned with who won the war and would be quite as happy with the Germans as with us. They were willing to sell anything to either side, including military information.

On his ship were some men who had been badly wounded before capture, so badly wounded that the Germans allowed them to be repatriated. The Germans had treated them very correctly, but they had had a bad time in hospital because of the shortage of anaesthetics—a result of the British blockade. The Germans had shown no resentment towards them, but whilst they were being carried through Belgian towns, the Belgians had spat on these desperately wounded men. A few years ago we had thought of the Belgians as only a little lower than the angels.

Next morning Ralph was helped into town by Phyllis and got to the Repatriation Office before it opened in the morning. He waited whilst others were escorted in by important people, he waited all morning. Just before lunch the office was empty of visitors, but he had not been called. He knocked on the door and entered. 'There seems to be one too many in the room', said the civil servant. Ralph said that he was very tired and had waited all the morning. 'I won't see you now, come back after lunch.'

After he had hobbled off to lunch and hobbled back, there was a notice on the door: 'No more cases will be seen today.'

Ralph really was nervy and this upset him so much that he had to go to bed for a week to regain his confidence. By the time he was able to return to his civil servant, the university term had begun and it was decided that he was too late.

Repatriation could not get him a job in which his training in chemistry, geology and mining was of any use, but he was offered a course in wool-sorting in the Working Men's College and told that if he did not take it, he would be crossed off the books. He did not take it. Nothing from Repatriation for him.

In some weeks he was fit enough to get a temporary job in the Commonwealth Patents Office and he stayed in it for over forty years. He made a remarkable recovery in the quiet of home and even the great hole behind his knee filled out. In time, he was able to play football again.

We got very friendly with the new people next door who had replaced the Rosenfelts, a widow with two little girls younger than I, nice people who got on particularly well with Ralph. One evening some few weeks after his return he limped in with his stick to feed their fowls—they were away for the afternoon. When he came back through our front gate someone had fixed a white feather on our letter box for him.

At first he had to attend hospital occasionally but at the end of March he had his last visit, was discharged from the army and his pension stopped. The army got rid of him very cheaply.

On his discharge he was given a lump sum to buy a civilian outfit and he stretched it to include a dinner jacket. This was a god-send to the rest of us for years. Previously, father's had been the only one in the family and if two brothers were going out at the same time, it was bad luck for one of them. Now there were two, but Ralph's was preferable.

It was not archaic like father's and although father and Ralph were shorter than the rest, still that dinner jacket looked pretty good. It was well worn before Ralph ever used it himself.

At the end of October 1917 Northcliffe's *Daily Mail* had made a bitter attack on Sir William Robertson, Chief of the General Staff, and on Lord Jellicoe, First Lord of the Admiralty. Robertson was blamed for not winning the war and Jellicoe for the result of the Battle of Jutland; after the battle the *Daily Mail* had said it had been a great victory, but it must have done its sums again. Both men were sacked.

That paper had viciously attacked Kitchener and we had been indignant; it had attacked Asquith as Prime Minister and had got him sacked, and we had not disapproved; but the Jellicoe affair was a different matter. Jellicoe had seemed to us to be just the right man as head of the navy, sober and solid, an organizer who would not panic. He was credited with the introduction of the convoy system which had already broken the power of the German submarines. It seemed that his policies were working and the German navy was in a bad way with mutinies every now and then. It might be that they had already been beaten without another great battle or further loss of life.

In March there was a fuss about Jellicoe in the House of Commons and the *Argus* made the most of it. Who had dismissed him? Sir Edward

Carson had recently been First Lord of the Admiralty and was still a member of the War Cabinet. Had he been consulted? 'Certainly not.' The first he had heard of it was a conversation between two farmers on a wayside railway station. It seemed that only three people knew anything about it: Lloyd George; Sir Eric Geddes, the new First Lord; and Bonar Law, the Conservative Leader, who had entered the room when the other two were discussing the matter.

Lloyd George's justification to Commons was that it was a government decision – so the government consisted of two men doing what Northcliffe told them. 'If Northcliffe is on our side, who then can be against us?'

The Commons attacked Lloyd George. There was a feeling that he was using the press to govern the country, but he denied that he had ever inspired any press attack on anybody. Perhaps he was speaking the truth: he may have only been doing what the press instructed him.

Lloyd George had rewarded the press. Northcliffe had been given the important job of representative of Britain in the United States; his brother, Lord Rothermere, who also owned papers, had been put in the Cabinet, as had Lord Beaverbrook, the owner of the *Daily Express*. It seemed odd that the great newspaper owners should be regarded as more efficient in running the war than men of other professions. It looked as if government policy coincided with press opinion and all public criticism was being stifled. Our own press had been important in shaping national opinion, but it had never dictated it. There was a nasty smell.

Then in May came a political crisis. Major-General Maurice, the Director of Military Operations, wrote to the press, but not to the Northcliffe press, stating that Lloyd George and Bonar Law had deliberately given false information on military matters in their speeches. There was no doubt they had. Bonar Law said that 'Government could not be carried on if an inquiry into the conduct of Ministers were considered necessary whenever their action was challenged by a servant who had occupied a position of great confidence'.

Asquith moved for an inquiry, and if his motion was carried, the government would have had to resign. The government organized its forces and the motion was lost.

Lloyd George again survived and General Maurice was sacked.

Up to this time we had trusted and respected British Prime Ministers as gentlemen and massive men: the Duke of Wellington, Peel, Gladstone, Disraeli and Lord Roseberry – all far greater and more impressive than our own. Now we could see that Lloyd George was shifty, more shifty than our own politicians. He never became a war hero to us.

We matched our Prime Minister against him and Billy Hughes stood as the bigger man.

Lloyd George never gained the confidence of the British Conservative Party. We had no party of that name here, but we had a lot of conservatives. They had confidence in Billy Hughes. No man could have been more conservative than our Mr McNab, the Senior Elder of the Armadale Presbyterian Church. That imposing and dignified figure was one of a group which met Billy Hughes at Spencer Street station on his return from England, tied ropes to the front of his car and pulled him in triumph through the streets of Melbourne.

It had seemed quiet in France whilst Britain was interested in her politics, and Russia in her revolution, but things had been building up there.

On 8 January: THE LAST HAZARD. OFFENSIVE IN MARCH. GERMANS MASSED IN WEST. '750,000 Germans from the Russian front have arrived'. On 10 January: IMPENDING BLOW. GERMANS MASSING MEN. ALLIES READY AND WAITING.

Then the war moved back to England. Sir Douglas Haig might not have been under fire in France, but he was under fire in the House of Commons. He was blamed for last year's reverse at Cambrai. Two days before the German attack he had certain knowledge that it was coming and he had disregarded repeated warnings from the units holding the front; he had made no preparations against the attack nor asked for help from the nearby French reinforcements. A member said that the Commander-in-Chief alone was responsible for any military disaster and urged the appointment of a new one.

The Undersecretary to the War Office said that no one in the higher command was to blame for Cambrai and that Haig was probably the most distinguished general of his time and that he had never lost the confidence of the Army Council or the War Office. As well as them, he still had the support of Northcliffe. He remained in command.

On 13 February we read: THE WESTERN FRONT. BIG ATTACK IMMINENT. On 20 February: GERMANY'S BLOW. DUE ANY MOMENT. OUR MEN WON'T FAIL. On 26 February: GERMANS PREPARING TANKS. On 28 February: GERMAN BLOW EXPECTED SOON. GENERAL FOCH CONFIDENT. 'ENEMY WILL FAIL'. On 8 March: WHEN WILL BLOW FALL? 'The strength of enemy divisions on the West Front is still increasing. They have a majority of some 16 divisions over the Allies'. Although the Allied divisions were larger, we were doubtful. The French might not be feeling too aggressive after the troubles of the past year, the Americans were inexperienced and, pro-British as we were, we thought that the German divisions might be better than the British. On 20 March:

Will Germans Attack? Doubt in Washington. On 23 March:
Germans Attack On British Front. Great Battle. Reassuring
News. Further Attacks Repulsed. On 25 March: British Fall
Back. New Line Occupied. Men and Guns Lost. But 'The British
retired in good order and the new British line holds everywhere'.

And on the same day: Shells Fall in Paris. The Germans had built
a prodigious gun which shot forty miles and fired every quarter of an
hour.

On 26 March: Optimism in London. 'Army has Saved Empire'.
But it hadn't, not by a long chalk. On 27 March: Bapaume Falls.
New British Line. Valiant Stand Made. If a stand had been made,
it was not for long, and any pockets of resistance were submerged in
the flood as the Germans chased the broken troops.

It hurt. Bapaume was the place that the Australians had captured
last year and they had got a lot of credit for doing it. In 'From the
Australian Front, Xmas 1917', there had been five pictures of the place
with an Australian band marching through the burning town the day
after its capture.

On 30 March: Albert and Montdidier Fall. Montdidier was a
familiar name and the Australians had fought and died there; Albert
was a sort of mascot and now the Germans had got it. Half the homes
in Australia had postcards of the Leaning Virgin perched shakily on
the top of the cathedral tower.

On 30 April: Fight for Amiens. It was the rock of our defence
and we had almost as many postcards of the cathedral as we had of
the tower at Albert. If the Germans got Amiens, we were in a mess.
It was the communications centre of the whole of northern France;
if it went, the whole line would dissolve. It would divide the British
and French armies, the one very concerned with its bases on the Channel,
and the other with the defence of Paris.

It was frightening. In a matter of days the Germans had advanced
about forty miles. Last year we had called it a victory when we had
taken months and suffered a million casualties to gain six miles and
even then there had been the nagging feeling that the Germans had
been deliberately falling back to strong prepared positions.

When this feared and expected attack broke, Haig was on leave in
England, and our General Monash, commanding the 3rd Division, was
on leave in the south of France; so was Keith.

Keith later wrote,

Monash wrote to me once or twice and seemed interested in Jimmy
Lewis's boys. I met Monash at Menton in the South of France when

we were both on leave. He had shed his uniform and was in mufti and had me tricked. He was tickled to death by the cheeky young lieutenants that pushed past the old man instead of springing to attention, saluting etc.

Then Monash's leave had a sudden end. His old friend, Brigadier-General Rosenthal, who commanded one of Monash's brigades, was convalescing after being gassed, and the two had gone off for the day together in the hills behind Monaco and then walked back to Menton, planning a trip to Italy for the next day.

The newspapers which arrived that evening gave the first news of the German attack. Then a telegram arrived from Jess, Monash's divisional Chief of Staff, telling that his division had been ordered east towards Ypres. Monash had to rejoin at once; he was able to pull rank and get a compartment on the Paris train the next morning.

Ten days later he wrote to his wife and a copy of the letter is in grandmother's papers. It is a terse account of what he and his 3rd Division did to save Amiens and so prevent the collapse of the entire Western Front. The account that follows is drawn from it.

He arrived in Paris on Monday morning, 25 March, the day after the Germans had first shelled Paris with their prodigious long-range gun. His A.D.C. and car were waiting for him; he had a quick breakfast and went off to Amiens to find the city 'in a state of frightful confusion. The Boche had been heavily bombing the town and civilians were evacuating it rapidly; there was great excitement. The railway square and the streets were full of war-torn troops of all kinds and excited officers'.

At the railway station he got a message saying that his division had been deflected from Ypres and was coming south, spending the night at Blaringhem prior to entraining for Doullens, which was 17 miles north of Amiens. He went on to Doullens to find the town in confusion and no one in authority. 'Streams of soldier-stragglers pouring in from the east with the most hair-raising stories that the Boche was almost on top of them'.

Then he went to his headquarters at Blaringhem to find it all packed up and ready for moving next day. He had a couple of hours' sleep and early next morning (26 March) he set out to look for X Corps headquarters – his division was then under X Corps. But all headquarters were on the run, divisional, corps and army, and telephone and telegraph communications had ceased to exist.

He eventually found his corps commander who said that he was trying to collect a few divisions to make a stand. He told Monash to concentrate his division on Doullens.

He returned to Doullens to find the confusion worse than on the previous day, masses of civilians and thousands of wild-eyed soldiers from lost units, streaming back in panic. The town hall was packed with British and French staff-officers in brilliant uniforms holding one of those urgent conferences.

Then he had a lucky chance. At the railway station the first instalment of his troops arrived under Brigadier-General Rosenthal, the friend who had been on leave with him a few days before. He ordered the train-load to take up a position to cover the detrainment of later arrivals. The Town Major ran up to say that German cavalry were within ten miles and there was nothing to stop them.

Then Monash went off to meet the first batch of his 10th Brigade as they detrained at Mondicourt. They too, were ordered to take up covering positions and to halt the Tommies as they streamed along the road, some with rifles and some without, and to form them into groups suitable for employment if needed.

Then he selected his headquarters and was able to establish contact with X Corps; he learnt that the Germans were not so close as the rumours had made out and that the Australian 4th Division was just about to arrive. But only one brigade was available and it was rushed off to plug a hole in the British line. Then he went back towards Doullens along a road crowded with all sorts of vehicles and the Germans near enough to drop an odd shell on it.

He got back to his headquarters at about 8 p.m. and an hour later a dispatch rider arrived with the news that his X Corps had passed from G.H.Q. Reserve to the Third Army. Another hour and another dispatch rider came with orders for him to report at Corps Headquarters at Corbie; as he set out, a third dispatch rider arrived to say that Corbie had been abandoned.

He set out to find his new superior, driving along a moonlight road crammed with the debris of a retreating army.

He found him at last – General Congreve.

'Thank heaven the Australians at last ... General, the position is very simple. My corps today was holding the line from Braye to Albert, when the line broke, and what is left of the three divisions after four days' heavy fighting without food or sleep are falling back rapidly. German cavalry have been seen approaching Morlancourt and Buire. They are heading straight for Amiens. What I want you to do is to get into the angle between the Ancre and the Somme as far East as possible and *stop him*'.

That was the whole of Monash's orders. He was given a room and a telephone and spent the night selecting positions for his units and arranging with the Third Army to bring the bulk of his infantry in buses as soon as possible.

Shortly after daybreak he went forward, and from the high ground he could plainly see the German cavalry operating. It would be a near-run thing. If the Germans got the Doullens ridge, Amiens was untenable.

As he watched, the first convoy, sixty old London buses crowded with men, arrived: two battalions, all armed and with ample ammunition. Off they went and took up position. At 10 a.m. another two battalions arrived. By 2 p.m. he had 5000 men under his hand manning the ridge between the two rivers and patrols out in front to contact the enemy.

The Germans checked when they met opposition and merely shelled odd villages in a casual sort of way.

That day (27 March) and on the following night, the rest of his infantry arrived, as did those who came by route march: his artillery, ammunition column, pioneers and odds and ends.

Athol was with the medium artillery and his letter home told about it. The horse-drawn guns pushed through a mob of men without rifles who yelled, 'Look out, digger, Jerry is just over the hill.' Off the road the infantry saw more. There was an English general hiding in the woods alone and crying. There were five junior officers lying in a hollow covered by a ground-sheet; when asked where their men were, one pointed nonchalantly with his finger 'Over there somewhere.' 'The men had lost all trust in their officers, and the officers, all interest in their men'.

In the past years men had been shot for 'desertion in the face of the enemy'; now nobody was staying long enough to shoot these deserters. Entire battalions were surrendering without a fight. It was blind panic. Panic like that of the Italians in the desert in 1940 when the British captured five times as many enemy as their own numbers. Panic like that in Malaya, when the Japanese routed and captured three times their number of British and Australians.

To return to Monash's account:

Hourly the position grew stronger. The tired and beaten men of the 35th, 21st and 9th British Divisions—now reduced to a mere handful, took up a line and further off the New Zealanders and 2nd Canadian Division arrived. We thus had a sprinkling of first-class divisions at various parts of the line and the effect of their arrival was electric and remarkable. The advent of my own division had an astonishing effect in stiffening everybody on both sides and the tendency to run

was checked. People began to regain confidence and measures for
re-organisation of the whole line were rapidly commenced.

During the night of 28 March, I pushed my line 2,000 yards until
they were actually in contact with enemy patrols and on the afternoon
the expected happened and he attacked me in considerable force.

Three German divisions attacked his single division, but the artillery
was ready 'and the battle was a walk-over for us. After an hour the
whole attack had petered out'.

It was the last of the drive to Amiens, the last splash of the German
wave which so nearly swept into Amiens where a few Germans would
have cut communications and divided the French and British armies
and brought the collapse of the entire strategic plan.

Four Australian divisions held the front previously occupied by an
entire British corps and their defence was probably the turning point
of the war. (Ludendorff thought the turning point came later when
the Canadians and Australians made the first substantial advance of the
Western Front campaign.) In the débâcle a couple of British divisions
stood firm, and so did the despised cavalry. 'The 12th Lancers went
a long way to neutralising the bad showing of the English infantry
regiments': that is the view of an A.I.F. officer who saw it at first-hand.

Monash's letter closes:

> As we Australians have so far lost no prisoners to the enemy and
> . . . from conversations with German prisoners I learned that they
> had no idea whatever that the Australians were in this part of the
> world. Our Press correspondents are forbidden even to mention the
> fact that the Australians are in this vicinity and several long cables
> which I know are ready to go to Australia have been held up in
> consequence – the full story therefore of what the Australians and New
> Zealanders have done to entirely retrieve the situation will probably
> not be known to the world at large until the news has become stale.

It was never widely known in the English-speaking world and there
was only a single report by Philip Gibbs in the *Daily Telegraph*. Haig
did not ever mention it. When Monash protested he said that his silence
was 'for the sake of British morale' and he gave the credit to the very
British divisions which had failed.

Even the Americans triumphed. When the Germans 'threatened the
city of Amiens. More than two thousand Americans were there'. Later,
'others were near Armentières, stemming the new German advance in
April'. In both cases the references are probably to those Americans
attached to the A.I.F. for training and held in the reserve. There is no
mention of their being in the fighting in either case. The first mention

of them fighting in appreciable numbers is in October, when the débâcle of two divisions was the direct cause of so many Australian deaths.

Haig's superior, Marshal Foch, behaved quite differently. 'You saved Amiens! You saved France! Our gratitude will ever remain, ever and always to Australia'.

The Bishop of Amiens: 'I owe you and your illustrious dead my heartfelt thanks because the land of my diocese has been your field of battle, and you have delivered it by sacrifice of your blood'.

In Athol's diary he records on 15 April 'Rumour says that the 3rd and 4th Australian Divisions have been awarded the privilege of wearing some shoulder tassle or similar distinction by the French for their defence of Amiens'. It is possible that the French really made such a proposal, although the British gave absolutely no recognition.

In Amiens cathedral is an ungainly wall tablet with the text in English and French, erected to the memory of the Australians who fell in defence of the city; there were 5995 of them 'who valiantly participated in the victorious defence of Amiens from March to August 1918'. Spattered about the walls are tablets to troops who had gained no honour by their performance. They are as appropriate as inscriptions scrawled in public lavatories, but time may transform them into historical evidence.

By 1918 the English felt an inferiority about the Australians and excused themselves with 'The Australians are wonderful in attack but not so good in defence owing to their poor discipline'. It was the Australian defence which saved the retreating British after their defence had collapsed. It was the failure of British discipline which turned their defeat into a rout: a failure due largely to the cleavage line between officers and men.

No more attacks towards Amiens, but other attacks and other retreats. On 11 April we read: THE CRISIS. EVERY MAN NEEDED. LLOYD GEORGE'S WARNING. FATE OF EMPIRE AT STAKE. CONSCRIPTION FOR IRELAND. In his speech Lloyd George said, 'The British retired but were never routed. Once more the cool courage of the British soldier, who refused to acknowledge defeat, has saved Europe'. He really said that.

Home Rule for Ireland, passed by the Liberal government in 1914 with Lloyd George as Chancellor, with no strings attached, was now to be at the price of conscription in Ireland and Ireland was in turmoil. 'The fate of liberty throughout the world is at stake', and the suppression of individual liberty in Ireland was to be the price.

The military age in Britain was to be raised to fifty years; it was doubtful whether those old blokes and the coerced Irish would have made better troops than those who had broken when the Germans attacked in March.

On 13 April: ARMENTIÈRES EVACUATED. Another mascot had gone. We all knew versions of 'Mademoiselle from Armentières', it had been one of the few light-hearted things coming out of France; now mademoiselle was being nice to the Germans.

On 15 April: HAIG CALLS 'HALT'. STIRRING ARMY ORDER. FIGHT IT OUT 'TO THE LAST MAN'. 'Every position must be held to the last man. There must be no retirement. With our backs to the wall and believing in the justice of our cause, each of us must fight on to the end. The safety of our homes and the freedom of mankind alike depend on the conduct of each one of us at this critical moment'.

That windy rhetoric went down well in England where it had a big audience, but I doubt if it was as good as our own 'Last man and last shilling' and it meant even less. If a worried battalion commander was silly enough to include it in his orders to his worried men, would it have heartened them? It was meant for home consumption. 'The safety of our homes', he said, but the homes were hundreds of miles away in safety. 'The freedom of mankind' could have meant little to those conscripted troops, or to the Irish.

It was about this time that Keith got into trouble; he did not tell us about it, but others did later. The 2nd Tunnelling Company had been isolated as the line was pushed back, but most of them tried to make their way back through the new German line. Keith was in a covered trench between the lines when two shells landed on either side of him and buried him. He took quite a time to dig himself out and it was a couple of days before he got back.

Despite Haig's order, on 17 April: BAILLEUL FALLS. BRITISH LOSE NEUVE EGLISE. Next day it was GERMANS TAKE WYTSCHAETE. On the 26th the Germans were using tanks for the first time.

On 27 April: GROUND REGAINED. IMPORTANT CAPTURE. AUSTRALIAN TACTICS SUCCEEDED. Haig announced that Australian and English troops had recaptured Villers-Bretonneux. It was something for Haig to mention the Australians, even if in conjunction with the British. The British had certainly been there: they had been hopelessly pinned down in front when the Australians had captured the town from the flank. The British were able to move into the captured town.

The recapture of Villers-Bretonneux was a victory in the continuing flood of defeat; some claim it as the turning point of the war, and it was certainly one of them. Amiens had been a defensive victory, this was offensive. It was a bastion regained when other bastions were falling, an isolated success.

On 27 April: KEMMEL HILL LOST. The Germans were still going on. On 30 May: THE AISNE CROSSED. On 3 June: THE MARNE REACHED.

Is Paris the Objective? The 'High Authority' said that 'the position was still anxious but there was room for hope'.

On 11 June: New German Attack. On the 12th: Advance in Centre. French Hold Flanks. On the 13th: French Counter Attack. Lost Ground Regained.

On 19 June Monash was put in command of the Australian corps, all five divisions, and Birdwood was moved on to temporary command of an army, taking the place of Gough who had been in command of the collapsed British front. Soon they were saying that Gough was being made a scapegoat; but if Gough was not to blame, it must be Haig, who knew of the attack, but thought that it would be somewhere else and refused reserves.

On 8 July:

BATTLE OF HAMEL

Brilliant Australian Success

ENEMY COMPLETELY SURPRISED

Tanks and Americans Helped

This time credit was being given to the A.I.F., for no British troops were there.

Monash had planned it. He intended to use 2000 Americans as support troops but just before the battle the American commander, Pershing, issued orders for their recall to become part of a solidly American force. Monash protested to his new Army Commander, Rawlinson, who took the matter to Haig; Haig took the matter further and the Americans were allowed to remain and the attack was able to go on.

It was a planned and co-operative venture. Monash consulted his brigade leaders and they, in turn, consulted their juniors; the process went on until each private knew what was expected of him and what he could expect from the next sections.

It was not a wave attack. From our papers we could not find when the new method started or who started it; it has been attributed to Monash but probably it evolved naturally by degrees.

The old method of a line of infantry moving slowly forward against an invisible wall of machine-gun fire had commonly been superseded by groups moving forward quickly and then diving for cover, whilst groups behind moved forward under their covering fire. Then the groups ahead took cover and gave covering fire in their turn. The machine-gun crews had to be quick to alter their aim as each group in turn took cover. When the attacking force got close enough a couple of individuals would edge sideways and get behind the gun, and machine-guns at close range were clumsy weapons. It was very unhealthy for a machine-gun crew with its gun pointing forward when men with grenades were coming from behind. The stories in our papers indicated that this method of attack was now common.

The Battle of Hamel was remarkable in that the attacking force had only the same numbers as the defence, and previously a three-to-one ratio had been regarded as a minimum; remarkable too, in that the attackers lost fewer men than the defenders.

In claiming the victory Haig said that his Fourth Army under Rawlinson had won this battle of Amiens. Rawlinson was more generous and told Monash, 'You have altered the whole course of the war, that's all'. He was right. In the years of fighting in France this was the first time that the Germans had been utterly routed.

The Australians had gained moral supremacy, and the Germans were shaken. The Australians' trench raids were common and feared. The German Commander, Von der Maritz, complained that entire units had disappeared in these raids and that the sight of a couple of Australians in a trench made the defence pack up. Volunteers were called for to stand opposite the Australians.

But the Germans were going ahead in other parts. On 8 July: GERMANS CLAIM 13,000 PRISONERS IN ADVANCE ACROSS MARNE. Now Paris looked shaky, but on 20 July: ALLIES ATTACK. DRIVING GERMANS BACK. EARLY MORNING SURPRISE. AMERICANS' FINE SHARE. This all happened on a 20-mile front between Chateau Thierry and Soissons, but it did not develop. Although the Americans had five times as many men as the Germans, they bogged down.

But the German advance had spent itself. It was not driven back by great counter-attacks; nor had it dashed itself to pieces against any wall of steel; it melted away in the captured food dumps. The German soldiers, exhausted after weeks of victory, were unwilling to leave the food and luxuries they had not seen for years, and impetus was lost.

20
Death in the Family

Death had been very considerate to our family and had never intruded. Of course relatives had died, but in a reasonable sort of way.

Grandfather, mother's father, had gone quietly along the sure path of old age. I liked him. He came up occasionally from Port Fairy, a ruddy-faced man with a white fringe of beard, and he had given me a shilling one evening in High Street. There was nothing very sad about his death and it had happened in Port Fairy. One of father's brothers had died ten years ago but I had never met him; he had been ailing for years and had died far away in Broken Hill. Before my time the dashing brother of the family had gone to Africa on a very romantic expedition which planned to cross the continent and look for gold on the way. The Portuguese would not allow them to leave Beira; fever attacked them and only one survived, and he died on the ship going home. This was the price of adventure, just as were deaths on the mine or in the bush, and was reasonable for the risks involved. Death had always been remote. Now it crashed into the middle of the family.

At Wesley Prep School, the geometry lesson was really interesting; we used compasses and set-squares, just as the ancient Greeks did, and they had started it all. They could use their compasses to bisect an angle and so could we; but they could not trisect an angle and no one had been able to in all the centuries between. Perry and I thought we might manage it and we would be the very first to do so, not bad for a couple not yet twelve. We tried it in all our spare time that day. Next morning I still had not managed it, but I thought I might if I gave full attention to the matter for a day. I had a bit of a cold; it was not really bad enough to keep me at home, but I wanted to trisect that angle and was allowed to stay.

I was sitting on my bed on the balcony in the morning sun still trying to trisect that angle. Phyllis rushed through the window. 'Owen has been killed', and collapsed on the bed and sobbed. A grown-up was crying, and so was I, we sobbed together on that bed. The foundation of our world had melted away. It was black tragedy. Of course it was happening to others every day, but this was to us, and this was Owen.

That day was a trial. We had to meet each other and we wanted to be by ourselves until the shock wore off. At lunch mother had red eyes, and Phyllis had to run out suddenly, and the maid was snivelling. It was a pity it was not Lilah; she would have been a comfort.

Neil was eating his school lunch beside the Front Turf when Bob Menzies found him and gently told him. Bob has done many things in his life, important things, kind things and cruel things, but none kinder than this.

I was lucky not to have been at school assembly when the Head announced that it had scored another death. The school was doing very well; Scotch and Grammar had more deaths, but they were bigger schools and we would like to think that our ratio was better.

O. G. Lewis had not been a brilliant success: he may have been dux of the school a year younger than his fellows, but he had not been in the crew or the football team. He was not quite a hero but he was passable.

Miss Kelly, the matron of the Prep boarding house, was a good sort, even if we were indignant with her when she walked into the pavilion when we were running about naked as we changed for sport. She was not really a teacher, but in the war-time shortage, she took our form for English. Miss Kelly asked the class where Lewis was. 'His brother has been killed', they replied. 'Poor little chap, I am glad that he is at home'.

I would not have stayed at home for that, I would have faced it out, even though it would have been impossible to hold back my tears in public, but trisecting the angle saved me. But it was bad enough in the weeks ahead and worst of all on Friday mornings with those maudlin songs: 'Somewhere in France there is a grave'. Yes, there was a new and particular one.

Mother had been proud to have four sons in the army: she wore a badge with four bars on it, which the government had issued to encourage recruiting. Now she was entitled to add a star to one of the bars. She never wore that badge again.

She did not wear any sign of mourning, nor did Phyllis; none of us wore those black bands on the left arm which had been so popular at the beginning of the war when a second cousin had been killed. Mourning was going out of fashion.

The aunts took it very well. They wore mourning and were happily sad that a near relative had been killed. Owen's portrait displaced that of General Monash from the central place on the little table in their sitting room.

Sorrow had been vulgarized by publicity. Every casualty list was pored over by those hoping to find the name of an acquaintance and the glory of knowing somebody 'who had laid down his life for his country'. Owen had not laid down his life: it had been snatched from him and from us. We had prayed that all the boys would survive, no matter how many others did not.

And what a rotten job for the Reverend David Millar to be forced to break the news. Mother had told Phyllis that if anything happened to the boys, she hoped it would not be the Millars who told her; there was nothing personal about it, but we would rather keep to ourselves. It was not Mr Millar who broke the news but her old friend, Mrs Shepherd. Her daughter, Vi., was married to Archie Sharpe who got all the London news and rumours before most others and he cabled the news to the Shepherds. The cable arrived on 17 April, five days after Owen's death. Mother called on Mrs Shepherd on her way home from her Religious Instruction class at the Armadale State School and she brought the news home.

Owen's name does not seem to have been in the casualty lists, perhaps the Flying Corps had some other arrangement. On 27 April under 'Deaths in Action' is LEWIS, killed in action, on 12th April. While flying in France, Lieutenant Owen Gower Lewis, R.F.C., aged 21 years, fourth beloved son of James B. and E. A. Lewis, "Remo" 41 Kooyong Road, Armadale'.

The very next day some fool of a woman, whom we hardly knew by sight, called on mother; 'she thought it must be one of her sons', and kept chattering away. A pity she was alive and Owen was not.

Friday evening, the usual Friday evening. Tea at 6 o'clock; meat, potatoes and a vegetable, and a pudding to follow. Then in comes the maid, she may be an economical war-time one, but she has to have her evening prayers like the rest of us. Tonight we miss Lilah.

Father gets out the big family Bible, opens it at the marker and reads a chapter, then we all kneel for the Lord's Prayer. That over, we clear away and wash up and then the evening is free. Friday, and we all go into the study; school homework will wait until father has read the usual Friday letters from the boys.

Keith's letter first; it is always breezy and he still makes no mention of having been buried and missing. Athol's is as lively as ever and talks of his becoming a legal officer at headquarters; his success as Prisoner's Friend may do him some good and he may become a lieutenant. Then

Owen's; father opens it and reads. It is cheerful, he is out of hospital and will soon be back with his squadron and all is going well. For five more Fridays those letters from the dead were read and filed.

Owen had one more thing to go in his file. One Saturday morning long after, I bring up the post to mother who is sitting on her low chair ready to begin her daily prayers. A big tidy envelope. 'Open it, Brian.' I open it. 'What is it?' I can't answer—and mother reaches across and takes it. It is a photo of Owen's grave with its tidy headstone. His file is complete.

A letter to father from John Monash. He may have signed hundreds of such letters, but this was no circular letter, it was one to his old friend written at a time when he was turning the course of history in France. Already with his 3rd Division he had thrown sand into the advancing German war-machine; soon with his new command of the five Australian divisions he would push the machine back until it was smashed beyond its last defences. Other British generals, corps and army, had had successes, but not continuing nor significant ones. I repeat, he was turning the course of history.

He did more. General Monash, commanding the 3rd Division, then holding the German advance, wrote to Lieutenant Keith Lewis of the 2nd Tunnelling Company, asking him to accept his sympathy and to convey it to Athol. All of us liked John Monash.

We did not know it at the time but Monash had already done something for Athol. Athol's diary and letters to Elsie told about it.

In April 1918 the three brothers had been only a few miles apart and often saw each other. One morning Athol heard that an Australian plane had crashed and felt uneasy; a little later his officer, Mr Thomas, called him over and told him that Owen had been killed and that all facilities would be granted him to obtain further information. Athol went across to Keith's billet and found him and both went to the aerodrome. The funeral was next day and Athol attended but Keith was in the line.

Exactly a week later Athol was called to battery H.Q. and told to fill in an application form for a commission. Now Athol was unpopular with his officers, perhaps because of his defence of prisoners at court martials and his C.O. had already refused to recommend him for a commission in the artillery, but Monash had sent a note explaining that the commission would be for legal work only. Three days later he was called for an interview with General Grimwade, who said that Athol had been doing well at court martials and that it was his, and Monash's wish to get him into a comparatively safe job for the sake of the family and that both had done the same thing in other cases. General Grimwade would recommend his commission.

A quarter of a million men in the A.I.F. might sound to be quite a lot of men but at times it seemed to be a cosy little army. Funny to think of two generals being concerned about a gunner in the artillery and his brother. The previous talk about a commission for legal work might well have come to nothing without their interest. I think Athol would have made a poor artillery officer in the field but he was to do well in his new job.

On 26 April, just three weeks after Owen's death, an orderly came and told Athol to report at H.Q. at 11. On the way an officer said 'Hullo, Lieutenant Lewis' and it was confirmed. He returned to his battery where his officer, Captain Foxton, took the news stolidly, then back to H.Q., then off to Abbeville to the Officers' Clothing Store at 5 to buy his officer's uniform. Back to H.Q. in time for dinner at 8, a dinner with wine and whisky on the table. After dinner Monash 'outlined very clearly and concisely the policy, the maintenance of discipline & a close scrutiny of all court martial proceedings, to advise on remission, suspension or reduction of sentences and to give up any idea of appearing as prisoner's friend! He spoke very kindly about Owen.' Athol was later told that the news had affected Monash very keenly, and I suppose it did, for with no son of his own, the elder brothers seemed something like his own family. At mess that night the conversation had been on the General and 'all had the highest opinion of his intellect & his power of discussing with each his own particular work.'

That morning Athol had woken as a gunner; that night he went to bed as a H.Q. officer between sheets in his own furnished room and next morning an orderly brought him hot shaving water and a glass of milk–just as at home where Lilah had always made a fuss of him and brought him milk to build him up.

Athol's uncomfortable war was over, but not Keith's. A fortnight later he wrote:

Keith came in. He wasn't looking as well as usual – he had had a very rough time at Riblmont – been there over a month & spent most of the time under shelter in cellars; his batman, Breen, had gone off his head & finally when Keith was getting full up with the thing, they sent up an officer to relieve him, the same officer was killed 5 hours later. They had left the billet & returning found it badly damaged by a shell – a little further down the road they heard a shell coming & threw themselves down; it landed a couple of feet from Keith who was stretched out flat; the other officer was on the other side of Keith but apparently hadn't got right down for he was killed on the spot. Keith was sent down for a week's rest as his nerves were badly shaken.

'In Memoriam' notices were no new thing in the English and Australian papers when the war started but they had become common by now. The bald statement in the casualty list might bring three or four 'in memoriam' notices from different members of the family or from friends showing their own personal grief. Next year on the same date similar insertions would be made, like the annual recutting of a name on a tombstone.

The war added a special section, 'On Active Service', which grew to dominate 'In Memoriam'. In it were the names of those we had expected to be our leaders in the new century. The Empire was at its most glorious and going on to even greater things, and our new Commonwealth was at a splendid dawning. Those we had expected to be our leaders had been obliterated but the names of some of them would be recalled on some particular day each year. There was no hint of any glory of war in the wording of these notices, but a sorry acceptance of the sacrifice of those willing to make it and a hope of reunion with them in a happy thereafter.

In the *Times* a notice still appears to the memory of some forgotten regiment wiped out in some forgotten battle more than sixty years ago. For decades the dates of Somme and Passchendaele could be established by the number of 'In Memoriam' notices.

Great figures, like Lord Kitchener, had their semi-official notices, but very humble people had theirs with verse especially composed for them; some of it was ridiculous, but we did not snigger at the deep feeling bundled up in the clumsy words.

We middle-class people were more reserved in our expressions. We shared 'Gone but not forgotten' but we relied more on texts and established poetry. 'Until the day breaks and the shadows flee away.' We looked forward to a new day when we would be together again and our present sorrow would have vanished in the hereafter. It may have come from our most beautiful erotic verse, but as it was from the Bible, we thought it very suitable.

There was so much suitable sentiment in Binyon's 'For the Fallen' that it was hard to decide on a suitable extract; 'They shall not grow old, as we that are left grow old'; 'At the going down of the sun and in the morning/We will remember them'; and 'As the stars that are starry in the time of our darkness/To the end, to the end, they remain.'

The family did not hold with public parade and made no insertion in the 'In Memoriam' column; all Owen got was the bare entry under 'Deaths in Action'. Phyllis did something personal and ambitious. She wrote an elegy of one hundred and fifty lines which, she admitted, owed much to Milton's *Lycidas*.

The young Milton was twenty-nine when he wrote it; Phyllis was twenty-two when she wrote '1918'. Milton was not deeply involved and used elegant words to record his conventional regret but her sorrow beat, imprisoned, against the bars of academic forms.

Father took the work to Archibald Strong at the University and he recommended publication; it cost £5, but father thought it worth the price. Of course it was not the sort of thing to sell, but it was favourably criticized and gave comfort to Phyllis and to others, and it was all that she could do.

She recalled the family excursions in the Tasmanian bush when she and Owen had looked down

> On sunny breadths of river, now concealed
> By hills and trees, now flashing into view.

She thought that Owen's hope of doing good for his fellows had not been dispersed into the void but remained as part of one great design, and that he had not lived for nothing.

Owen returned to her in dreams:

> Your voice approaching laughs. It was not true,
> I never felt death's pangs nor went from you.

She waited surely for eventual reunion at the end of her own life, and closed with a shot at the spiritualists:

> Take your dark powers to others; we can wait
> To know the whole of what you tell in part.

Spiritualism was booming in England and Australia; like reincarnation, it had some justification in the Bible. Very respectable church people were going to seances and getting in touch with those killed in France. There was a little new Spiritualist church on the way to school near the Chapel Street corner.

Our second cousin, Archie Sharpe, had moved to London and the brothers often stayed at his Chiswick house when on leave. Archie went to a seance and wrote to us about it.

Owen had spoken through the medium and it was very convincing. He gave a description of a girl, clearly identifiable as Phyllis, standing in front of our apricot tree, just as in a photo of her; it was too detailed to have been invented and apricot trees were unknown in England. Archie asked if mother wanted him to go on with the matter. She did not; neither did Phyllis.

Of course Wesley suggested a £5 memorial chair, but even if we had had a lot of fivers, the family did not like the idea.

Owen did get a personal memorial a couple of years later. Those old enemy neighbours of ours, the Austrian Rosenfelts, were living in Sydney and they donated a tree in a memorial avenue at Hunter's Hill, dedicated to their old friend, Owen Lewis.

Those were grey months, but Tassy was bright and cheerful. There had been splendid dogs in the past, but distemper and violence had finished them. But Tassy was my own dog, a spaniel from Tasmania. My dog, who jumped up to welcome me when I came home from school each day; Tassy, who sat down and looked into my face and talked yearningly to me.

Tassy was killed in High Street. The maid with the little girl had taken him shopping; she was not very good with dogs and a car got him. No Tassy to welcome me that afternoon, just a tattered heap which I had to bury under the apricot tree. There could never be another Tassy.

I knew that some day I would meet Owen again, even though it might be years away and we might not recognize each other at first, but there was no after-life for dogs.

In bed each night I cried for Owen; now too, I cried for Tassy.

That night I died. I died. There was no terror, no agony, a comfortable sleep after a busy day. The light faded and I was happily dead. Then the first light of a new life. It was still grey and something was jumping on my legs, yes, it really was Tassy. The light brightened and there was Owen grinning in welcome.

Things seemed much better in the morning.

School assembly now was morbid to me and many others. We felt no pride when it was announced that another batch of Old Boys had been killed; it might add to the school's score but we knew that more people were sad.

We were tired of the victories which disappeared, and we were not very excited by the horrible things the Germans still did.

'On this day, so and so died for the cause of righteousness and freedom in the World's War'; every now and then a new name would be announced which would have the same thing said about it next year.

'Somewhere in France there is a grave'. De Lacey still sang his solo with the same exaggerated pathos but now we felt irritation. There were too many graves in France with no nice wild flowers on them and no grasses waving over them. There were too many with no graves. Some might still enjoy the photographs of dead Germans littering the ground, but we knew that there were many more of our own people in the same condition. Perhaps some of the Germans were quite decent people who had families just like us.

We sang of our dead Old Boys:

> Far on his breast the purple lies
> And on his brow, the sunset gold.

It was nice that the school colours worked in so well, but we did not enjoy singing it, and it was not the most banal of our Friday songs.

The letters from the front which the Head read after his summary of the war news no longer gave a feeling of high adventure, but of a waiting for casual death.

One letter. The brother of the captain of the football team had been killed. He and another officer had gone out at night to investigate a report of a Belgian spying for the Germans. (Who would have thought of a Belgian spying for the Germans in the early days?) A bomb dropped and he was killed. It must have been well behind the lines, for the next day he was given a very respectable funeral. 'There were three public schools represented at the funeral—I placed a small bunch of Purple and Gold flowers on the grave'.

In World War II the much smaller number of burials was prosaic. I know of no flowers on a grave except on one, and even then it was not a real grave. It happened when an English special unit—they were good people—was on one of the Greek islands towards the end of the war. It was a spick-and-span unit. There was no pissing about the place: they used a tin funnel draining off into the ground, surrounded by a rectangle of white stones. On Sunday, up from the village came a procession. There were acolytes in front, someone carrying a cross, the village priest, and behind him, the villagers. They came to the rectangle of white stones and grouped around it; the priest recited the burial service, and a woman came forward and put a bunch of flowers in the tin funnel.

Twenty years later I went to see how Owen was getting along. He and those with him did not expect visitors from twelve thousand miles away, but they made no fuss about it. They were not even surprised that a youngster they had left in Australia should be older than they were. Nothing could surprise them.

Owen was out of the Flying Corps, grounded for good, back in the army; it was an army all of infantry, the greatest infantry force the world had ever seen. That army was marching irresistibly over the rolling hills outside Amiens, moving like a tide out of history, nothing could stop it. It was amazingly accurate in its drill formation and superbly neat in white uniforms with square shoulders; only a badge on the chest showed whether the man was from Britain, Canada, Newfoundland, South Africa, New Zealand or Australia. It was a quietly happy army. Each of them had once thought he might be in it; now he was sure. A happy army of privates, N.C.O.s, lieutenants and captains. There were no brass-hats made lethal by years of military training, no dainty staff-officers, no base-area troops, no military police. This was an army of picked men.

Owen's lot were happy enough and happy to be together. They were decent people. The rogues had been sorted out before they got to France, and if an occasional one slipped through, he had given himself a self-inflicted wound so cleverly that it could not be proved and he had then been transferred to the provosts, the military police, the Judas-sheep who led the others to the slaughter and then stepped safely aside.

All around Owen were others in their twenties, old enough to accept the risks that their community had asked of its men but not old enough to gain the birthright of every man, the triumph and peace of surrender in the surrendering arms of the woman he loved.

There is a pleasant Jewish story that a couple of months before the birth of a man-child, the name of his future wife is announced in heaven. But the names of these young men had been blotted out and they left unmarried widows.

In the Armadale Presbyterian Church we had been lucky and had only five red stars on the honour roll. Most girls met their husbands at church; there were five missing husbands. In fact there were six, because Alan Gibbs' lively brother, Maurice, returned with an English wife. Of course the really attractive girls would look after themselves—or so you might think. But it was precisely these who missed out: Alan's bright sister, Lois, with blue eyes, black hair and a lovely complexion is still Miss Gibbs. The two Shedden sisters, Grace and Marion—'Merny'—as dewy as a fresh spring morning with the promise of a golden day, they are now silver old ladies, still going to the Armadale Church fifty years on, and still sitting in the same pew.

We once thought that Owen was interested in Grace, but he did not commit himself. Possibly he did not want to involve her in what he seemed to expect for himself.

It would be nice to think that those unmarried widows and widowers would come together in some other life.

The race is not to the swift nor the battle to the strong. Those attractive and intelligent girls may have been too reserved to compete, and they remained single. The unattractive ones had no inhibitions, they fought and they fought dirty.

In 1918 Ralph, although badly damaged, was lonely in his prime eligibility. He was assailed by a remarkably unattractive girl, sallow and angular, looking like a tired old horse. She was so unattractive as to make her efforts seem ludicrous, but she battled. The more Ralph dodged her, the harder she came at him. Ralph told me about it a couple of weeks ago, all those years later.

She wrote to him saying that she was pregnant but not hinting that Ralph had anything to do with it; it is possible that she was so well brought up that she did not know how pregnancy was managed and was only interested in it. Ralph was willing to marry her to cover up. Mother did not know of the letter but intervened with such tact that she saved Ralph and avoided a row between the two church families.

Next year the troops started returning from France and that girl had learned a lot. Once again she said she was pregnant and this time she spread the news. The congregation was surprised, for it could not believe that any man could have been so reckless or so drunk as to be responsible, But she said she was pregnant; the news was so widely spread that even I heard it, and it was not the sort of thing talked about in front of a thirteen-year-old. Marriage was inevitable and she was married. Nine months passed, enough for most people; two years passed, enough for an elephant, but there was never a blessing on that union.

On 4 May we read: JEWS IN JERUSALEM. ZIONIST MISSION ARRIVES. We had liberated, or conquered, Jerusalem and in the preceding November, the Balfour Declaration of a Jewish national homeland had been made. It had not been as easy as all that. There was sympathy for Jewish aspirations but fear of offending the Arabs and the Moslem world, and France had expectations of getting Palestine. In the plans for cutting up the Turkish Empire after victory, Britain was to have got the Euphrates valley, and the French, Syria; they had already staked a claim there, and regarded Palestine as part of Syria, but we had won it.

The future of Palestine had been settled in 1916 when Asquith was Prime Minister. He was a middle-aged and middle-class man who was then having a notorious affair with Venetia Stanley, a rackety aristocrat in her twenties. On Cabinet matters he was as indiscreet with her as Lloyd George was later with his Miss Henderson. Asquith wrote to her:

> in carving up the Turk's Asian dominions, we should take Palestine, into which the scattered Jews could swarm back from all quarters of the Globe, and in due course obtain Home Rule. What an attractive community. Curiously enough, the only other partisan of this proposal is Lloyd George, who, I need hardly say, does not care a damn for the Jews or their past or their future, but who thinks it would be an outrage to let the Christian Holy Places—Bethlehem, Mount of Olives, Jerusalem etc., pass into the possession of or under the protectorate of 'Agnostic Atheist France'.

It was not flattering to the Jews. But then Venetia dumped Asquith, she had found his attentions embarrassing; she turned Jewish.

If she had declared herself to be an atheist it would have passed quite unnoticed by us or the official Church of England, but to declare herself a Jew? In the past it had been regarded as quite proper that a Jew should become Church of England for financial reasons but now it seemed most improper that the process should be reversed. She had decided to marry young Montagu for his substantial inheritance, which was conditional on his marrying a Jewess.

Venetia Stanley's conversion was important enough to be printed in our papers, and we were interested, but we would have taken more notice if our papers had told us that she was the sister of the Governor of Victoria, Sir Arthur Stanley.

On 7 May we read: MEN FOR WAR. ENLISTMENT OF MINORS. PARENTS' CONSENT UNNECESSARY. So now boys who had just turned eighteen could enlist and their parents could do nothing about it. Those boys who were not allowed to vote as citizens nor make a normal contract were allowed to make the most important contract of their lives.

Unlikely soldier as he would have been, Ronnie certainly would have already enlisted if father had given his consent. That consent was not now needed and he was free to go—but he didn't. It would have been far easier for him to make the sacrifice of enlistment rather than to accept the insults for non-enlistment.

We had been proud of Keith when he joined up; we had accepted Owen's unworldly altruism; we had regretted Athol's and Ralph's feeling of inevitable duty. Owen had been killed; Ralph had been maimed; and Keith and Athol were still in danger. We did not want Ronnie to add to our anxieties, none of the family did. Athol wrote to Elsie saying that it would be unfair to mother and that there were many who should go before Ronnie. Mother did not want him to go and he agreed to finish his university year, but it was a nasty year for him.

He was just twenty and President of Queen's College Students Society and host at their annual dinner. The chief guest was Harold Stewart, assistant headmaster of Wesley, and in his thank-you speech he attacked Ronnie for not having enlisted.

Stewart was a bachelor with no one dependent on him and had been under forty when the war started; if he had been keen to go, he had needed nobody's consent. Others older than he had enlisted.

STUDENTS AND SLACKERS. In the State parliament Dr Malone asked 'is compulsion being used at the Melbourne University to cause students to enlist under penalty of exclusion from University studies?'

Well, not actual compulsion, but the Medical Students' Society would not admit anyone who could not give a satisfactory reason for not being in khaki. And Presbyterian Ormond College would allow no eligible man over twenty years of age to remain in residence. The Presbyterian General Assembly, previously the most sane of the Protestant church bodies, approved the ruling of the Master of Ormond, MacFarlane, formerly the most tolerant of the leaders in the University. Ironically, Mac-Farlane's stand was opposed by Dr Rentoul, previously the most rabid of the Presbyterians.

The war was dreary. We did not rush for the paper before breakfast to read of the latest victory, for we just did not believe in victories any more. Good and bad things were happening in France, but we did not care; all we knew was that the same killings were being made as in the past years and it would probably get worse when the Germans brought still more troops from Russia. Now it was a matter of lasting out in the hope that things would get better and hoping that no more brothers and friends would be killed before the end—the end was not in sight.

Now we strongly resented the Jones brothers when they marched loudly into church in their tidy uniforms.

One Sunday about this time they did not march in; the three of them slipped in quietly behind their parents, in civilian clothes, just as they had before August 1914. We were not the only ones tired of fancy-dress uniforms, and action had been taken. All members of the Instructional Corps and the Citizen Forces who were unwilling to enlist must hand in their resignations. The Jones boys, who once had been heroes in uniforms, were now shirkers in civilian clothes, and taunts were common in 1918.

We had been very disappointed in one young chap at the church. He was a nice chap, everybody had once thought; but not any more, for he had not enlisted. What made it remarkable was that he had been a keen peace-time soldier, first in the volunteers and then as a captain in the Citizen Forces. He came of a very respectable church family; I think his father was an elder.

In 1914 his father sometimes did not come to church because he was off-colour; he may have later turned up occasionally, but we got used to his not being there. The mother and sisters came with the captain-brother, but he seemed to avoid us, as well he might.

Now, in the middle of 1918 the story drifted around the church. His father was now as mad as a coot and in an asylum and the son had the full responsibility of looking after his mother and sisters. It was shameful to have a father in an asylum and should be kept a secret. We could not tell him that we knew about it and fully approved of his stand; there was nothing we could do about the silent insults of past years.

It was hard for a man to be forced into the army when he did not want to go, but much harder for a man who wanted to go but could not reveal his reason for staying out. I fancy Bob Menzies was one of these. He now had to resign his captaincy in the Melbourne University Rifles.

Phyllis and Bob seemed to be showing even less enthusiasm for each other. Owen had been killed and Bob was safe at home. Ralph was home too, and Ralph, always close to Phyllis, did not like Bob. Perhaps he felt that the war had treated him badly while Bob was doing well out of it.

If Phyllis was meeting Bob in town, of course she could not go by herself so Ralph escorted her and they both waited about until Bob's late arrival. He showed no sign of regret and gave the impression that he expected people to wait for him.

Phyllis broke off the engagement. We were all relieved for it had seemed so matter-of-fact, but strangely enough, we had a lot of sympathy for Bob. We were used to Phyllis dominating all of us brothers and she had shown no sign of being willing to enter into an equal partnership.

We only knew later that they had long ago decided that they would not marry but Bob had wanted it kept quiet so as not to cause talk. His immediate reaction was less to his credit. His dignity had been disturbed; he, Robert Menzies had been rejected; he did not want to tell his parents and asked Phyllis to do so.

21
The Coming of Peace

The Germans had been held; now was the time to hit back at them. There was to be an attack by the new Australian Corps, the whole five divisions working as a unit, with four Canadian divisions and two British. The Germans opposite had six divisions and we had 435 tanks.

The accepted method had been weeks of bombardment with all the guns and shells which could be scraped together and tanks and supplies obvious behind the lines. The ground in front of the lines would be churned into mud and great shell-holes filled with water. Then just before dawn the shelling would stop, whistles would be blown and close lines of men would stagger forward. The German machine-gunners would come up from the shelters and mow them down.

But this August attack would be different—more like Hamel, but even better. The men would head for some particular point, not just out into the featureless devastation. Forty draftsmen were gathered to make maps—John Gawler was one of them. These maps would be available to everybody, completely modern maps with all local features shown. Huge models of the land in front would be made and every man in the attack would come along with his unit to see where he was meant to go. No man would be so tired that he could not move on, no man so over-loaded that he would be useless when he met the enemy. There would be aircraft to drop supplies and ammunition. The first attack would move forward to recognizable positions and there consolidate and a fresh second wave would move through them to renew the attack. There would be no preliminary barrage lasting days to give notice of intention so that the Germans would have reinforcements ready. All rear preparations would be carefully hidden. The noise of the tanks being brought up at night would be masked by the noise of low-flying aircraft, and the tanks would be hidden during daylight. It was to be a secret attack.

A sudden fierce barrage, a line of fire moving forward in fixed steps, and an unexpected attack by remarkably few troops. It was not like real war at all, it was the application of intelligence to a military problem; it was, at last, common sense applied when thousands of lives were at risk.

A hole nearly twelve miles wide was punched in the German defences; penetration, with all the military resources blotted out and our troops still going ahead.

This was what the Germans had done to the Russians, the Romanians, the French; only five months earlier they had done it to the British. Now it had been done to the Germans and they did not like it. The last advance of the war had begun and it was to break the Germans. Ludendorff said,

> August 8th was the black day for the German army in the history of the war . . . The British, mainly Australian and Canadian divisions . . . broke between the Somme and the Luce deep into our front . . . it was a gloomy situation . . . six or seven divisions that were quite fairly described as effective had been completely battered . . . August 8th made things clear for both army commands, both the Germans and for that of the enemy.

A British account says, 'The Australians, as so often, had the easiest passage', but what was meant was that they could succeed in an operation and suffer fewer casualties than other troops. This time the Canadians were almost as successful, but not quite, and they suffered more; the two flanking British divisions were almost passengers, but they suffered most.

This time the Australians had 776 casualties, including walking-wounded, and they captured 1500 prisoners. The casualties did not seem so bad when there was so much to show for them. Perhaps there was some splendour in the war at last; perhaps it did not feel so bad to be wounded if you were sharing in something that justified it.

On 11 August Eddy Shemilt from the church got his wound. We knew that he had enlisted very young but it was only later that we learned that he had been wounded just after his seventeenth birthday and had been in the army for eighteen months.

We got the news of the battle on 10 August. HAIG'S ATTACK. MANY TOWNS TAKEN. THOUSANDS OF PRISONERS. AUSTRALIANS ENGAGED. Those were the *Argus* headlines. In Haig's dispatch, just at the end in small type, was 'Australian troops took part'.

Monash and his 3rd Division had first stemmed the British retreat; now Monash and the Australian Army Corps had won the first great Allied victory in France which started the slide of the Germans into defeat. Not Haig in his polished riding boots, nor any of the generals of the five armies, but a colonial Jewish civil engineer had made history. Good for Monash.

On 15 August Monash was knighted by the King at a great parade of Australian troops in France. On 16 August: MONTDIDIER FALLS. ALLIES SWEEPING ON. PRISONERS 25,000. AUSTRALIANS IN LEAD. Montdidier was well known to us, things sounded good. On 20 August: ROYE FALLS. The French had done that, but we had never been very concerned with the place. The New Zealanders had never got much mention in our papers but now, in small print, they had outflanked Bapaume. And the A.I.F. was back in Pozières, where it had all started for them, and they were visiting the graves of 1916 and finding that they were in quite good order.

On 23 August: BYNG ADVANCES NORTH OF ALBERT. FRENCH ENTER LASSIGNY. On 24 August: FALL OF ALBERT. AUSTRALIANS TAKE PART. This was really good, Albert really did mean something to us. On 26 August: GOOD NEWS FROM ALL POINTS. On 31 August: BAPAUME FALLS. FRENCH TAKE NOYON. AUSTRALIANS NEAR PÉRONNE. Bapaume and Péronne; two places we knew.

On 3 September:

PERONNE FALLS

Taken by Australians

Further Advances Elsewhere

Heavy Toll of Prisoners

On 4 September: HINDENBURG LINE BROKEN BY BRITISH. This was premature; an outlying defence spur had been taken but the main line stood solid as the last defence work in France. On 14 September: AMERICANS ATTACK. IN ST MIHIEL SECTOR. ADVANCE OF FIVE MILES. But it did not work out too well, for although they had five times as many troops as the Germans, the attack crumpled and stopped.

On 18 September: SALONIKA FRONT. ALLIES ATTACK BULGARIA. After a couple of safe years, all those idle troops were moving at last. On the same day we read that it would be 'A Great Day for Empire if Hughes Accepts Seat in Commons'. So they would squeeze up the five hundred and more M.P.s and squeeze in the Australian Prime Minister; once he was in, they might promote him to something. It was exactly a month since Sir George Reid had died. He had been almost as prominent a figure in Australian politics as Hughes now was, but he had made little impact as a member of the House of Commons except on the one occasion when he had moved a motion on Ireland which was in violent disagreement with Australian government policy. He had sent back the most encouraging and unbelievable reports on the war. It might be that to be Prime Minister of Australia was as important as being a British M.P.

On 23 September: HINDENBURG LINE. AUSTRALIANS NEARER. AT ST QUENTIN CANAL and VICTORY IN PALESTINE. TURKS OVER-WHELMED. The next day it was TURKS DEMORALISED. OVER 10,000 PRISONERS. On 25 September: BULGARS FLEE. PURSUIT BY SERBIANS ON 100 MILE FRONT. The same day it was PALESTINE VICTORY. 'FINAL AND COMPLETE' TURKISH ARMIES SMASHED. If the same effort had been made on Gallipoli in 1915 it might have happened then.

On 30 September: SEEKING PEACE. BULGARS APPROACH ALLIES. The next day Bulgaria had surrendered. The first enemy country had gone.

The Germans asked for an armistice. They might have lost Bulgaria and Turkey might be shaky but they had recovered on the Western Front. They had held Foch's general offensive; the American attack in the Meuse-Argonne had been stopped and the attacks by the British, French and Belgians in Flanders were not going well, but they approached President Wilson and this gave a hint that they thought they were beaten.

This was embarrassing, for already in August they had agreed to give all that we had said we were fighting for. Germany had asked for her colonies back and that Belgium should be neutral and not in the Anglo-French bloc, but she had agreed on reparations for damage. Wilson ignored the German plea. His terms were unconditional surrender and the abdication of the Kaiser.

All this was happening without any help from the Russians. Now we were actually fighting them and liked them less than we did the Germans; they were now savage and nasty people and no longer our gallant allies. There had been little news about Russia in our papers whilst all the big things were happening in France, and what news there was, was hopelessly confused.

On 28 June it had been RUSSIA. SENSATIONAL REPORT. BOLSHEVIKS OVERTHROWN. COSSACKS SEIZE MOSCOW. General Korniloff was dictator; evidently he had superseded the previous leader, Kerensky.

Perhaps the Russian armies were still fighting on our side. IS BLOW IMPENDING? GREAT OFFENSIVE EXPECTED FROM RIGA TO THE BLACK SEA. 'The Russo-Roumanian armies were in a high state of efficiency'. There was a war between the Finns and the Russians, and the Germans were helping the Finns. On 16 July the British troops in north Russia captured some little town, so both we and the Germans were fighting the Russians although we had been told that the Germans were leading the Bolshevik troops. Puzzling; we had been fighting the Germans for the rights of small nations (except Ireland), and now the Germans were doing the same thing by helping the Finns.

And the Czecho-Slovaks were marching about in Siberia and capturing towns from the Russians; they had deserted the Austrian armies to join the Russians and now they were fighting them; everybody was fighting the Russians and even the Americans had landed in the north.

Then it was official: EX-CZAR SHOT. The Bolsheviks were afraid that the town where he was a prisoner would be captured by the Czechs. There had been rumours before, but this time it was true. We did not approve.

Our Billy Hughes in London listed the type of man he hated: 'A Bolshevik, a pacifist, a Russian or a German'; it was strange that he left the Irish out, for now all Irish were classed as Sinn Feiners, just as all Russians were lumped in with the Bolsheviks. Now the Bolsheviks declared war on us, Lenin did it on 16 August. And they kept killing people, like the German ambassador to the new nation of Ukraine—a nation which did not last very long after German help dried up.

But in August: BOLSHEVIK FAILURE. LEADERS PREPARE TO FLEE and next day, COUNTER-REVOLUTION SPREADS. In Siberia it was ANTI-BOLSHEVIK SUPREMACY. Things were not going too well for the Bolsheviks. On 3 September: LENIN DEAD. SHOT BY A WOMAN. Unfortunately, next day he was not dead; only desperately wounded. In September a Bolshevik mob invaded the British Embassy and murdered the attaché. Korniloff was killed and the Tsarina was murdered a week later. BOLSHEVIK REIGN OF TERROR, MURDER AND ANARCHY.

Improbable stories were coming out of Russia, but on 28 October came one as good as any. A Salvation Army Commissioner reported from Russia that the Tsarina, who had always been regarded as pro-German, actually 'had a private telegraph line from the Winter Palace in Petrograd to Potsdam and she told the Kaiser all the war plans'. When she heard that Kitchener was coming to Russia, 'she gave the fullest details, which resulted in the sinking of the vessel'.

The war was going very well without any Russian help and with us actually fighting the Russians. The agreement to give Constantinople to the Russians had therefore lapsed; as the Greeks had not been very helpful, there was really no one to give it to.

The line on the Western Front was back where it had been before the rout of the Fifth Army in March and in front were the tremendous works of the Hindenburg Line–the Germans called it the 'Siegfried Line'. Between it and the Australians was the deep cutting of the St Quentin Canal as it approached a tunnel through the hill, and over the tunnel was the country across which the attack would be made.

Winter was not far off, and if the line was held, there might be time for the Germans to consolidate and to draw resources from their con-quered territories in the east–they already had Romanian oil and they might get wheat from the Ukraine. Things were unsettled there, but it was to be expected that there would be stores of wheat which had been bottled up by the Turkish command of the Bosporus.

The Hindenburg Line was the greatest defence line of the war, an immense defence with thick forests of barbed wire, concrete emplace-ments and prodigious dug-outs where the troops could wait in comfort during the unpleasant preliminaries of an attack. All this was known, for complete plans had been captured in the advance and the attack could be planned in conformity with the knowledge.

An unexpected bit of luck or well-earned good fortune; on the left the British had managed to get across the St Quentin Canal.

On 1 October: ENEMY LINE BROKEN. ALLIES REACH CAMBRAI. GERMANS RETREAT ON AISNE. Then in little print, 'the Australians and Americans have stormed the canal on both sides of Bellicourt'. They went ahead with the tanks towards the next organized line of German resistance. AUSTRAL-AMERICAN BLOW. HINDENBURG LINE CROSSED. Not much of a fuss about the smashing of the last German defences our side of the Rhine.

Two Australian divisions were in the line and it was planned that two American divisions would go through them to take the open defences in front of the Hindenburg Line, and consolidate. Then two Australian divisions would pass through the Americans to the main attack, go to a certain point, and then the last two Australian divisions would pass through them and they would be through the Hindenburg Line. It would go like clockwork, just like the previous attacks. But it didn't.

Off went the Americans with gallantry and swept over the outer German lines, but then something went wrong. No signals came back.

On 3 October: AMERICANS OVERSHOOT MARK. HARD TASK BRAVELY FACED. 'There is not the slightest doubt but that the Americans yesterday in their first assault reached Gony.' They had got there but they had not mopped up, they were too busy winning victories. Up came the Germans from their safe shelters, set up their machine-guns and were as good as new; those Germans should have been prisoners or dead.

Not a word from the Americans; they had just disappeared. They had done nothing; they had done worse than nothing. In addition to the main attack, the Australians had to repeat the preliminary attack on an alerted enemy and without artillery, for it could not be used with the Americans out there somewhere in front. They were heavy losses in getting to what had been planned as the starting point.

A note left in a machine-gun post: 'Dear Tommy, from this place I shot 60 Americans with my machine-gun; they came like sheep'. When the Australians reached Gony there were no Americans; the Germans had captured 1200 there.

These were the Americans who were going to win the war for us. All this lot had done was to cause needless losses; no estimate was published as to how many, but it rankled.

The Australian deaths in front of the Hindenburg Line should not have occurred; in the A.I.F. there was loudly expressed resentment of American ineptitude, which became part of our oral history. Some years later, when my turn came for compulsory training, four of the senior officers of my battalion had been there and told us youngsters about it. We accepted their views in World War II; after our time the same views persisted in Korea and Vietnam.

There was heavy fighting after this bad start but the Hindenburg Line was breached, the last defence line in France, and it was now to be open fighting against a demoralized enemy. The advance went on, on to the village of Monrehain and there it was the end of the war for the A.I.F. They were pulled out of the line and the Amercians took over.

The Armistice was signed just before they were due to go into the line again. The war would have finished for many of them anyway, for some had already been selected for home-leave after four years of active service. All divisions had been in the line since April—128 days against the usual 14. Napoleon's Hundred Days had been dramatic but those 128 days were quite as important; the changing of defeat into victory, the holding of the Germans outside Amiens, the first advance on the Western Front at Hamel and the smashing of the Hindenburg Line. National bias we had, but still the A.I.F. was not too bad.

The *Argus* of 12 October printed a letter from an Australian sergeant-major being repatriated after two years as a prisoner of war in Germany. It would have been written about the beginning of September.

> Do you know that I have come away from Germany tremendously impressed with a sense of her power and will to win the war, or, at least, to bring the whole world down with her in case of defeat . . . the people have suffered untold misery in the shape of starvation . . . I have seen the guards of our camp steal about when they thought that no prisoners were looking and gather up the mouldy bread and crusts which we had thrown into the refuse-box. And whenever prisoners pass through any village or town they are simply besieged with children asking for bread or biscuits—and they don't generally ask in vain—soap, for instance, is unprocurable—for a pair of new boots they will offer you from 5 to 8 pounds. . . The best fed man in Germany is today the British prisoner of war—his Red Cross parcels arrive regularly'.

In 1926 I met Egremont, an English architect who had been working in Berlin in 1914. After some months he was interned but his firm paid him half-salary throughout the war. His English wife remained free and visited him in his camp at Ruhleben and smuggled food out of the camp for herself and her German friends.

So they were starving, and it did them no good to say that the British blockade of foodstuffs was against the Law of Nations, not after what they had done with their poison gas, submarines and Nurse Cavell. Their adult food ration of 1000 calories a day was half the essential, and the infant mortality figures were double the pre-war ones. The pictures of a German family sitting down to a meal of one tiny scrap of food were really funny. Yes, we were winning the war.

It had been a sordid war and still was. It was nothing like what we had imagined in 1914: no dashing about waving swords in the sunlight, just a grey war of starvation and promiscuous death and far too many stars on our honour boards.

Victories. This year we really had victories but we did not cheer. We had celebrated so many fantasy victories that we could not believe in real ones. We just wanted it all over and tidied away.

The war looked as if it were lurching to its collapse and we in Upper I at the Wesley College Preparatory School were bewildered. We had been part of Mr Adamson's 'School at War' and what would happen when there was no war for the school to be at? The war had been our absorbing interest and what we remembered of life without the war seemed remote and unreal. No war, and there would be great emptiness. We could not remember our papers without a war to fill them. We could not remember school assembly without the war as its centre. What could the Head talk about if there was no war?

We had been proud of the Head as the great leader of our pack—not only the Wesley pack, but the whole great pack of Victoria. Now we had doubts which we were too timid to express. The pathos of his war now looked ridiculous and artificial; the leader we had revered for years now seemed to be an isolated figure posturing and gesticulating remote from us; we had dropped away behind him. Death for our country, which he had set as our highest goal, now looked like something which might be avoided, if luck ran your way.

Those Old Boys who had gone away so gloriously at the beginning were nearly all dead and their high adventure now looked like over-optimistic romanticism; those later ones, like Owen, who had enlisted as a spiritual sacrifice, now looked as if they might have been deluded; those now going as an unavoidable duty enforced by public opinion, had our sympathy rather than our admiration.

We knew that God was on our side—He had made it obvious when He personally intervened at the retreat from Mons—but now He seemed unenthusiastic about helping us and had done nothing much recently.

Were the Germans really so bad? Many believed they were, but a lot of us had doubts. Many still believed in their corpse factories, and if you thought about it, they had many more of our bodies available than their own. This was 1918 and the stories of 1914 were still believed by some. There was a letter from an A.I.F. man in France: 'Kultur exhibited, which violates women, stuck babies on bayonets and displayed them outside butchers' shops'. But another letter from the A.I.F. said,

Everyone here is 'fed-up' of the war, but not with the Hun. The British staff, British methods and British bungling have sickened us. We are military socialists and all overseas troops have had enough of the English . . . I feel disaster in my blood. Curse all the powers that bungled us to defeat.

This was from a man who had 'heard the cry of England' in 1914.

We had lost our reverence for England. We no longer gloried in the Empire and the army that Kipling wrote about before the war. His army had been a jolly rollicking lot; his army was now senselessly brutal and our Kipling showed a sadistic delight in its brutality. He wrote of the shooting of a sentry for sleeping at his post:

> I sleep because I am slain.
> They slew me because I slept.

and of the shooting of a coward:

> I could not look on Death, which being known,
> Men led me to him, blindfold and alone.

This was written before the great retreat of early 1918, when quite a few merited the same treatment.

We did not like all this shooting of cowards, sentries, Irish and conscientious objectors. Haig might think that the A.I.F. was inferior because it did not allow capital punishment; we thought it was good and that Haig was inferior.

In 1914 we had learned to hate the Germans heartily and we enjoyed it. It had been our Christian duty to hate them and it had seemed proper that the whole evil race should be wiped out. Now we hated others more: the Bolsheviks, the Sinn Fein and the I.W.W.; now we ranked the Germans at about the same level as the Pacifists. We were beginning to think that they were men, women and children, rather like us, even if, as Germans, they were inferior.

Peace was in the wind and we had relented, but not Kipling. He thought the Germans were beaten and in October he wrote:

> Evil incarnate is held at last
> To answer to mankind
> And cold, commanded lust
> . . . A people with the heart of beasts.

We were confused. We no longer pretended to believe what once we had believed. Our nation had been ignoble and noble; it had been selfish and had offered a selfless sacrifice. It was all too much, we were sick, utterly sick of the war.

On 14 October we read: MOMENTOUS NEWS. GERMANY READY TO YIELD. On 16 October: NO ARMISTICE EXCEPT ON OUR TERMS. WILL GERMANY GIVE IN? On 18 October: EXCITEMENT IN ADELAIDE. 'There was the wildest excitement in Adelaide today at the report that the Kaiser had abdicated and that Germany had unconditionally surrendered . . . the bells of the town hall were rung, flags were hoisted throughout the city and suburbs . . .'. But it was premature.

On 21 October, not the usual notice of the weekly prayer intercession in the Melbourne Town Hall, but WAR TIME INTERCESSION AND THANKSGIVING. On 23 October: GERMAN REPLY 'UTTERLY UNSATISFACTORY'. On 24 October: PEACE NO NEARER.

So there might not be an armistice and the fighting would go on and more people would be killed, although we and the Germans were tired of it all. The fighting was still in France where we had fought for four years within forty miles of Paris. How long would the desperate Germans fight over the hundreds of miles to Berlin? They were on the run but they were not going so far or so fast as we had done in 1914 and last March. It might go on for years: the German army was still intact and it was where it had been at the opening battles of 1914.

Then a rush of events. Ludendorff resigned on 26 October. We did not like him nor Hindenburg; they were like our Dr Mannix, they might be clever but we hated them. They seemed bigger men than our leaders. On 2 November: TURKEY TO SURRENDER. AUSTRIAN COLLAPSE. Revolution was spreading there and her navy had surrendered to the Southern Slavs and the country was to be divided into republics.

Bohemia was now part of Czecho-Slovakia. The Germans in the northern part of Bohemia wanted their own republic, but republics were unacceptable if they were composed of the wrong sort of people. These Germans were lumped in with Hungarians and Ruthenians as minorities in the synthetic Czecho-Slovakia and would later give trouble as Sudeten Germans.

Austria had surrendered, but that did not stop the Italians from doing their last ridiculous act of the war. They attacked the troops pouring back home and captured 300 000 of them.

The Kaiser was to be replaced and the German princes would decide on his successor. The Turkish armistice had been ratified; the Allies had entered the Dardanelles three years late and the forts were to be garrisoned by Anzacs. There was a German naval mutiny and another premature report of an armistice with Germany. Europe was in a mess.

Peace might come and how good it would be. Dull, yes, but it would rid us of the fear which had been behind our shoulders for all the past years. Peace and safety for Keith and Athol, and Ronnie would not have to join them; peace and father would be earning again; peace and I would have the same sort of clothes as the others as school; peace and we would be a family again.

There was a lot of chatter about the end of the war at school, but not as excited as it had been some days ago. Why should we have peace with Berlin hundreds of miles beyond our troops?

Home from school. Tea; homework in the cold breakfast room; red lines ruled under the headings; ready for bed. Turn out the gas in the central fitting and go across to the warm study–father, mother and Ralph there. Kiss mother goodnight, say goodnight to the others and go upstairs. Feel in the dark for the matches and candle in the big cold dormitory–I am the only one using it now–light the candle and read a chapter of the Bible open on top of the chest-of-drawers, too high for comfort but the best position available; undress, fold my clothes and put on pyjamas and along to the bathroom for a cold wash.

Back to the dormitory, blow out the candle, cross the room and open the window and out to my bed on the balcony, sit on it, looking out into the night. Tonight is 11 November, nothing funny about that; it's a starry night, milky around the horizon.

Lights in the front room of the Lees' house opposite, lights in the upper windows of the Morans' house down the road—early for them to be upstairs.

Up Kooyong Road there is a pool of light where St George's Road butts in with the dark Church of England on the corner, that church with its primitive bell on a scaffold, the one that Bob Menzies rang the only time he did anything ridiculous, the street corner where he stopped an egg at the anti-conscription meeting.

All the usual lights in the windows all the way to the Malvern Town Hall. A moving light blinks where a tram goes up High Street. The usual quiet night.

A church bell. Funny time for a church bell, and it is ringing fast. It is to the left—St John's, Toorak.

Another bell begins far away to the right in Caulfield. A factory hooter blows very faint back towards town. This must mean something. This must mean peace.

I run down the dark stairs to the study and into the warm light. 'The war is over'.

Father stands up: 'How do you know'?

'The church bells are ringing, come up and hear them'.

By the time we are on the balcony the bells are ringing all round. Then someone comes and fiddles with the rope of the Church of England bell on the other side of the road and it joins in.

The war is over.

· · · · · · · · · · ·

Sources

The main source is personal memory of the war, reinforced and confirmed by those of other contemporaries. Family memories are nearest in parallel, particularly those of the brothers, Keith and Ralph. The war at Lawside kindergarten is clearly remembered by Gelda and Polly Pyke, Ellison Harvie and Marion Schneider (now Mrs Erswell). Professor Hartung supplied a detailed written account of the treatment given to him, to his father and others of German descent. Peter Hooks has supplied writings and a recording of his father's account of the New Guinea landing made when he revisited the place in 1975. Chief Petty Officer Hooks was the first Australian to set foot on enemy territory and may well have been the first British.

The Melbourne newspapers, the *Argus*, *Age* and *Herald*, gave us the news of the war and shaped our opinions, particularly the *Argus*, as the most respectable for respectable people such as ourselves. The Sydney *Bulletin* almost ranked as a Melbourne paper and had more radical views. We middle-class people saw the London *Punch* and *Illustrated London News* when we went into town to the dentist and more affluent people took other London journals as status symbols, but they were of minor importance compared to the other two.

All three daily papers published extracts from the London press, particularly from the *Times*, which we accepted as a sure and unpolluted source. The official handouts were printed most prominently and if they contained any reference to the Australians, that section was advanced in prominence. Our own war correspondents gave less stilted accounts and all our dailies printed 'Letters from the Front'—letters which had passed only the field censor and were often very free in criticism of British generals and troops. There were official British complaints about the Australian press. The letters showed no hatred for the Germans, for hatred seemed to increase with distance from danger. They did not show many things which later were revealed in diaries of the time, an admiration for German generalship and German fighting qualities and the despondency and expectation of defeat, particularly in 1917.

In the huge and growing pile of writings on the war it is remarkable that no consensus of opinion yet exists on important elements. Most still hold that 60 000 Ausralians died for the belated succour of Gallant Little Belgium, despite the 1918 opinion that the Belgians were a grubby lot not worth fighting for. Many still believe in the Angel, or Angels, of Mons.

In later writing, the great figures have gone up or down; usually the Germans have gone up and ours have gone down. The Kaiser now has an appreciative press; Hindenburg remained for years as the figure-head of Germany and other generals are now given appreciation not granted in the war years; even Ludendorff's final lapse is the only one attributed to him.

Haig is right down: he dived there himself when he published his private papers. Northcliffe is down. He died as a dangerous madman in 1922 as a logical conclusion to his war-time activities. Lloyd George still has admirers. He entered the war as the bright boy of the Liberal Party and was leading it as it shrank to a mere rump. Many of the claims he made for himself during the war are still believed by some and recently a prominent authority on the period has credited him with the introduc-tion of naval convoys to combat the U-boats, a claim which even Lloyd George never made.

Billy Hughes is still regarded as having done what he set out to do – to express and direct Australian majority opinion. Monash stepped down from his high international position to work for a salary for the Victorian government and made no fuss about it. In all the writings of the war his letters to his wife are as vivid as any, more vivid than his formal account of his campaigns. Perhaps he was too modest. There is a long letter telling of the Victory Dinner at Buckingham Palace where he went as Australia's representative. That immense figure of the war seemed to be impressed by the condescension of the titled flunkeys of the court.

The main references are of varying dependability; the most useful, the *Encyclopaedia Britannica*, 14th edition, 1936, still includes some war-time distortions. The *Times Illustrated History of the War*, compiled at the time of the events, merely petrifies contemporary views. C. E. W. Bean's *Official History of Australia in the War of 1914-1918* is remarkable for its modesty and balance, as are the writings of B. H. Liddell-Hart.

Tom Hazell of the University of Melbourne has supplied important material on Archbishop Mannix; Dr Julie Hickford, Phyllis's friend, has described the war years at the University. Three individual librarians have generously given noteworthy help: Mr P. D. Singleton of the University of Melbourne, Mr John Thompson, formerly of the La Trobe Library, and Mr Peter Wilkie of the Wesley College Library.

Central Army Records Office has supplied individual military histories. The Minutes of Council of the University of Melbourne have been studied and the Wesley College Chronicle has provided contemporary appreciations of the war years. The Royal Australian Institute of Architects and the Institution of Civil Engineers, London, have helped; and even the Melbourne and Metropolitan Tramways Board has done its bit.

Memory deludes itself by believing that things it hoped would have happened actually did happen; the same foible can be recognized in post-war scholarly writings.